A Future
Built on
Remembrance

The 2023 Basque Law on
Historical and Democratic Memory

Basque Politics Series #25

A Future
Built on
Remembrance

The 2023 Basque Law on
Historical and Democratic Memory

EDITED BY
Xabier Irujo and Unai Belaustegi

CENTER FOR BASQUE STUDIES
UNIVERSITY OF NEVADA, RENO
2023

This book was published with generous financial support from the Basque Government.

Center for Basque Studies
University of Nevada, Reno
1664 North Virginia St,
Reno, Nevada 89557 usa
http://basque.unr.edu

Copyright © 2024 by the Center for Basque Studies and the University of Nevada, Reno
ISBN-13: 978-1-949805-87-1
All rights reserved.

Library of Congress Cataloging-in-Publication Data

Names: Irujo Ametzaga, Xabier, editor. | Belaustegi, Unai, editor.
Title: A future built on remembrance : the 2023 Basque law on historical and democratic memory / edited by Xabier Irujo and Unai Belaustegi.
Description: Reno : Center for Basque Studies Press, University of Nevada, 2024. | Series: Basque politics series; 25 | Includes bibliographical references and index. | Summary: "Contemporary Basque society can only be understood in conection to the consecuential events of the fleeting twentieth century. They had a lasting impact on the phyches of the Basques. A clear example of this, in the case of the Autonomous Community of the Basque Country (BAC), is that (part of) society still refer to the period beginning in 1936- or even further back, in 1931- to justify, understand, and explain present-day circumstances"-- Provided by publisher.
Identifiers: LCCN 2024013176 | ISBN 9781949805871 (paperback)
Subjects: LCSH: Law--Spain--País Vasco--History. | Constitutional history--Spain--País Vasco. | País Vasco (Spain)--History--Autonomy and independence movements. | País Vasco (Spain)--Politics and government.
Classification: LCC KKT5671.A197 F88 2024 | DDC 342.46/6009--dc23/eng/20240326
LC record available at https://lccn.loc.gov/2024013176

Printed in the United States of America

Contents

1. LEGISLATING AMNESIA: MEMORY OF THE SPANISH CIVIL WAR AND THE FRANCO DICTATORSHIP IN THE BASQUE COUNTRY (1975–2014) BY *UNAI BELAUSTEGI* 1

2. THE HISTORICAL MEMORY ACT OF 2022 OF THE AUTONOMOUS COMMUNITY OF THE BASQUE COUNTRY BY *XABIER IRUJO* 24

3. MEMORY POLICIES IN NAVARRE: THE INSTITUTE OF MEMORY OF NAVARRE BY *JOSÉ MIGUEL GASTÓN AGUAS* AND *CÉSAR LAYANA ILUNDAIN* 42

4. HERITAGIZATION OF SITES ASSOCIATED WITH CONFLICTS: AN ANALYSIS OF UNESCO'S CURRENT DEBATE BY *MAIDER MARAÑA* 67

5. MASS GRAVE EXHUMATIONS: A TESTAMENT TO REPRESSION IN THE SPANISH STATE: AN OVERVIEW OF THE EXHUMATIONS CONDUCTED BETWEEN THE YEARS 2000 AND 2021 BY *LOURDES HERRASTI* 95

6. PRIMAL VIOLENCE BY *ANTONI SEGURA I MAS* 115

7. THE "GERNIKA" CASE IN THE GERMAN HISTORICAL MILITARY WRITING OF THE POSTWAR YEARS AND THE DENIAL OF CULPABILITY BY *ÁNGEL VIÑAS* 127

INDEX 140

ABOUT THE AUTHORS 149

one

Legislating Amnesia

Memory of the Spanish Civil War and the Franco Dictatorship in the Basque Country (1975–2014)*

Unai Belaustegi

Contemporary Basque society can only be understood in connection to the consequential events of the fleeting twentieth century. They had a lasting impact on the psyches of Basques. A clear example of this, in the case of the Autonomous Community of the Basque Country (the BAC), is that (parts of) society still refer to the period beginning in 1936—or even further back, in 1931—to justify, understand, and explain present-day circumstances.

The whole of Basque society was involved, directly or indirectly, in the Spanish Civil War of 1936 and suffered firsthand the consequences of the conflict. After Gipuzkoa's (Guipuzcoa) capital city of Donostia-San Sebastian fell in the hands of the insurrected in September 1936, most of the province fell in a chain reaction. With Bilbo-Bilbao's defeat in June of the following year, the rebels against the Spanish Republic won permanent control of the territory. The act of June 23, 1937, put it plain and simple: those who had *mistakenly* joined the wrong side would be punished. Not long thereafter, General Francisco Franco seized power and established what would be a nearly forty-year-long dictatorship. Although the military conflict lasted short of fourteen months in the BAC, its shock waves reverberate to this day.

What the faction had won by force, the law perpetuated. This formula helped cement the winner-loser narrative. An unrelenting propaganda campaign condemned all who had erred in their choice. In Franco's Spain, only one Spanish identity was accepted, and it did not accommodate *rojos* (leftists), separatists, freemasons, and traitors; unless they became of use to the dictatorship, that is.[1]

After the dictator's death, the political era between Franco's regime and the constitutional state known as the Transition held the country back in several ways. The pre-constitutional act promulgated in 1977, in the process led by Spanish president and reformed Francoist public official Adolfo Suárez, set the pattern for all future policymaking, including that of the BAC. The Amnesty Act was pivotal in shaping society's view of its recent past.

Warmly welcomed, and even championed, by most of the political parties of the time, the new act granted an amnesty to all victims of punitive measures of a political nature during the dictatorship, and it provided the perfect opportunity to liberate from prison or exile the family members and friends who had suffered the consequences of the oppressive Francoist regime. On the flip side, attempts to elucidate the events of the preceding forty years would be indefinitely muzzled, and the perpetrators of the 1936 coup, the Civil War, and the dictatorship were spared from facing justice; none of them would be prosecuted. As the transition period came to an end and Spain immersed itself in the early years of democracy, the Amnesty Act became the yardstick by which to judge any decision related to the war or the Franco regime.[2] All bills, acts, and political decisions regarding the Civil War and the dictatorship stemmed from it up until at least the year 2000.

After 1977, ignoring the past became the primary stance of society as well as of the political sphere: *both* sides had done *terrible* things. Other acts and decrees, such as the decree of 1978, which were enacted to reinforce the Amnesty Act, fostered this narrative. The decree of 1978 reformed the Official Secrets Act of 1968, which banned access to archives and documents over national security concerns and the fundamental interests of the nation.[3] As a result of this two-page act, any information that may cast light on what happened between 1936 and 1975 remains mainly inaccessible. It has meant an almost insurmountable obstacle for many victims.

Three months later, in a chamber of Congress still showcasing Francoist symbols, the Spanish Constitution was approved. To add insult to injury, the first version of the actual constitution featured the Francoist eagle on the first page. Unfazed by the fascist motif, most Spaniards voted in support of the Magna Carta. In the BAC, the greater part of the community did not turn out to the polls.

After years of pain and punishment, victims of Francoist oppression witnessed how their own institutions buried every path toward recognition. Perpetrators would not stand trial or face a sentence. Nor would victims be granted public recognition or monetary reparations. The actors behind these ruthless actions would be allowed to remain anonymous. They would not have to answer for their roles in the coup, the war, or the executions, nor for their involvement in any act of violence against sympathizers of the Spanish Republic such as the *paseos* (people were walked outside of town to be executed), the repression, the torture, the belittling, the punishments, or the misappropriation of property. The memory of this passage of Spanish history would be lost in oblivion or remembered only through an amnesic lens.[4] The dictator's shadow loomed over Spanish democracy beyond his death, hampering all attempts to dig up memories of what had happened. Collective amnesia spread across the country and began to cast a gentler light on the era that had been left behind. It may have been beneficial in the construction of the post-Franco society. But, at the same time, it is inarguable that, for years, amnesia was central to the way Spanish society understood, explained, and legislated the present.[5]

FROM MONETARY REPARATIONS TO MORAL RECOGNITION (1975–2004)

During the Transition, Spanish institutions showed no interest in unearthing memories of the dictatorship; they did little to promote moral, historical, or economic initiatives of such nature.[6] On top of that, the initial batch of reparations were exclusively monetary and directed at communities that had lost their rights during the war. Such measures were introduced through the acts and decrees enacted between 1976 and 1979 to regulate the pensions that members of the military and civilians were to receive in compensation for their war wounds or mutilations. But they failed to grant equal recognition to combatants of one side or the other, and to those killed extrajudicially. Later, a 1984 act "recognized the service provided by and the rights" of those who fought for the Spanish Republic in the armed forces, law enforcement, and the Customs Guard during the Civil War. It complemented the acts of 1978 and 1980 but missed by regarding all combatants as equally deserving of recognition yet again: it only rewarded members of statutory forces that had been under the rule of either one of the two governments. And, as mentioned, the only type of recognition offered by this act were monetary reparations.[7] An act passed months before recognized prison time—served for reasons contemplated under the Amnesty Act—as worked time, for Social Security contribution purposes.[8]

After the promulgation of the constitution and the approval of the Statute of Autonomy of the BAC in 1979, the Basque government faced the task of building its own legal framework from the ground up. Largely, the legislation introduced up until the 2000s, both at the regional and national levels, would be mainly known for granting only monetary reparations and for having to undergo several amendments and additions in response to victims' complaints of discrimination and of the impossibility to claim recognition.

During the first legislative term of the democratic era, from 1979 to 1982, the Spanish Congress discussed and approved several bills to help the widows of military men mutilated or killed in the war. The bills talked about the "discrimination" suffered by this community. The two most important acts of the second legislature of 1982–1986 were enacted in 1984 and were related to "the military members of the Spanish Republic," on the one hand, and, on the other, to the political prisoners protected by the Amnesty Act.[9]

These pieces of Spanish legislation provided the backdrop for the first set of regional acts conceived within the BAC's legal framework. The Basque Parliament introduced its first act in 1983, three years after its first session and four years after the Statute of Autonomy was approved. The act revolved around the recognition of labor rights and the right to a pension for the personnel who had worked for the Basque government during the war and the dictatorship for a period of at least one year, between October 7, 1936, and January 1978. It allowed the possibility to grant recognition to the personnel who had to abandon their jobs because of the war or endure imprisonment for a period of at least eight months. The act was remarkably limited. The only beneficiaries were those stipulated in the act of 1981: high-ranking government officials, key personnel, the president and the council members who had comprised the Basque government between 1937 and 1979, as well as their next of kin.[10] The time periods and positions specified in the act left out the bulk of victims involved in the Civil War and the Franco dictatorship, including numerous civil servants and administrative workers of the Basque government.

The act stood out for the tone of the arguments put forth to support it. They painted the Basque government as a "victim" of the war. Because the Basque regions had not been able to install or certify a regional government during the war, "the specific provisions contained in the Spanish act" concerning the recognition of civil servants who had been victims of war reprisals never included the workers at the service of the Basque government. The purpose of the Basque 1983 act was to compensate for this legislative gap.[11] But, because of its deficient content, the act had to be reformed and completed two years later.

In 1985, the Basque Parliament thought it necessary to introduce another act meant to reinforce four different aspects of its predecessor. The new act admitted that "only the survivors of high-ranking government officials had benefited from the older act," which "had failed to meet certain expectations." But, besides extending eligibility to spouses and "some family members" of key government officials and providing health care and prescription drug assistance to victims, the act did not offer any new alternatives.[12] The benefits were kept to a minimum, and a large portion of the population affected by the war and the dictatorship was excluded from the protections of these measures.

Both acts were "reformed" by a new decree published by the Basque government in 1986. Among other announcements, the new resolution stated that the presidency of the Spanish government had interpreted the acts of 1983 and 1985 as unconstitutional and had sent the case to the Constitutional Court for review, where the acts were pending a decision. It acknowledged for the first time, albeit indirectly, that failure to satisfy established "expectations" had doubly victimized the victims. To amend mistakes, financial assistance programs were expanded to "anyone who had worked for the Basque Public Administration during that period of time."[13]

Except for several mentions in an act of 1994, the Basque Parliament approved almost no significant piece of legislation on the matter until after the turn of the century. Not even between 1986 and 1989, when the fiftieth anniversary of the Civil War and the third Spanish legislature—led by the Spanish Socialist Party (PSOE) after a majority victory in Congress—overlapped from beginning to end. Spain accomplished little; during this period, the country only passed an act and a royal decree on "historical memory," which addressed highly specific communities, and a decree concerning union assets, which touched on the subject indirectly.[14]

The royal decree modified two rules of 1984 and 1985 about the pensions of former military and Customs Guard members of the Republic. Barely half a column long, the decree, announced in the Official State Gazette (BOE), confirmed that the government kept missing the mark on the design and implementation of memory-related public policies. The announcement mentioned the "complaints" made against the rule, along with the "challenges" of the implementation process. By then, some victims had already been receiving benefits for a year.[15] The decree admitted that the Amnesty Act and the acts of 1978 and 1980 had unfairly favored professional military personnel by immediately granting them "retired" status.[16] Announcements aside, perhaps what is most remarkable about this decree is that it marks the first time that voices advocating for moral reparations were heard in Congress, following the proposals of Catalan representatives.[17]

The fourth Spanish legislature from 1989 to 1993 with Socialist Felipe González as president had a minimal impact on the BAC in the short term. In the long term, however, the consequences of an unsuccessful legislation burdened the autonomous communities for a full decade. In 1990, President González allocated a portion of the budget to monetary reparations directed at people older than sixty-five years who had been imprisoned during the war and the Franco dictatorship. The ramifications of this measure are only comparable to the high percentage of rejected applications it produced. Of the more than one hundred thousand applications submitted, more than half were rejected, leaving 41,162. Ninety-two percent were rejected because of insufficient evidence of victimhood. Under these circumstances, more than half of the Spanish autonomous communities decided to create regional legislation to address the problem, including the BAC in 2002. But the rejection percentage remained high across the board. In the autonomous community of Aragon, 53 percent of the applications were rejected, and 48 percent in Castilla la Mancha.[18]

As mentioned, the BAC's institutional inaction about memory in the 1990s was rattled only by the approval of an act in 1994 in the fifth Spanish legislature (1993–1996). Congress passed several "historical memory" acts, including the act related to union assets; the act concerning political prisoners; the act on Spanish nationality of members of the International Brigades; and, lastly, the act that came into effect as a result of a motion introduced by a senator representing the Basque Nationalist Party EAJ (Euskal Alderdi Jeltzalea) and which sought to mend "the awful situation of the so called 'children of the war' " in Russia. A year after the motion was discussed in the Senate, the BAC passed an act to address the needs of Basque communities in foreign countries. In the preamble, the act contended that many Basques had been forced into exile during the Civil War. Starting from the eighteenth century, the act briefly summarized the history of Basque exile, cited war as the main contributor to the creation of Basque communities outside of the Basque Country, and concluded by pointing out that the defense of "freedom and democracy" had driven Basques to exile.[19]

In spring of 1996, things began to change dramatically. The conservative party Partido Popular (PP) won the general elections, and José María Aznar became president of Spain.[20] The new political environment sparked concerns over the treatment of Spain's recent past and the issue of victim reparations, which have kept mounting to this day. Although the 1996–2000 legislature was not prolific in terms of historical memory legislation, it predetermined the course of future regulations on the matter. Only three decrees and one act were approved; two of the decrees complemented each other, and the third one expanded on the act related to "the Spanish emigrant community."

The decree of 1999 granting people access to the General Archive of the Spanish Civil War was the most important. It reflected the growing interest in historical memory among scholars and the public, and it expressed the need to reclassify all documentation tied to a key episode in modern history. Additionally, it argued that the war and its far-reaching consequences had profoundly altered the history of the country. The decree was best remembered, however, for having heightened tensions existing since at least 1979 between the Catalan and the Spanish governments over documents confiscated from the Catalans during the war.[21]

In the same legislature, the Spanish Parliament enacted the first act acknowledging wartime repression, proving that designing an act of such characteristics was actually feasible. The Act for the Restitution of and Compensation for the Assets and Rights Seized to Political Parties between 1936 and 1939 was approved in 1998, and it was followed by a complementary decree a year later.[22] The resulting legal proceedings were in place until 2006 and pertained to the reparations owed to wartime political parties, as prescribed by the act. The scope of recognitions set by this rule was broader than any previous act addressing the whole of society. Thanks to it, fourteen political parties, including some with representation in the Basque government, received substantial financial compensations.[23]

The conversation over the recognition of victims of repression started gaining traction during PP's first legislature and intensified by the second legislature, with a stronger presence in parliamentary debates and in the streets. The issue began to be explored from a new more purposeful perspective, and the victims and/or their family members became central figures of the social and public conversation. These situations originated in a context of frustration against PP's policies and the conservatives' treatment of Spain's recent past.[24]

ETA was an additional player to consider in the Basque and Spanish social and political arena. Short for *Euskadi Ta Askatasuna* (Basque Country and Freedom), ETA was a Basque separatist organization that sought an independent Basque state by means of terrorism.[25] When PP's member Miguel Ángel Blanco was kidnapped and murdered, "the response from the community was unprecedented." ETA victims "turned into political subjects" and achieved a level of social relevance unlike any other group of victims had before. Legislators proceeded in accordance with the new context. The anti-terrorist pact signed between PP and PSOE in 2001 was a clear example of the shift: "Victims of terrorism are our chief concern."[26] Within a short period of time, this change in focus produced a new legal framework inclusive of "all" victims: victims of the war, the dictatorship, and of "terrorism." It has yet to consider all groups of victims equally, however.[27]

PP's majority in both chambers of Congress after the general election of early 2000 only triggered increased demands for change on this subject and disapproval toward the government's memory policies.[28] The role of PSOE as an opposition party changed, too. Scant legislation on historical memory was passed during this legislature. Only two acts were approved: one tied to the General Archive, in 2001 and the other, in 2002, concerning the documentation centers of the Civil War, which the Memory Act of 2007 ultimately repealed.

Because of their majority in Congress, PP blocked almost every one of the bill proposals initiated by the other political parties. EAJ's non-legislative motion to "condemn" the 1936 coup was introduced in the Lower House in 2001 and approved by Congress in November 2002. So was a proposal regarding the Valley of the Fallen. But, overall, the conservative bench smothered most of more than a dozen bills.[29]

Meanwhile, in the BAC, a new era of institutional support for memory policies was ushered in after Basque Nationalist Juan José Ibarretxe took over the presidency of the Basque government in January 1999. During his second legislature from 2001 to 2005, Parliament promulgated three decrees related to repression during the war and the dictatorship. The fourth decree was enacted in 2006. The decrees captured a change in how the community and the institutions perceived historical memory by including, along with other things, several legal aspects related to social recognition. Note that the BAC was quicker to grant this kind of recognition than the central government of Madrid.

In November 2001, the Basque Parliament revisited a case pending resolution since 1990. Through the unanimous approval of a non-legislative motion, the Basque government was compelled to provide benefits and social recognition to those who were imprisoned or persecuted during the dictatorship and could not benefit from the national legislation.[30] As a consequence of this agreement, the Basque government enacted two rules, one in 2002 and the other in 2003.[31]

The act of March 27, 2002, stipulated that the teachers of *ikastolas* (schools in which the educational program is fully taught in Basque) who had worked until the school year of 1967/68 should receive "recognition" and "monetary reparations," arguing education in Basque would not have been possible without the dedication of professional and volunteer instructors, who worked in a context of danger, scarcity, and harsh secrecy. The applicants, or their surviving spouses, had to show proof of at least one school year of teaching in Basque. As strange as it may seem, the amount of the monetary reparations was not specified in the same act of 2002, but in the decree published by the Basque government in 2003.[32]

Designed as a development of the act of 2002, the decree of May 6, 2003, reemphasized the courageous and dangerous work of *ikastola* instructors and their precarious working and living conditions. It allocated 3,000 euros to each former instructor per school year, 2,000 of which would make up for their inability to contribute to Social Security during their working years. Ways to furnish proof of teaching experience were significantly simplified: instructors needed either "affidavits from two witnesses," these could be teachers, students, or parents, or an official report of sanction, arrest, or police statement against them "as a consequence of their occupation."[33] Arguably, the writers of the 2003 decree learned to elude the obstacles faced by the preceding act related to political prisoners.

In November 2002, between the first and second pieces of legislation on *ikastola* teachers, the Basque government introduced a decree announcing monetary reparations for political prisoners of the war and the dictatorship. It was rooted in profusely rebuked national legislation and was influenced by a 1995 Navarrese decree. In it, the Navarrese ombudsman exhorted all autonomous communities to offer support for this group of victims from within their own territories. In the opening statement, the Basque government declared "respect" for the victims and stated that "never will any reparation be able to restore what victims and their families lost to repression and imprisonment in their quest for freedom." The decree was thoroughly developed in the following four years.

No other previous Basque act had included such a statement. The decree also meant to provide monetary reparations to the individuals who had been "unable to benefit" from national legislation, which was nearly all the victims. With it, the government acknowledged failure. Under this new code, victims had to have been sentenced "to a penal or correctional institution or a concentration camp" for a minimum of six months. The only caveat was that applicants had to be sixty-five years of age or older by December 31, 1990. Spouses and children with disabilities were also eligible candidates. The Basque government apportioned a total of 3.6 million euros to the measure and established a maximum sum of 10,000 euros per applicant.

Although it was a well-intentioned act on paper, requirements proved difficult to meet. Victims were asked to provide, among other documents, a certificate specifying their confinement dates issued by a civil or military penal authority; and a certificate of the "judgment of court or administrative resolution" that interpreted the charges leading to imprisonment to be within the scope of the Amnesty Act of 1977. The resolution of the call for applications, published in May 2004, showed that 71 percent of the applications had been rejected.

The outcome pointed, once again, to a clear double victimization of the victims of the war and the dictatorship. Forty-seven percent of the rejected applications were not accompanied by the required documents[34] because most of the victims could not have access to them. The massive number of appeals filed against the resolution, however, forced the government to grant benefits to close to a half of the total of applicants. The allocated budget for the first call for applications had to be increased to 21 million euros. The decree may have been in itself the best example of the failures of preceding jurisprudence. Legislators seemed oblivious to the faulty cycle of memory legislation where, time after time, a newly introduced act failed to meet the established expectations, left many victims out, and, ultimately, had to be replaced by a more complete and further developed act.[35]

That year, the Basque government, in collaboration with the scientific association *Sociedad de Ciencias Aranzadi*, created and tasked an interdepartmental commission with locating and identifying execution victims of the Civil War. The project meant a great step forward in the process of exhumations, and it opened the door to sharing the worries and experiences of pain of victims and their families with society at large. After this first agreement, Basque and Spanish institutions engaged several times in collaborative agreements with other associations to exhume the remains of Civil War victims.[36] Thanks to this agreement, the BAC has witnessed fifty successful exhumations, the majority of which happened in Bizkaia (Vizcaya), and the recovery of 110 victims.[37]

The next decree was published in 2006. Like several others before, it was designed to offset the deficiencies contained in a previous act. In particular, the 2006 decree revamped the 2002 act concerning political prisoners. It protected individuals sent to the *Batallones Disciplinarios de Soldados Trabajadores* (Disciplinary Battalions of Working Soldiers, BDST) by granting them the same benefits and reparations that the victims protected by the 2002 act had received.[38] An additional 10 million euros were allotted to the program, and victims had a three-month window to apply.

The rule was drafted because legislators could no longer ignore the growing dimensions of the issue. The 2006 decree, which filled the legislative gaps of the acts of 2002 and 2004, acknowledged past failures and included the following statement: "Factors such as age and difficulty in obtaining the required documentation may have forced applicants (. . .) to submit their applications past the deadline, which defeats the rule's fundamental purpose of moral recognition."[39]

"MORAL" RECOGNITION FOR "ALL" (2004–2014)

The new Spanish government of April 2004 led by Socialist José Luis Rodríguez Zapatero was transformative for the historical memory movement and brought sweeping changes to national memory legislation.

In September, Congress endorsed the creation of an interdepartmental commission to "study the circumstances of individuals who suffered reprisals during the war and the dictatorship as punishment for their commitment to Democracy." The eventual report included a draft bill that sought "to adopt the appropriate measures to provide moral recognition and reparations to the victims."[40]

Because of its strong emphasis on the need to understand the situation of the victims of the war and the dictatorship, to counteract the consequences of ineffective past policies, and, especially, to grant moral recognition to individuals who had been overlooked by previous similar efforts, the bill rose above prior memory legislation, even when its main purpose differed from the rest. It could be argued that public institutions started listening to the demands of different social factions.

Legislation on historical memory achieved unprecedented status after this bill. The coinciding celebrations and commemorations in connection with the Spanish Republic and the Civil War, such as the seventieth and seventy-fifth anniversaries of the proclamation of the Republic and the beginning of the war, or the sixtieth anniversary of the universal declaration of human rights raised the visibility of these historical events. As a result, the public had the chance to engage in a more thorough examination of its recent past. The acts introduced during this period mentioned such dates.[41] All the more so when, on March 17, 2006, representatives of forty-three countries signed an agreement at the Parliamentary Assembly of the Council of Europe to "strongly condemn the extensive and wide-ranging human rights abuses committed by the Franco regime in Spain from 1939 to 1975," and declared "July 18 the official day of condemnation of the Franco regime."[42]

While not the first, the exhumation in 2000 in the small town of Priaranza del Bierzo (León) of thirteen corpses dating back to 1936 attracted enormous media attention. Spanish society was deeply impressed by the discovery and the way the remains had been exhumed: a relative of one of the victims initiated the process, and a group of volunteers disinterred the bodies. Priaranza del Bierzo represented a breakthrough in Spain's recent history: it was the point of departure for recovering the scores of bodies everyone knew were buried and hidden on the side of the roads. Institutional obstacles shrank in importance. Society started to mobilize. In the BAC, too, where several grassroot movements made and keep making invaluable progress on the matter.[43]

The last years of the twentieth century and the first of the twenty-first saw the political coming of age of the younger generations.[44] The so-called grandchildren of the war, born during or soon after the Transition,[45] were critical of the agreements reached during that era and demanded a reinterpretation of the events. In addition, as social tensions built up in the aftermath of the global financial crisis of 2008, many members of the grandchildren generation led the protests that eventually spawned the 15M anti-austerity movement and Podemos, a new party to the left of the Spanish Socialist Party. In an increasingly inquisitive society, many struggled to fathom how all Francoists had been *forgiven* and allowed to continue controlling some state powers; how a monarch imposed by a dictator remained in power; how certain streets were still riddled with Francoist symbols; or how dictator Franco could still be buried in a mausoleum he had built for himself.

Spain's need to reopen the debate and fix its mistakes became especially dire after the arrest of Chilean dictator Augusto Pinochet in London on October 16, 1998, following an arrest warrant issued by a Spanish judge.[46] At that point, the country was at a crossroads: Spain was about to prosecute a Latin American dictator, but was unable to try any actor who had participated in the Franco dictatorship.[47] The intersection of multiple consequential events in a brief period of time helped rally the population and prompted a reconsideration of the status quo.[48]

In the BAC, Ibarretxe's administrations laid out the foundation of new public policies, which bore plenty of fruit during Zapatero's presidency. This thriving period was perhaps best embodied in President Ibarretxe's Plan for Peace and Reconciliation, introduced in June 2005 and approved by the Governing Council in May 2006.[49] The plan was conceived in the new scenario of ETA's permanent ceasefire of March 2005. Based on fundamentals such as respect of human rights and "the right to live," the plan introduced the idea of "politically motivated violence" and included a recognition of "victims of Francoism" and their "memory."[50] Following the public awareness campaign for human rights launched in December 2005,[51] the BAC adopted a human rights approach in the treatment of all victims, regardless of type or historical period.

On the seventieth anniversary of the constitution of the first Basque government and the failed coup against the Republican government of Spain, the Basque government directed its focus to the memory of the victims of the Civil War, the Franco dictatorship, and that of the victims of the state, in general, with a program meant to "commemorate and honor victims of Francoism." A number of commemorative events were scheduled as part of the plan and several tribute sculptures were built and placed throughout the autonomous community.[52] One objective of the plan weighed in on "the debt" incurred during and owed since the Transition, and stated that "Spain had the duty to mend a historical injustice" and to help "repair the moral and financial damages caused to the victims as a result of repression and the Franco dictatorship."[53] It also mentioned the future "Historical Memory Act" several times. The Basque government was well aware of the need of a national memory act since 1990, by means of a series of reports.

Regulation on the memory of the war and the dictatorship gained momentum between 2005 and 2010 with the approval of about thirty acts and decrees at the national level and twenty at the regional level. Still, some of the acts, decrees, and regulations introduced in the first three years of this prolific period were revisions or updates of prior regulation, whether they were on the rights of exiled Spaniards, the assets of unions and political parties (2007), the individuals who were deprived of their freedom, or Spanish citizenry. Of particular significance was the act of July 7, passed in 2006 in commemoration of the "75th anniversary of the Spanish Republic," because it designated the year 2006 as "the Year of Historical Memory."[54] The aim of an ensuing royal decree of 2007 was to create the Historical Memory Documentary Center.

But, clearly, the most important decision of President Zapatero's first legislature was the Historical Memory Act, of December 26, 2007. Of strong symbolic name, the rule was the product of an almost three-decade-long process. Under this act, monetary reparations no longer sufficed; it aspired "to recognize and expand rights to the victims who were persecuted and/or suffered violence during the war and the dictatorship due to their political, ideological, or religious ideas and beliefs; and sought to foster the moral recognition of the victims and the restoration of their and their families' memories."[55]

Besides overtly addressing issues such as collective and individual "recognition," "reparations," and private and public memory, the Historical Memory Act also denounced persecutions for ideological reasons, and the illegitimacy of the courts and the "administrative-penal bodies" instituted during the war, along with the sentences and sanctions pronounced by them. At the same time, the text called for the revision of past legislation and talked about those who had died "defending democracy" as well as "freedom and democratic rights" until 1977. For the first time, the narrative that the Transition had been a peaceful reconciliation process was put into question.[56] Victim advocacy associations working to restore dignity to the victims of Francoism were acknowledged for their crucial role in the advancement of historical memory issues.

After two legislatures in power, PP's conservative government was unexpectedly defeated by PSOE, and now the stakes were high for Zapatero's Socialist government, and its memory act. The president's family was directly affected by the war, and he recalled his grandfather—executed during Spain's Second Republic—several times during his presidency. While it is undeniable that the Historical Memory Act made a substantially broader and more comprehensive interpretation of the events than any other act before it, it is also true that the act was heavily criticized by members of the opposition and memory associations alike. The UN special rapporteur may have been the most critical of it. Pablo de Greiff visited Spain "to know and evaluate the measures adopted" to redress the violations of human rights perpetrated during the war and the dictatorship until 1975. He asserted that, in his twenty years of professional experience, he had "never" come across a similar situation.[57] The report exhorted the state to "show a firm commitment" on this issue, while simultaneously highlighting the need to "extend the recognition and coverage of reparation programs to" all victims.[58]

In hindsight, considering none of the established expectations or goals were ever met, it is unequivocal that the Historical Memory Act never stood a realistic chance to change the partialities deeply embedded in the system since at least 1975. The act was the consummation of a long and complex process, and, while unsuccessful in many regards, it represented a milestone on the matter. To put it in numbers, the act inaugurated a fertile period between 2008 and 2009 in which almost twenty acts, decrees, provisions, and ministerial provisions were introduced. Collectively, they set nearly all previous measures right. The act of 2007 was used as the frame of reference for the majority of these (new) regulations.[59] Two ministerial provisions were perhaps the most relevant of the set: one mandating the removal of all Francoist symbols from government property,[60] and another ordering the opening of a bureau for the victims of the war and the dictatorship.[61] The Spanish Parliament promulgated two other resolutions in 2010: a decree regulating the military judicial archives, and a resolution that further developed the act of 2007 on citizenship eligibility by extending the original two-year period by a full year.[62]

The Historical Memory Act was at the basis of every decision on the issue in the BAC. The Basque Parliament did not promulgate any legislation on the victims of the war and the dictatorship while Socialist Francisco López was in charge from 2009 to 2012. The only exception was the decree on "victims of human rights violations and of other unjust distress inflicted in a context of politically motivated violence" passed on March 31, 2011.[63] The bill rebuked the "unjust" nature of the victims' suffering and underscored the BAC's long-standing commitment to "provide reparations" and restore "dignity" to the victims. Yet, a study of memory legislation in the BAC points to rather inconsistent outcomes. The bill, turned decree on June 12, 2012, introduced some innovative aspects and configured a chronological and ideological frame that would inform subsequent regional decisions. The text argued that victims from 1960 to 1978 had been equally victimized by "institutional oblivion" and urged them to submit their application to an assessment commission for evaluation within an eighteen-month submission period. Applicants could receive up to 135,000 euros in monetary reparations, and those applying on behalf of victims who had died because of human rights violations were eligible for the maximum amount.

The bill, however, does not explain the rationale for the proposed chronology. While December 28, 1978, marks the last day before the Spanish Constitution entered into force,[64] the year 1960 seems unjustified within the context of memory. The only historical event of significant memory value that year was the death of twenty-two-month-old Begoña Urroz after a bomb explosion at the train station of Donostia-San Sebastian. The fact is that, in the initial stages of the decree, part of the historiographical community together with several political sectors placed the blame for the bombing on ETA, even when it was already publicly known that the anti-fascist armed organization *Directorio Revolucionario Ibérico de Liberación* (Iberian Revolutionary Liberation Directory, DRIL) had been the perpetrator of the act.[65]

On that account, the rule would come to be the first in the BAC to remember Franco's era through a "terrorist" or an "anti-fascist" event, rather than by the dictatorship itself.[66] The 2017–2020 Action Program presented by Gogora, the Institute for Memory, Coexistence, and Human Rights, made it plain that the mindset behind the design of memory policies concerning Francoism centered on "terrorism": the timeline starting in 1960 "is marked by the historical period rife with the terrorism meted out by the different factions of ETA, by different chapters of illegal counter-terrorism and by breaches of human rights caused in a context of political motivation."[67] Apparently, that "terror events (. . .) before 1968 (. . .) were rare" is irrelevant.[68]

As mentioned, the decree informed (and misinformed) future political decisions and projects commissioned by Basque public institutions.[69] Consequentially, the centrality of the forty-year Francoist dictatorship on the BAC's recent history was dismissed and relegated to the background. The presence of ETA, as the main actor in the violation of human rights in the recent history of the BAC, is pivotal in the foundation of Gogora: "That framework of the end of terrorism in the Basque Country has been a context of opportunity."[70]

EPILOGUE (2014–PRESENT)

Memory legislation in the BAC really came of age in November 2014, when the Basque Parliament approved an act to create Gogora. The first board of directors was formed in October 2015. The backbone of the 2014 act was captured in the following observation from the text:

Public policies on memory must fuse and harmonize two fundamental principles: on the one hand, it must take ethical and political responsibility to remember, commemorate, share, and transmit a democratic memory; and, on the other, it must reflect in its structure the expression and participation of a plural society.[71]

Ever since its inception, Gogora has been entrusted with the management of memory projects. Although the institute dates its beginnings to as recently as 2007, the reality is that Gogora is the culmination of a long legislative history. The board of directors is formed by the president of the Basque government, the director of the institute, about twenty public officials, and three independent members "renowned for their successful promotion of memory and the defense of civil liberties." Their duties as board members include stewarding the project proposals previously brought forward in Parliament and fostering the completion of an array of projects to meet the goals set by memory policies. In its short life, Gogora has already become a success story both regionally and nationally for its work in the field of memory and in the research of human rights violations.[72]

Gogora has launched several action programs since 2015, all bound by the underlying theme of human rights violations.[73] The 2017 program unveiled eleven development initiatives to be implemented until 2020, and it established a distinction between Historical Memory (1936–1975) and Recent Memory (1960–2011). The 2017 program brought about several noteworthy projects, including awareness campaigns, DNA banks, exhumations of victims from the Valley of the Fallen, and the controversial school initiative *Herenegun*. The 2021 action program designed the activities for the following four years, from 2021 to 2024.

The bill on the Historical and Democratic Memory of the BAC, explored in the next chapter of this book, became a law in September 2023.

As observed throughout this chapter, a lot has changed regarding the legal framework for the regulation of the memory of the Civil War and the dictatorship since the Spanish Parliament first covered the subject. Lawmakers, too, faced a steep learning curve when answering the demands of social agents to reinstate the rights of victims became inevitable. Gradually, the issue of memory permeated society and acquired a more complex and broader meaning. Needless to say, thousands upon thousands of victims were neglected and forgotten by public officials and institutions before a mobilized society put a stop to their inaction. In the BAC, the massive marches censuring ETA that started in 1995, coupled with the support offered by public institutions to ETA victims, steered the design of major legislation on the memory of the war and the dictatorship in another direction. The only thing that remains unaltered are the restrictions imposed by the Amnesty Act of 1977.

The beginning of the new millennium clearly welcomed a more humane and moral legal framework that resulted from new legislation that placed human rights violations at the heart of every decision on the subject of memory. What started as exclusively monetary reparations progressively transformed into increased awareness for the needs of the victims, and it finally redressed the damages inflicted and granted the victims meaningful social recognition. However great these steps may be, not all victims who suffered human rights violations during the dictatorship are considered equal in the eyes of public institutions.

BIBLIOGRAPHY

Aguilar Fernández, Paloma. 2002. "Justicia, política y memoria: los legados del franquismo en la transición española." In *Las políticas hacia el pasado. Juicios, depuraciones, perdón y olvido en las nuevas democracias*. Edited by Alexandra Barahona de Brito, Paloma Aguilar Fernández and Carmen González Enríquez, 135–194. Madrid: Istmo.

———. 2008. *Políticas de memoria y memorias de la política*. Madrid: Alianza Editorial.

Baby, Sophie. 2012. *El mito de la transición pacífica*. Violencia y política en España 1975–1982. Madrid: AKAL.

Beaumont Esandi, Edurne and Mendiola Gonzalo, Fernando. 2004. "Batallones disciplinarios de soldados trabajadores: castigo político, trabajos forzados y cautividad." *Revista de Historia Actual* 2: 31–48.

Belaustegi, Unai and Irujo, Xabier. 2022. "Making Public Memory: The Public History of the Spanish Civil War and the Francoist Dictatorship in the Basque Country (1936–2015)." *The Public Historian* 44, no. 2: 8295.

Encarnación, Omar G. 2014. *Democracy Without Justice in Spain. The Politics of Forgetting*. Philadelphia: University of Pennsylvania Press.

Espinosa Maestre, Francisco. 2015. *Lucha de historias, lucha de memorias*. Sevilla: Aconcagua Libros.

Gómez Calderón, Guillermo. 2021. "El uso del pasado reciente del PNV en el congreso de los Diputados. 1977–2015." *Brocar* 45: 153–181.

Hernández Castrillo, Santiago ed. 2010. *Recopilación de normativa sobre Memoria Histórica*. Madrid: Ministerio de Justicia.

Ipiña Bidaurrazaga, Aritz. 2017. *Represión y terror franquista en la Diputación de Bizkaia: fusilamientos y depuración (1936–1976)*. Bilbo-Bilbao: Pamiela.

Landa Gorostiza, Jon-Mirena. 2018. "Políticas de víctimas de la violencia política en España y el País Vasco: una reflexión a la luz del holocausto." *Revista General de Derecho Penal* 29: 1–50.

Levi, Primo. 2014. *Los hundidos y los salvados*. Barcelona: Península.

López Romo, Raúl. 2014. Informe Foronda. Los contextos históricos del terrorismo en el País Vasco y la consideración social de sus víctimas. 1968–2010. Eusko Jaurlaritza-Gobierno Vasco, Instituto Valentín de Foronda, UPV/EHU: Vitoria-Gasteiz.

Rivera, Antonio. 2021. "La amnistía de 1977 y los debates sobre el pasado." *Clio & Crimen* 18: 155–171.

Urquijo, Mikel. 2006. "La memoria negada: la encrucijada de la vía institucional en el caso del Gobierno Vasco y las víctimas del franquismo." *Hispania Nova: Revista de historia contemporánea* 6 http://hispanianova.rediris.es/6/dossier/6d002.pdf (Accessed July 7, 2002).

Urquijo, Mikel. 2007. "Memoria y olvido de las víctimas del franquismo. Una propuesta para Bilbo-

Bilbao." *Bidebarrieta* 18: 41–60.
Various Authors. 2022. BegiradaK. Bases compartidas para la construcción social de la memoria en Euskadi. Bilbo-Bilbao: Gogora.

ANNEX: COMPLETE CITATIONS OF THE LEGISLATION REGULATING THE MEMORY OF THE SPANISH CIVIL WAR AND THE FRANCOIST DICTATORSHIP.

Act No. 48/1978, of October 7, which Amends the Official Secrets Act of April 5, 1968.
Act No. 7/1981, of June 30, on the Government Act.
Act No. 11/1983, of June 22, on the Labor Rights and Right to Welfare of the Personnel who Worked for the Basque Government.
Act No. 18/1984, of June 8, which Recognizes Prison Time Served for Reasons Stipulated under the Amnesty Act of October 25, 1977 as Time Worked, for Social Security Contribution Purposes.
Act No. 37/1984, of October 22, which Recognizes the Service Provided by and the Rights of Those who Fought for the Spanish Republic in the Armed Forces, Law Enforcement and the Customs Guard during the Civil War.
Organic Act No. 9/1984, of December 26, Against Actions by Armed Associations and Terrorist Groups, and in Continuation of Article 55.2 of the constitution.
Act No. 8/85, of October 23, which Complements Act 11/1983, of June 22, on the Labor Rights and Right to Welfare of the Personnel who Worked for the Basque Government
Legislative Decree No. 1/1986, of May 13, Approving the Recast Text on the Labor Rights and Right to Welfare of the Personnel who Worked for the Basque Government.
Royal Decree No. 255911986, of December 12, which Amends Article 11, number 2 of Royal Decree /03311985, of June 19.
Act No. 24/1986, of December 24, on the Reinstatement of Professional Military Personnel.
Act No. 14/1988, of October 28, on Payments to Senior Officials.
Act No. 8/1994, of May 27, on Relations with Basque Centers and Basque Communities Outside the Autonomous Community of the Basque Country.
Royal Decree No. 426/1999, of March 12, on the Creation of the General Archive of the Spanish Civil War.
Royal Decree No. 610/1999, of April 16, to Approve the Regulation of Act 43/1998, of December 15, on the Restitution and Compensation for the Assets and Rights Seized to Political Parties as a Result of the Act of Political Responsibilities Implemented between 1936 and 1939.
Act No. 3/2002, of March 27, on the Recognition and Reparations to *Ikastola* Instructors who Taught in Basque Schools before their Legalization.
Decree No. 99/2003, of May 6, which Develops the Act on the Recognition and Reparations to *Ikastola* Instructors who Taught in Basque Schools before their Legalization.
Decree No. 75/2004, of May 4, a Third Amendment of the Decree on Monetary Reparations to Individuals whose Freedom Was Curtailed for Reasons Prescribed in the Amnesty Act.
Royal Decree No. 1891/2004, of September 10, on the Creation of the Interministerial Commission to Study the Circumstances of the Victims of the War and the Dictatorship.
Decree No. 22/2006, of February 14, which Establishes Provisions to Provide Monetary Reparations to Individuals who were Deprived of their Freedom, Including those Sent to the Disciplinary Battalions of Working Soldiers, under the Same Conditions and Requirements Prescribed on Decree 280/2002, of November 19, on Reparations to People who were Deprived of their Freedom by Suppositions Appearing in the Amnesty Act, Except for the Procedural

Amendments Foreseen in this Rule.

Act No. 24/2006, of July 7, on the Declaration of the Year 2006 as the Year of Historical Memory.

Act No. 52/2007, of December 26, which Recognizes and Expands Rights, and Establishes Measures to Support Victims of Persecution or Violence during the Civil War and the Dictatorship.

Order CUL/3190/2008, of November 6, which Announces the Agreement of the Council of Ministers, of October 31, 2008, which Mandates the Removal of All Francoist Symbols from the Property of the General State Administration and its Subsidiary Public Agencies.

Order PRE/3749/2008, of December 22, which Announces the Agreement of the Council of Ministers on the Creation of a Bureau for the Victims of the Civil War and the Dictatorship.

Resolution of March 17, 2010, of the Undersecretary, Announcing the Agreement of the Council of Ministers of January 22, 2010, which Extends by One Year the Application Period to Request Spanish Citizenship Established in the Additional Provision n. 7 of the Act 52/2007, of December 26, which Recognizes and Expands Rights, and Establishes Measures to Support Victims of Persecution or Violence during the Civil War and the Dictatorship.

Decree No. 1/2011, of January 11, Amending Decree 31/2009, of February 10, on the Creation and Regulation of the Advisory Council for Human Rights Education and for Peace.

Decree No. 107/2012, of June 12, on the Recognition and Reparation to Victims of Unfair Suffering, as the Result of the Violation of their Human Rights, between 1960 and 1978, in the Context of the Politically Motivated Violence Experienced in the Autonomous Community of the Basque Country.

Act No. 4/2014, of November 27, on the Creation of the Institute for Remembrance, Coexistence and Human Rights.

Act No. 12/2016, of June 28, on the Recognition and Reparation to Victims whose Human Rights were Violated, between 1978 and 1999, in the Context of the Politically Motivated Violence Experienced in the Autonomous Community of the Basque Country.

Act No. 20/2022, of October 19, of Democratic Memory.

Bill on the Historical and Democratic Memory of the BAC (Accessed December 12, 2022): https://www.euskadi.eus/proyecto-ley/27-proyecto-de-ley-de-memoria-historica-y-democratica-de-euskadi/web01-s2enple/es/

NOTES

- Project: COD. PGC2018-095712-B-100.
1. Aritz Ipiña Bidaurrazaga, *Represión y terror franquista en la Diputación de Bizkaia: fusilamientos y depuración (1936–1976)* (Bilbo-Bilbao: Pamiela), 2017.
2. The comments of Xabier Arzalluz, the then-leader of the Basque Nationalist Party (EAJ) in the Spanish Congress, are illustrative of such compromise: "It is a critical step towards forgetting our past conflicts and in the direction of achieving some minimal harmony." Journal of Sittings, Congress of Deputies (CD), September 14, 1977 n. 8, 201. Ramón Jáuregui, a member of the Spanish Socialist Party (PSOE), shared a similar sentiment. See Omar G. Encarnación, *Democracy Without Justice in Spain: The Politics of Forgetting*, (University of Pennsylvania Press: Philadelphia, 2014), 50.
3. *Ley 48/1978, de 7 de octubre* [Act No. 48/1978, of October 7] (see bibliography for complete citations of the acts and decrees referenced in this article).
4. In *The Drowned and the Saved* (*I sommersi e i salvati*), Italian author Primo Levi talked about "deliberate oblivion" as something that occurs when the act of remembering turns too

	complex or painful and leads to the denial of the events. *Los hundidos y los salvados* (Península: Barcelona, 2014).
5	Juliá, Santos: "Echar el olvido" *El País*, June 15, 2022.
6	Professor Mikel Urquijo expanded on the matter: the payments issued by Spanish institutions during the first years and even decades [of democracy] are to be interpreted as social assistance payments rather than monetary reparations. The concept of reparations "implies an acknowledgement that the authorities who imposed those sentences were illegitimate, (. . .) which institutions have failed to do." Perhaps, the first time Spain assumed responsibility for such actions may have happened only recently when the government declared the dictatorship illegal. Legislation did evolve, though, in its understanding of victim recognition. Mikel Urquijo, "La memoria negada: la encrucijada de la vía institucional en el caso del Gobierno Vasco y las víctimas del franquismo," *Hispania Nova: Revista de historia contemporánea* 6 (2006), http://hispanianova.rediris.es/6/dossier/6d002.pdf (Accessed July 7, 2022).
7	Ley 37/1984, de 22 de octubre [Act No. 37/1984, of October 22.]
8	*Ley 18/1984, de 8 de junio [Act No. 18/1984 of June 8].* This article by Paloma Aguilar Fernández offers helpful insights on the matter: "Justicia, política y memoria: los legados del franquismo en la transición Española" in *Las políticas hacia el pasado. Juicios, depuraciones, perdón y olvido en las nuevas democracias*, ed. Alexandra Barahona de Brito, Paloma Aguilar Fernández y Carmen González Enríquez (Istmo: Madrid, 2002), 135–194; Paloma Aguilar Fernández, *Políticas de memoria y memorias de la política* (Alianza Editorial: Madrid, 2008). The Asociación para la Recuperación de la Memoria Histórica (Association for the Recovery of Historical Memory) offers valuable information on their site: https://memoriahistorica.org.es/2-2-pensiones-e-indemnizaciones/ (Accessed November 11, 2022).
9	Informe general de la comisión interministerial para el estudio de la situación de las víctimas de la guerra civil y del franquismo. July 28, 2006; 5.
10	*Ley 7/1981, de 30 de junio, 10.* [Act No. 7/1981, of June 30, 10.] Article 37 of the 1981 act referencing a 1983 act was repealed in 1988. *Ley 14/1988, de 28 de octubre.* [Act No. 14/1988, of October 28.]
11	*Ley 11/1983, de 22 de junio, 2268* [Act No. 11/1983, of June 22, 2268.]
12	*Ley 8/1985, de 23 de octubre* [Act No. 8/1985, of October 23.]
13	"Quienes en su día formaron parte de la Administración Pública Vasca, en cualquiera de sus niveles" *Decreto legislativo 1/1986, de 13 de mayo.* [Legislative Decree No. 1/1986, of May 13]
14	Santiago Hernández Castrillo (ed.), *Recopilación de normativa sobre Memoria Histórica* (Ministerio de Justicia: Madrid), 2010.
15	*Real Decreto 2559/1986 de 12 de diciembre.* [Royal Decree No. 2559/1986 of December 12.]
16	*Ley 24/1986, de 24 de diciembre.* [Act No. 24/1986, of December 24.]
17	Informe general de la comisión interministerial para el estudio de la situación de las víctimas de la guerra civil y del franquismo. July 28, 2006; 5.
18	Source: *Comisión Interministerial para el estudio de la situación de las víctimas de la Guerra Civil y el franquismo. Informe General* (Madrid, July 28, 2006), Annex 2: Actuaciones de las Comunidades Autónomas. See also Mikel Urquijo, "Memoria y olvido de las víctimas del franquismo. Una propuesta para Bilbo-Bilbao" *Bidebarrieta* 18 (2007); 48.
19	*Ley 8/1994, de 27 de mayo.* [Act No. 8/1994, of May 27.]
20	PP's victory was possible thanks to the endorsement of EAJ, among other political parties.
21	*Real Decreto 426/1999, de 12 de marzo.* [Royal Decree No. 426/1999, of March 12.]
22	*Real Decreto 610/1999, de 16 de abril.* [Royal Decree No. 610/1999, of April 16.]

23 Informe general de la comisión interministerial para el estudio de la situación de las víctimas de la guerra civil y del franquismo. July 28, 2006; 65.
24 Francisco Espinosa Maestre describes the events between 1996 and 2002 as "a rebirth of memory" in *Lucha de historias, lucha de memorias* (Aconcagua Libros: Seville, 2015); 108 and ss.
25 Britannica (last seen on August 24, 2023): https://www.britannica.com/topic/ETA.
26 Raúl López Romo, Informe Foronda. Los contextos históricos del terrorismo en el País Vasco y la consideración social de sus víctimas. 1968–2010 (Eusko Jaurlaritza, Instituto Valentín de Foronda, UPV/EHU: Gasteiz, 2014); 92.
27 An act explicitly mentioning "victims of terrorism" was promulgated in 1984: Ley 9/1984, de 26 de diciembre. [Act No. 9/1984, of December 26]. See the contrasting exercise between legal frameworks related to victims in Jon-Mirena Landa Gorostiza's "Políticas de victimas de la violencia política en España y el País Vasco: una reflexión a la luz del holocausto" *Revista General de Derecho Penal* 29 (2018); 19 and ss.
28 Such as the endowments provided by Mr. Aznar's administration to the Francisco Franco Foundation. A total of 150,841 euros were furnished between 2000 and 2003; *Público*, May 24, 2017.
29 Guillermo Gómez Calderón, "El uso del pasado reciente del PNV en el Congreso de los Diputados. 1977-2015" *Brocar* 45 (2021); 167. The Spanish newspaper *El Mundo* published an article on February 14, 2001, under this revealing headline: "El PP rechaza la condena al franquismo y a ETA propuesta por PNV, PSOE e IU." [PP rejects a proposal by PNV/EAJ, PSOE and the left-wing party Izquierda Unida (IU) to condemn Francoism and ETA's actions].
30 According to Mikel Urquijo, this agreement ended a process initiated in 1998, when the recognition of victims was brought forward for the first time: "La memoria negada: la encrucijada de la vía institucional en el caso del Gobierno Vasco y las víctimas del franquismo," *Hispania Nova: Revista de historia contemporánea* 6 (2006), http://hispanianova.rediris.es/6/dossier/6d002.pdf (Accessed July 7, 2022.)
31 The Basque provincial councils of Bizkaia, Araba (Álava), and Gipuzkoa enacted a series of regional acts addressed to the wounded or imprisoned during the war concerning individual income tax exemptions; *Informe general de la comisión interministerial para el estudio de la situación de las víctimas de la guerra civil y del franquismo*. July 28, 2006.
32 *Ley 3/2002, de 27 de marzo*. [Act No. 3/2002, March 27.]
33 *Decreto 99/2003, de 6 de mayo*. [Decree No. 99/2003, of May 6.] Navarre approved a similar regional rule in 2007.
34 Mikel Urquijo, "La memoria negada: la encrucijada de la vía institucional en el caso del Gobierno Vasco y las víctimas del franquismo," *Hispania Nova: Revista de historia contemporánea* 6 (2006), http://hispanianova.rediris.es/6/dossier/6d002.pdf (Accessed July 7, 2002.)
35 *Decreto 75/2004, de 4 de mayo*. [Decree No. 75/2004, of May 4.] Lack of foresight cannot justify this behavior because several historical memory associations tried to educate and caution the Basque government on the matter. That memory affairs were under the management of the Department of Housing and Social Affairs should be a revealing fact. Ararteko (the Basque ombudsman) "condemned" Minister Javier Madrazo (IU) for the "mistreatment" of the victims. *El País*, March 15, 2005.
36 See *Plan Vasco 2015-20 de investigación y localización de fosas para la búsqueda e identificación de personas desaparecidas durante la Guerra Civil*. Eusko Jaurlaritza: Vitoria-Gasteiz, 2015.
37 An additional forty-two remains of mostly Franco detractors were identified in the exhumation performed at the cemetery of Begoña, Bilbo-Bilbao. The last exhumation took place in

Mutriku on October 2, 2022, just as we were finishing this chapter; the remains found in the grave belonged to a Franco detractor. and his identification was possible thanks to the accounts of locals.

38 Edurne Beaumont and Fernando Mendiola's research work played a decisive role in this decision. They demonstrated that these battalions (Battalions of workers or BBTT and BDST) were, in fact, recruitment and punishment spaces, and never, as the Basque government posited, spaces for military service. "Batallones disciplinarios de soldados trabajadores: castigo político, trabajos forzados y cautividad," *Revista de Historia Actual* 2 (2004): 31–48.

39 "La edad de muchas de las personas solicitantes y las dificultades de obtención de documentación han dado lugar a que muchas personas, (. . .) hayan entregado su solicitud fuera del plazo previsto para ello dando lugar a que la reparación moral que la norma pretendía no haya podido llevarse a cabo en estos supuestos, siendo éste su objetivo primordial" *Decreto 22/2006 de 14 de febrero*. [Decree No. 22/2006, of February 14.]

40 "Estudiar la situación de los que, como consecuencia de su compromiso democrático, padecieron actuaciones represivas durante la guerra civil y el franquismo" "Regular medidas necesarias para ofrecer un adecuado reconocimiento y satisfacción moral a las víctimas" *Real Decreto 1891/2004, de 10 de septiembre*. [Royal Decree No. 1891/2004, of September 10.]

41 Several acts and decrees directly mention these special dates.

42 *El País*, March 18, 2006.

43 Unai Belaustegi and Xabier Irujo, "Making Public Memory: The Public History of the Spanish Civil War and the Francoist Dictatorship in the Basque Country (1936–2015)," *The Public Historian* 44/2 (2022): 82–95.

44 Paloma Aguilar Fernández wrote a thought-provoking article on the "generational issue" in relation to the Civil War; *Políticas de la memoria y memorias de la política* (Alianza Editorial: Madrid, 2008), 30–35.

45 Informe del Relator Especial sobre la promoción de la verdad, la justicia, la reparación y las garantías de no repetición, Pablo de Greiff, July 22, 2014.

46 "¿Qué cambió realmente con la detención de Pinochet en Londres?" *BBC Mundo, Cono Sur*, October 15, 2013.

47 Not long after, on April 14, 2010, Argentinian judge María R. Servini opened the case concerning the Francoist murders of 1937. In 2020, Servini took a statement from Rodolfo Martín Villa, former Francoist politician and former minister of interior during the Transition.

48 See, among others, Antonio Rivera's "La amnistía de 1977 y los debates sobre el pasado," *Clio & Crimen* 18 (2021): 155–171.

49 "Plan Integral en favor de la Paz y la Reconciliación, que contemple y aglutine todas las actuaciones a desarrollar por el Ejecutivo en el ámbito de los derechos humanos" Gobierno Vasco, June 22, 2005. This plan contained manifold mentions to the "70th anniversary." In 2007, the Basque government promoted the "Plan vasco de educación para la paz y los Derechos Humanos (2008–2011)" which was later broken into several other plans, including the "Plan de Paz y Convivencia 2013–2016," Gobierno Vasco, November 2013.

50 See, Jon-Mirena Landa, Informe sobre Víctimas de Vulneraciones de Derechos Humanos derivadas de la Violencia de Motivación Política, Eusko Jaurlaritza, Vitoria-Gasteiz, 2008.

51 See, for instance, *Decreto 1/2011, de 11 de enero* [Decree No. 1/2011, of January 11.]

52 *Decreto 22/2006 de 14 de febrero*. [Decree No. 22/2006, of February 14.]

53 "Estado tiene que reparar esta injusticia histórica" "reparar, moral y económicamente, el daño causado por la represión y la dictadura franquista." "Plan Integral en favor de la Paz y la

Reconciliación, que contemple y aglutine todas las actuaciones a desarrollar por el Ejecutivo en el ámbito de los derechos humanos" Gobierno Vasco, June 22, 2005; 46–49.

54 *Ley 24/2006, de 7 de julio.* [Act No. 24/2006, of July 7.]

55 "Reconocer y ampliar derechos a favor de quienes padecieron persecución o violencia, por razones políticas, ideológicas, o de creencia religiosa, durante la Guerra Civil y la Dictadura, promover su reparación moral y la recuperación de su memoria personal y familiar" *Ley 52/2007, de 26 de diciembre.* [Act No. 52/2007, of December 26.]

56 Interesting revisions of the Transition in Sophie Baby's *El mito de la transición pacífica. Violencia y política en España 1975–1982* (AKAL: Madrid, 2012) and Omar G. Encarnación's *Democracy without justice in Spain: The Politics of Forgetting*, (University of Pennsylvania Press: Pennsylvania, 2014).

57 *El País*, February 3, 2014.

58 Report of the special rapporteur on the promotion of truth, justice, reparation, and guarantees of non-recurrence, Pablo de Greiff, July 22, 2014.

59 Memory legislation related to the war and the dictatorship is still being built against the baseline of this act to this day, including the most recent Democratic Memory Act and the bill on Historical and Democratic Memory of BAC.

60 *Orden CUL/3190/2008, de 6 de noviembre.* [Ministry of Culture's Provision CUL/3190/2008, of November 6].

61 *Orden PRE/3749/2008, de 22 de diciembre.* [Ministry of the Presidency's Provision PRE/3749/2008, of December 22].

62 Resolution of March 17, 2010.

63 *Decreto 107/2012, de 12 de junio.* [Decree No. 107/2012, of June 12.]

64 About these chronological boundaries, the act suggested to leave "the extension of this victim support policy for a later legislative period." *Ley 12/2016, de 28 de junio* [Act No. 12/2016, of June 28, 2016.]

65 Check the stimulating discussion on historiography between historians Emilio Majuelo and Antonio Rivera on *Segle XX: revista catalana d'història*, n. 13 (2020).

66 Note that victims of state violence—whether it was at the hands of the Franco regime or of the constitutional state—feel disregarded by this act, citing a diminished definition of their victimhood over that of the rest of the victims. The act defines them as victims of "police abuse." See Vv.Aa. *BegiradaK. Bases compartidas para la construcción social de la memoria en Euskadi.* Gogora: Bilbo-Bilbao, 2022.

67 "Está marcada por el tiempo histórico protagonizado por el terrorismo de las distintas ramas de ETA, así como el terrorismo del GAL y otros grupos de extrema derecha y vulneraciones de derechos humanos causados en un contexto de motivación política," *Action Program 2017-2020. Consejo de Dirección del Instituto de la Memoria, la Convivencia y los Derechos Humanos,* Gogora-Gobierno Vasco, s/f, 41.

68 "Hechos de terrorismo (. . .) con anterioridad a 1968 (. . .) fueron aislados," Raúl López Romo, *Informe Foronda. Los contextos históricos del terrorismo en el País Vasco y la consideración social de sus víctimas. 1968–2010*, Eusko Jaurlaritza-Gobierno Vasco, Instituto Valentín de Foronda, UPV/EHU: Vitoria-Gasteiz, 2014.

69 Two clear examples of this: Forensic Paco Etxeberria's and his team's work on torture analyzes cases occurred after 1960. Similarly, the research team who authored the 2022 document "Bases compartidas para la construcción social de la memoria en Euskadi" set the year 1960 as

the starting point of their chronological frame, even though the call for projects did not specify a date, it mentioned only "recent memory."

70 "Este marco de final de terrorismo en Euskadi representa un contexto de oportunidad," *Action Program 2017–2020. Consejo de Dirección del Instituto de la Memoria, la Convivencia y los Derechos Humanos*, Gogora-Gobierno Vasco, s/f, 8.

71 Ley 4/2014, de 27 de noviembre. [Act No. 4/2014, of November 27.] See Gogora Institute's Articles: Decreto 204/2015, de 3 de noviembre, de Estatutos del Instituto de la Memoria, la Convivencia y los Derechos Humanos. [Decree No. 204/2015, of November 3, of Articles of Association of the Institute for Remembrance, Coexistence and Human Rights.]

72 See Various Authors BegiradaK. Bases compartidas para la construcción social de la memoria en Euskadi, Gogora: Bilbo-Bilbao, 2022.

73 This action program was built upon previous plans designed by the Basque government. The first one was executed between 2013 and 2016.

two

The Historical Memory Act of 2022 of the Autonomous Community of the Basque Country

Xabier Irujo

After the demise of the dictatorship in the wake of General Francisco Franco's death in November 1975, the Congress of Deputies and the Senate enacted the Spanish Constitution on October 31, 1978. Ensuingly, the Autonomous Community of the Basque Country (the BAC) was constituted and its Statute of Autonomy approved by virtue of Organic Act 3/1979, of December 18.[1] In a short time, starting in 1983, the Basque Parliament began to introduce legislative initiatives on historical memory meant to redress the painful consequences of the Civil War and the repressive measures of the Francoist dictatorship. Such initiatives were developed per Article 9 of the Statute of Autonomy which enables Basque public authorities to "watch over and guarantee the proper exercise of the citizens' fundamental rights and duties, and to adopt measures aimed at promoting favorable conditions and removing obstacles in such a way that the freedom and equality of the individual and of the groups of which he forms part may be effective and real."[2]

Public policies concerning the recognition of Franco-era victims and the efforts to elucidate the past entered a bountiful era in 2000, twenty-five years after the death of Franco, through a plan to locate and exhume mass graves. The plan put the BAC at the European forefront of historical memory matters. On December 10, 2002, the Governing Council of the BAC created an interdepartmental commission to investigate and locate the graves of those who disappeared during the War of 1936. A few months later, in 2003, the Department of Justice of the Basque government signed a collaboration agreement with the scientific association *Sociedad de Ciencias Aranzadi* (Aranzadi), a nonprofit organization trailblazing the exhumations of mass graves of the Francoist dictatorship (1936–1975).

In 2007, the Spanish Parliament, headed by the Spanish Socialist Party (PSOE), approved Act 52/2007, of December 26, which recognized and expanded rights for victims, and established measures to support victims of the Civil War and the dictatorship who were persecuted or subjected to violence because of their political leanings, ideology, or religious beliefs. The act, formed by twenty-two articles and eight additional provisions, addressed ten aspects of historical memory that urgently needed attention:

a. Recognizing victims to acknowledge and denounce the "unjust nature of all convictions, sanctions and expressions of personal violence produced, for (. . .) political, [religious] or ideological reasons."[3]
b. Proclaiming the illegitimacy of the courts, juries, and bodies of any administrative nature constituted during the dictatorship from 1936 to 1978.
c. Recognizing the right to obtain a declaration of personal reparation and recognition to those who were subjected to the rulings mentioned in the preceding articles during the war and the dictatorship.
d. Compensations:

- It established a monthly pension of 132.86 euros for all nondisabled orphans over the age of 21 whose circumstances had been caused by personnel other than civil servants as established by acts 5/1979, of September 18, and 35/1980, of June 26.
- It compensated political prisoners for their time served during the dictatorship: 6,010.12 euros for over three years of prison time, and 1,202.02 euros for each additional three-year period served.
- It provided financial assistance to correct the tax burden derived from the compensations issued since January 1, 1999, to individuals who had been deprived of their freedom in the cases listed in Act 46/1977, of October 15, of Amnesty.
- It acknowledged the right to be compensated with 135,000 euros to beneficiaries of individuals who had lost their lives between January 1, 1968, and December 31, 1977, while defending and proclaiming democratic rights and freedoms.

e. Developing measures to encourage collaboration in the task of locating and identifying victims between public agencies and individuals.
f. Removing Francoist symbols and monuments.
g. Banning all events praising the War of 1936 and/or Francoism.
h. Recognizing victim advocacy associations.
i. Creating a General Archive of the War of 1936 and a Historical Memory Documentary Center.
j. Granting Spanish nationality to children of exiled nationals and to volunteer members of the International Brigades.[4]

In the plenary session on March 31, 2011, the Basque Parliament passed Non-Legislative Motion 61/2011 in support of victims who had suffered human rights violations and unfair distress in a context of politically motivated violence. This motion prompted the Basque government to adopt measures and initiatives to recognize these victims and redress their suffering.[5] A year later, the Basque government signed Decree 107/2012, of June 12, on the recognition and reparation to victims subjected to unfair suffering because of the violation of their human rights between 1960 and 1978, in a context of politically motivated violence in the BAC.

Act 4/2014, of November 27, which created Gogora, the Institute for Remembrance, Coexistence, and Human Rights, significantly aided in the institutionalization of memory-related public policies in the BAC. With this law, Gogora became the official agency through which to further, in a comprehensive and articulated manner, all Basque public policies related to historical memory.[6] The institute was born with the fundamental mission of channeling, promoting, and shaping an open community dialogue that would couple memories with past experiences of social and political trauma. Gogora aimed to help build a dynamic, productive community based on shared values, with the goal of achieving greater equality. As established in Article 3 of the law, Gogora was to design, develop, promote, and execute public policies related to the ethical values and democratic principles that best embodied the protection of human rights, the democratic harmony of Basque society, and the memory of the fight for freedom. The institute would be a proactive supporter of the political and social values that push society to understand and be aware of the sustained efforts made throughout the decades to defend freedom and the development of democracy. In addition, it would watch over the preservation, development, and transmission of the collective heritage of the BAC, which involves the memory of those who defended the principles and values that underpin democratic harmony today—and the precious first-hand accounts of victims of historic events. Lastly, Gogora would disseminate and defend human rights and values of peace.[7]

As per the new law, Gogora came to be "a memory center," an agency commissioned to work with the community on an ethical road map toward memory. The makers of the act justify the need for a memory center by reasoning that, while the right to memory extends to the whole of society—citizens being as they are the inherent builders and heirs of history, remembrance, and memory—oblivion impedes recognition, imposes a particular version of the past, and induces an ethical vacuum.[8] Following this idea, the public policy on memory and social harmony did not have only victims in mind but society in its entirety.

The law of November 2014, which constituted Gogora, grouped memory policy-making under the umbrella of an institutional subject and configured its responsibilities in terms of promoting memory policies at a structural level. The board of directors of Gogora approved its first action program for 2015–2016 on October 19, 2015, and the 2017–2020 program on October 23, 2017. This last one incorporates six initiatives that have currently put in place a wide-ranging set of public policies concerning historical memory, including a report on the human rights violations that occurred between 1936 and 1978 prepared by the institute in partnership with the general secretariat of human rights, social harmony, and cooperation; the University of the Basque Country; and the Aranzadi Society of Sciences. Since its formation in 2015, Gogora has launched an assortment of educational and research projects on historical memory and celebrated several events to recognize and pay tribute to victims of the Civil War and Francoism.

As a continuation of the 2012 decree, the Basque Parliament approved Act 12/2016, of July 28, 2016, on the recognition and reparation to victims whose human rights were violated between 1978 and 1999 in a context of politically motivated violence in the BAC. The third additional provision granted retroactive protection to those individuals who, even when they met the eligibility criteria established in Decree 107/2012, had not requested recognition or reparations, or had done so out of the application period. The Spanish government, at the time led by Mariano Rajoy, a member of the conservative party Partido Popular (PP), appealed several articles of the law to the Constitutional Court.

The law was paralyzed for several years between 2011 and 2017, coinciding with the two legislatures of Rajoy. Then, PSOE brought a non-legislative motion to Congress for the effective enforcement and development of the Historical Memory Act (162/000327), which was signed into law in May 2017, passed on a 198–1 vote, with 140 abstentions.[9] The law was designed to amend some major deficiencies of Act 52/2007. Several proposals were put forward for consideration: first, that the state should take over the duties of locating, exhuming, and identifying the remains found in mass graves; second, that DNA banks should be created; and third, that a bureau for the victims of the war and the dictatorship should be opened to coordinate all memory-related efforts through one central agency. The motion aimed to revise regulation on archive accessibility, for standardization and increased research purposes. Family members and victim advocacy associations received greater institutional, legal, and financial support, while associations glorifying the dictator or anti-democratic values were excluded from public grant programs. The last two proposals entailed the establishment of a truth commission and the proclamation of November 11 (the European Day Against Fascism) as the Remembrance Day of Franco-era Victims.

A compromise amendment to the Non-Legislative Motion 10/2018, on the legal instruments related to public policies concerning historical memory, was tabled in the Basque Parliament on February 15, 2018. In response, Parliament gave Gogora eight months to prepare a report to evaluate the need for a Basque historical memory law. Gogora was additionally asked to commission a report to analyze the strengths and weaknesses of the current legal and institutional frameworks to correct any identified deficiencies. The non-legislative motion introduced by the Basque Nationalist Party (EAJ) and the Basque Socialist Party (PSE-EE) was endorsed by all the political parties except for the PP, which stood against drafting a future Basque law on historical memory.[10]

Gogora commissioned this report to researchers Francisco Ferrándiz and Marije Hristova from the Spanish National Research Council (CSIC) on April 10, 2018. The conclusions of their research were presented to the Basque Parliament on October 29, 2018, in a report titled *Valoración comparada de las políticas públicas de Memoria Histórica en Euskadi (2000–2018)* (Comparative assessment of historical memory public policies of the BAC (2000–2018)). The report encouraged Basque institutions to build a new legal framework that would lay the groundwork for the legal consolidation of the bundle of initiatives put into effect thus far, and for their promotion, expansion, and judicial development.[11] A historical memory act would mainly seek to complement the Gogora act of 2014, because the latter defined only the "who," namely, the institutional subject and its responsibilities in the development of memory policies, but failed to stipulate the "what," the scope of action for such policies in the BAC. The creators of the report contended the new law would fill this void and ultimately confer consonant purpose to public policies and reinforce their legal entity. Driven by their conclusions, Gogora requested an initial draft of the Historical Memory Act from expert adviser Eduardo Barrera.[12]

After the three-year interim caused by the COVID-19 pandemic, Iñigo Urkullu, the *lehendakari* (president) of the BAC, addressed the Basque Parliament during a plenary session of June 2022 to endorse the bill on Democratic and Historical Memory of the BAC. Regarding the victims of the War of 1936 and the ensuing Francoist dictatorship, Urkullu underscored that the act aspires to "restore the dignity of the forgotten victims, reinstate violated rights and mend injustices." The draft bill received the support of EAJ, PSE-EE, and the Basque Democratic Socialist parties EH Bildu and Elkarrekin Podemos-IU. Vox, the party of the far right and the coalition of the conservative parties PP and Ciudadanos each tabled amendments rejecting the draft bill entirely, but they were unsuccessful and the project moved forward.[13]

According to Article 3 of Presidential Decree 36/2019, of November 26, which mandates the writing of the draft bill on the Democratic and Historical Memory of the BAC, this rule seeks to "promote moral reparations and recover the personal and family memories of those who experienced persecution or violence during the Civil War and the Dictatorship due to their political affiliation, ideology or religion; and tries to raise awareness of democratic values and principles by providing access to education on the events that unfolded during the time period comprising the Civil War, the Francoist dictatorship and the transition to Democracy, up until the Statute of Autonomy was enforced."[14]

Through Decree 4/2020, of February 13, Urkullu signed the draft bill on the Democratic and Historical Memory of the BAC. Advocates claimed in the bill's explanatory statements that:

> this law, which hopes to recover, in a firm and final way, the historical memory of the Civil War and Francoism, will be conceived in a context of maturity thanks to the over 40 years of democracy in the BAC and the more than 15 years institutions have spent trying to recover the democratic and historical memory of the BAC. We create this law without losing sight of the victims who suffered the unjust consequences of these historical events, which should have never happened and should never happen again. Reclaiming our memory will transform our future. The democratic legacy that comes with memory should be viewed as the building blocks of the democratic society of today and tomorrow and as the driving force of ethical values and democratic principles.[15]

Constructing the BAC's democratic memory upon the memory and rigorous knowledge of the historical events of its recent past secures a common democratic future and constitutes the best way to strengthen its democratic culture against negationist narratives, and narratives of exclusion and intolerance.

The law intends to integrate principles of international humanitarian law into the policy framework of the BAC. Some examples include the underlying principles of the 1948 Universal Declaration of Human Rights and the 1966 International Covenant on Civil and Political Rights and on economic, social, and cultural rights. One of the most impactful codes to help build the framework is Resolution 60/147, which was enacted by the United Nations on December 16, 2005, regarding the principles and guidelines on the right to a remedy and reparation for victims of gross violations of international human rights law and serious violations of international humanitarian law.[16] This resolution considers access to and protection of the truth to be a highly effective measure in the eradication of human rights violations. Ascertaining facts and publicly revealing the whole truth are the most valuable tools to help victims and prevent violations from reoccurring. Resolution 60/147 defines the right to truth, justice, and reparation as a set of principles to instill democratic values and values of the law in a society devastated by the violation of its fundamental rights.[17]

A common thread emerging from these proposals is that of transitional justice. As manifested in the report of the secretary-general of the United Nations entitled *The Rule of Law and Transitional Justice in Conflict and Post-Conflict Societies,* justice, peace, and democracy are not mutually exclusive objectives, but rather, mutually reinforcing imperatives. Transitional justice stands for a broad range of processes and mechanisms whose goal is to tackle the issues faced by societies that have undergone serious conflicts, wars, dictatorships, and periods of repression and abuse to serve justice and achieve reconciliation.[18] Judicial and nonjudicial mechanisms may accompany these processes, including the pursuit of truth, prosecution initiatives, reparations, and measures to keep human rights violations from happening again. Some of these measures include constitutional, legal, and institutional reforms, and the furtherance of civil society and memory recovery efforts. Similarly, measures concerning culture initiatives, archive preservation, and education reforms are incredibly relevant. As a step toward reconciliation and a manner to prevent future violations, transitional justice aims to grant appropriate recognition to victims, build up citizens' trust in national institutions, inspire greater respect for human rights, and promote the rule of law in society.

The *lehendakari* said: "Nothing we are trying to fix is unfixable; we are trying to figure out what happened to avoid repeating history. Truth, as an emerging right in the international arena, will help victims and the whole of society, as the catalyst of a new social contract based on the teachings of the rule of law."[19] In a similar vein, the Human Rights Council of the United Nations approved, on September 29, 2011, Resolution 18/7, relating to the mandate of a special rapporteur on the promotion of truth, justice, and reparation as guarantees of nonrecurrence of gross violations of human rights and/or serious violations of international humanitarian law. The draft bill on the Historical Memory Act of the BAC functions within the same scope of action, in accordance with the responsibilities established in Article 9 of the Statute of Autonomy.

The draft bill on the Democratic and Historical Memory Act was not created to formulate any new public or institutional policies on the matter, but rather to strengthen and expand the legislation developed since 1983 in the BAC.

The structure of the draft bill is divided into twelve chapters and a collection of additional provisions.

The first chapter lists the general provisions, synthesizes the essential objectives, and the goal of the law; it frames the principles on which the law stands and defines the beneficiaries of the law. Additionally, this first section outlines the necessary measures to bring about three fundamental rights of historical memory: the right to truth, the right to justice, and the right to recognition. At foundation are the principles of truth, justice, reparation, and guarantee of nonrecurrence, and the democratic values of freedom, defense of human rights, and a culture of peace, equality, and diversity. Beatriz Artolazabal, the minister of equality, justice, and social policies of the Basque government, underscored that the law had two main purposes: to promote the memory, recognition, and reparation of victims, and to foster ethical values and principles. In July 2022, Artolazabal characterized the draft bill as forward-looking and highlighted that "while it looks to the past, it is mostly concerned with the BAC's future. A future that remembers its past; because truth warrants justice and ensures nonrecurrence. And memory, truth, justice, and nonrecurrence are the democratic legacy for the entire Basque society." She also asserted that "memory cannot and must not be used to divide and confront; memory, truth, and the recognition of victims are and will be a legacy for the entire Basque society."[20]

Under Article 3 of the first chapter of the draft bill entitled "Beneficiaries," the following individuals and groups are considered "victims" and fall under one of the categories below, in the new legal framework:

a) Victims of fatal injuries because of bombings or extrajudicial or summary executions; victims who died in prison; all individuals who died or disappeared while fighting for a democratic rule and against the military coup and the Francoist dictatorship.

b) Individuals who underwent imprisonment, torture, deportation, or forced labor or were sent to concentration or extermination camps, inside or outside of the Basque Country, because of their defense of the Republican government or their fight against the Francoist regime in their quest to reinstate a democratic regime.

c) Individuals who went into exile to escape the military coup or the Francoist dictatorship.

d) People who faced economic repression, fines, or confiscations.

e) All public servants and public officials who were victims of reprisals or purges because of their work for the government of the Second Republic.

f) Political parties, unions, and feminist and other social movements that fought for freedom and democracy and against the dictatorship.

g) Masonic lodges and other organizations tried by The Court to Repress Freemasonry and Communism under a homonymous emergency law.

h) Victims of repression because of their ideology and occupation, in particular, teachers.

i) Victims of repression because of their sexual orientation or because they belonged to a minoritized ethnic group.

j) Individuals who suffered persecution and repression because they used,

promoted, disseminated, and taught the Basque language (Euskara), which was banned under the Francoist regime.
k) Women who experienced humiliations, violence, or punishment for exercising their freedoms or for simply being related to other victims.
l) Individuals who suffered persecution and repression for defending workers' labor rights.
m) Other groups that may be included later in Gogora's four-year plans.

Chapter two addresses the legal concept of "the right to truth." As defined in the draft bill, the right to truth consists in the right to know and investigate the human rights violations committed during the Civil War and the Francoist dictatorship, and the effort to defend freedom and democracy, even in the worst of circumstances. It stipulates that the right to truth applies to society in general and to victims and their families in particular; it also stipulates that all of them have the right to know what happened during the war and the dictatorship. The text contains several potential initiatives to accomplish these goals, including a report on the human rights violations perpetrated in the BAC between 1936 and 1978 and a census recording victims of fatal injuries of the Civil War in the BAC. To that end, Gogora and other public institutions will steward research projects to elucidate the events and identify victims.

Chapter three applies to the development of the principles of the right to justice. As established in the Spanish Constitution of 1978, the central state holds exclusive responsibilities in matters related to the administration of justice, meaning the public bodies of the BAC face major limitations when it comes to developing initiatives directed toward that end. To effectively serve justice, it is of essence that the Ertzaintza (the BAC's police), the district attorney's office and the appropriate judicial bodies coordinate efforts to find evidence to substantiate the crimes committed during the war and the dictatorship. With a view to defending the right of victims and the whole of society to equity, Gogora, as the agency in charge of historical memory matters, will cooperate with institutions of justice in the untangling and solving of the crimes and will be ready to take legal action when needed, among other things.

Chapter four regulates the right of victims to recognition and reparation. According to the legal text, the right to recognition and reparation must be full, effective, and proportional to the severity of the violation or the damages suffered. This implies that measures of moral reparation, restitution, compensation, reinstatement, and satisfaction must be applied collectively and on a case-by-case basis. In view of this, the draft bill plans to evaluate whether it would be appropriate and feasible to adopt additional compensations to supplement existing ones.[21] The draft bill recognizes the right of victims and their families to obtain an official personalized certificate of recognition issued by the Basque government that is meant to reinstate their honor and provide a righteous moral satisfaction. But collaborating with victims and their families to obtain the declaration prescribed by Article 4 of Act 52/2007, of December 26, is still binding, nonetheless. The law additionally calls for the institution of a remembrance holiday to honor the victims of the war and the dictatorship.[22] The law entrusts Gogora with the planning of events to recognize and honor victims. Parallel to these events, Gogora will steward an interagency declaration supporting the restoration of historical memory to preserve the memory of victims and champion freedom and democratic values.

Only a well-informed and educated society can have a judicious understanding of the past. Chapter five explores measures to achieve that end. It also stresses the importance of promoting historical research and of holding conferences, seminars, exhibits, and other educational activities to impress historical memory upon Basques. The law plans on founding and consolidating Gogora's library and documentary center. Two projects will naturally accompany this initiative: a documentary and audiovisual collection mostly focused on the first-hand accounts of victims of the war and the dictatorship, and the improvement and modernization of several museums of the BAC, especially, the Gernika Peace Museum.

The law compels Gogora to partner with the education department so that, together, they can devise the appropriate educational tools to start incorporating historical memory in the core curriculum of Basque schools. They will also organize complementary school activities such as cultural visits, trips, and exhibits.

Chapter six stipulates that all efforts to locate, exhume, and identify the remains of the disappeared during the war should be channeled through Gogora, and it also stipulates that identification measures should adhere to the protocol for scientific and multidisciplinary action described in Article 12.1 of Act 52/2007, of December 26. The protection of columbaria, as designated spaces of tribute and remembrance of the disappeared, will also be in the custody of Gogora. Since it is responsible for personal data treatment, Gogora has custody of the database containing DNA information from the exhumations. All mass graves will be marked in a map to be included in an integrated map of the entire territory of Spain, in accordance with the proceedings established in Article 12 of Act 52/2017, of December 26. The law urges joint efforts through agreements with other autonomous communities or the central government to garner the maximum amount of information and recover as many remains as possible. It places special focus on the bodies interred at the valley of Cuelgamuros that families have requested to be exhumed. This valley was formerly known as the Valley of the Fallen, and it is where General Franco was buried along with 33,833 fighters from both sides.

Chapter seven lays out the rules for the administration of places, itineraries, and spaces of memory. The law calls for assembling a catalog and regulating the protection and preservation of such spaces. As prescribed by the law, a place of memory is any space, building, or site where events of special significance for the community took place, whether for their historical or symbolic meaning or for their lasting effect on a community's collective memory, and they are associated with the defense of democratic freedoms and values. Itineraries of historical memory are spaces enclosing two or more memory places with shared criteria in terms of legal interpretation.

Although most institutional symbols, distinctions, and honors paying tribute to individuals, institutions and events of the Francoist regime have been removed throughout the last decade, some vestiges remain and should be permanently eliminated. Chapter eight discusses steps to remove these symbols that conflict with the historical memory and the dignity of victims. Gogora, in alliance with municipal and provincial councils, should work to remove from public spaces all elements or mentions put up by groups or individuals to honor, exalt, or elevate the coup of 1936, the war, or the dictatorship, or any of their leaders or organizations supporting the regime. Examples of such elements include plaques, coats of arms, emblems, inscriptions, and anagrams displayed on public buildings or on the street. Similarly, name changes are mandated for streets and public spaces once designated in honor of politicians or members of the military endorsing the military coup or the dictatorship. To bring these initiatives to completion, the municipal councils of the BAC have a full year after the enactment of the law to submit a report detailing to what extent they have met the requirements established in this chapter.

Chapter nine applies to the acquisition and safekeeping of documents concerning the preservation of historical memory in the BAC. Under this law, a "document" is any primary or secondary source of information produced by any physical or legal person, such as first-hand accounts or historical sources of other kinds. In accordance with the proceedings established in Act 7/1990, of July 3, on Basque cultural heritage, Gogora has the authority to request that documents not currently considered Basque documentary heritage be certified as such by the leading department on the matter. Article 21.1 of Act 52/2007, of December 26, defines as Basque documentary and bibliographic heritage all documents related to the war and the dictatorship belonging to both private and public archives. As prescribed by the law, documentary collections, first-hand accounts, and, specially, confiscated documents, should be reclaimed and preserved at Gogora's Historical Memory Documentary Center. The center, under Act 7/1990, of July 3, on Basque cultural heritage, oversees collecting, recovering, studying, disseminating, and providing easy access to this information.

The BAC and Catalonia are at the leading edge of restoring historical memory and promoting democratic and ethical values, thanks to the efforts of the several associations and institutions working toward the recovery of memory. Chapter ten focuses on a public registry of entities advocating for historical memory, which all associations, foundations, and social and nonprofit organizations registered in the BAC will be able to join. Through it, entities will have a way to draw attention to their activities and establish a direct rapport with Gogora as well as with one another. The law plans to create and affiliate an advisory commission, constituted by a collegiate body of experts, with Gogora to provide advice to such entities and help them on their mission.

Chapter eleven sets the rules for the administrative organization and approach of Gogora's duties. It is Gogora's responsibility to ensure that the measures established by the law and stipulated in Act 4/2014, of November 27, which created the Institute for Remembrance, Coexistence and Human Rights, are applied. Act 4/2014 and Decree 204/2015, of November 3, establishing the statutes of the Institute for Remembrance, Coexistence and Human Rights, outline the institute's structure, functions, organization, and legal and economic frameworks. As mandated by Article 38, Gogora is responsible for the development and promotion of the measures established in the act and is required to produce four-year action programs at the beginning of every legislature. These programs, prepared by the board of directors of Gogora, set forth the public policies to be implemented over a span of four years and determine the budget allocated for their execution.

Finally, chapter twelve establishes the penalty system. The law introduces sanctions against whomever may praise the military coup or the dictatorship, utter offensive and belittling statements against the dignity of the victims, or destroy war graves.[23] Under this rule, excavations failing to comply with Article 17.1 and the destruction and concealment of graves, other places of memory, and relevant documents are considered "very serious" offenses with fines ranging from 10,000 to 150,000 euros.[24] Finding human remains and failing to report it; removing human remains without the proper authorization stipulated in Article 17.3; and alterations or construction work made on a place, space, or itinerary of historical memory significance in the BAC fall under the category of "serious" offenses. Likewise, any demonstration exalting Francoism or any offensive, belittling or menacing statement used or uttered in the media, in public speeches or on digital platforms against the dignity of the families or the victims of the war or the dictatorship will be penalized as a serious misconduct, whenever these acts do not constitute a crime of incitement of hatred. The penalty system imposes fines ranging from 2,000 to 10,000 euros for "serious" offenses. Noncompliance with Article 23, on the obligation to allow public visits of historical memory places of the BAC, and damage to spaces or property located on places, spaces, and itineraries of historical memory significance in the BAC carry fines ranging from 200 to 2,000 euros.

For fines not exceeding the 100,000-euro limit, the authoritative power to impose the sanctions provided in chapter twelve will be Gogora; the Governing Council will assume responsibility for fines ranging from 100,000 to 150,000 euros; the city will sanction infractions stipulated in Article 41.3.e), providing the violated resolution is a municipal one.

This chapter has stirred up some controversy, particularly, among the far right.

As the political journalist Josean Izarra pointed out in a piece for *El Mundo*, Ignacio Camuñas, an ex-minister for Vox, publicly refuted the fact that the armed revolt had been a coup d'état, but rather a necessary attempt to save and defend political and social values, as Francoists have generally contended. Although his assertion may be untenable—after all, all armed insurrections against lawfully constituted governments are, by definition, coup d'états—it is not considered a crime nor a punishable act under this law. It is not considered a crime because, first, Camuñas resides in Avila, not in the BAC; and second, because the bill stipulates sanctions "for any public display exalting Francoism," not for promulgating interpretations of history. What it punishes is the praise of state terrorism and the use of violence or values that violate the normal exercise or the protection of human rights.[25]

During the discussion in the Basque Parliament over the draft bill on the memory act, Carmelo Barrio, in representation of the conservative coalition of Partido Popular and Ciudadanos, approved of "most of the text," yet tabled an amendment to the entirety of the bill, alleging that the rule's omission of ETA victims and of victims of the "repression" exerted by the Republican government from 1936 to 1939 divided "victims into first- and second-class victims." In a similar vein, Amaia Martínez, the only representative for Vox in the Basque Parliament, admonished the rule, claiming it "disregards ETA's actions" and "cloaks the atrocities perpetrated by the Republican side" to "brainwash society and perpetuate the confrontation between the two sides."[26]

In response to Barrio's statement, PSE-EE representative Eneko Andueza stated that specific laws on the matter in the BAC have provided recognition to ETA victims throughout the years they have been and continue to be in place. As a matter of fact, recognition and restitution of ETA victims has been largely provided for in the legislation meant to alleviate, to the extent possible, the effects of terrorism. The assistance program directed at victims of terrorism is currently regulated by Decree 313/2002, of December 30, which is an amended version of Decree 214/2002, of September 24. The latter stems from Decree 221/1988, of August 4, amended in 1991, 1993, and 1995 and replaced in 2000 by Decree 107/2000, of June 3. Concurrently, Act 4/2008, of June 19, has been providing recognition and reparations to victims of terrorism for fourteen years, and, at a national level, Act 5/2018, of October 17, grants protection and recognition, and honors the memory of victims of terrorism. Never, however, had a Basque law recognized and provided reparations to victims of the violence inflicted by the Spanish state during the dictatorship. As it happens, PP voted in favor of such previous measures and not once showed any concern over the law acknowledging only ETA victims and neglecting the rest of individuals who had suffered violence in the BAC, which, effectively engineered "first- and second-class victims," as Barrio put it. In reaction to Vox's opposition, Andueza remarked that "no political party that considers itself democratic can reject" a bill whose purpose is precisely to promote and cement values of peace, harmony, and democracy.

Barrio's allegations that the bill neglects victims of "Republican repression," such as those who perished at the storming of the prison of Larrinaga in Bilbao-Bilbo during the Civil War, were refuted by EAJ representative Inigo Iturrate. Iturrate reminded the conservative that the act acknowledges "all" victims of the war, including those who died in extrajudicial executions. Iturrate further contested Barrio's arguments by clarifying that the law explicitly refers to the victims who had suffered in their defense of the Republican legality, because, up until then, they had been forced to ostracism and oblivion, as opposed to the victims mentioned by Barrio, who had been recognized with monuments and even a crypt at the cemetery of Vistalegre in Bilbao-Bilbo. It is worth observing that acts such as the storming of the prison of Larrinaga, in which individuals acting on their own behalf were brought to justice by Republican authorities, sit in stark contrast to the violence of the insurrected, which was planned, organized, and executed by the bodies of the illegitimate regime and carried out by the security forces and the army of General Franco's government.

Vox and PP have consistently stood against memory legislation and refused to participate in the events of Remembrance Day of November 10, claiming the date was originally thought to remember victims affected exclusively by ETA's violence. But, as Julen Arzuaga, Basque parliamentarian for EH Bildu (Euskal Herria Bildu: Basque Country Unite), avows, the actual reason why they oppose these measures is because they feel and, indeed, are the "political heirs of Francoism." Consequently, they find it inappropriate to reproach the excesses and transgressions committed throughout the more than forty years of war and dictatorship. In fact, a memory law in the BAC became vital in great part because any time the right (PP and Ciudadanos) or the far right (Vox) took control of the central government, the national memory law would not be properly enforced. In fact, while conservative Mariano Rajoy was in power between 2011 and 2017, the Basque Parliament repeatedly decried the infringement of the Historical Memory Act 52/2007, of December 26.[27]

Historical memory laws are undeniably beneficial for societies coming out of scarring cycles of violence; but, when, in the aftermath of such periods of violence, societies are denied justice, these laws become utterly necessary. Such is the case of Basque and Catalan societies, and even of Spanish society, too. Although not without controversy, the denazification process of West Germany has had an impact well beyond its borders, favoring not only German society but the whole of Europe, and the world. When respect for human rights and the democratic principles of freedom, justice, and peace lie at the heart of a country's internal and international relationships, societies around the world benefit from their positive consequences. On the opposite end, the Spanish and Italian states failed to educate society in democratic values and, therefore, similar concepts to "denazification," such as "defascification" or "defrancoification" never crystallized. The concerning repercussions of such actions, or lack thereof, stretch to present-day Europe with the resurgence of openly neo-fascist movements in Italy and neo-Francoist movements in Spain through political parties such as the pro-Fascist Fratelli d'Italia (Brothers of Italy) or the pro-Francoist Vox.

Iturrate mentioned in the Basque Parliament that the law could not have been introduced at a better time. Negationist and reductionist narratives and narratives of exclusion—revisionist narratives—are spreading across the country, justifying the Francoist uprising and the War of 1936, exalting the forty-year- long Francoist dictatorship, and denying or minimizing the human rights violations perpetrated throughout. It is critical to approve a law whose foremost purposes are to recover memory, to provide recognition and reparations to victims, and to strengthen the democratic and ethical values in society.

Laws can transcend regulation and help enlighten society. They can help foster democratic values of respect—and even devotion—for human rights in places where the law is not yet a staple of the political culture of its community, only a political principle. Iturrate said the law on memory will accomplish "a crucial educational mission" after forty years of extreme injustice. The Historical Memory Act of the BAC defines the principles of truth, justice, reparations, and recognition, and the transmission of ethical and political values as the cornerstones of a society with a healthy political culture, where the body of laws and the representative institutions are fully democratic, which is the best antidote against corruption.

NOTES

1   The Basque Country, *Euskadi* or *Euskal Herria* in the Basque language (*Euskara*), is a nation politically divided into two nation-states and three different administrations. Within the Spanish state, it is broken into the *Comunidad Foral de Navarra* (Regional Community of Navarra, CFN) and the Autonomous Community of the Basque Country (BAC) which comprises the historical regions of Araba (Álava), Bizkaia (Vizcaya), and Gipuzkoa (Guipuzcoa). Within the French Republic, the *Communauté d'Agglomération du Pays Basque* (the Agglomeration Community of the Basque Country) is the intercommunal structure administering the historical territories of Lapurdi (Labourd), Baxe Nafarroa (Lower Navarre), and Zuberoa (Soule). This chapter will examine the policies on historical memory developed in the BAC.
2   *Ley orgánica 3/1979, de 18 de diciembre, de estatuto de autonomía para el País Vasco. BOE, No. 306, diciembre 22, 1979.* [Organic Act 3/1979, of December 18, regulating the Statute of Autonomy of the BAC. Official State Gazette (BOE) n. 306, of December 22, 1979]. https://www.basquecountry.eus/contenidos/informacion/estatuto_guernica/en_455/adjuntos/estatu_i.pdf.
3   Ley 52/2007, de 26 de diciembre, por la que se reconocen y amplían derechos y se establecen medidas en favor de quienes padecieron persecución o violencia durante la guerra civil y la dictadura. BOE, No. 310, diciembre 27, 2007. [Act 52/2007, of December 26, which recognized and expanded rights for victims, and established measures to support victims of the Civil War and the dictatorship who were persecuted or subjected to violence. BOE, n. 310, December 27, 2007.] https://reparations.qub.ac.uk/assets/uploads/Ley-52-2007-Spain-EN.pdf.

4   Ley 52/2007, de 26 de diciembre, por la que se reconocen y amplían derechos y se establecen medidas en favor de quienes padecieron persecución o violencia durante la guerra civil y la dictadura. BOE, No. 310, diciembre 27, 2007. [Act 52/2007, of December 26, which recognized and expanded rights for victims, and established measures to support victims of the Civil War and the dictatorship who were persecuted or subjected to violence. BOE, n. 310, December 27, 2007.] https://www.boe.es/buscar/act.php?id=BOE-A-2007-22296.

5   Decreto 107/2012, de 12 de junio, de declaración y reparación de las víctimas de sufrimientos injustos como consecuencia de la vulneración de sus derechos humanos, producida entre los años 1960 y 1978 en el contexto de la violencia de motivación política vivida en la Comunidad Autónoma del País Vasco. [Decree 107/2012, of June 12, on the recognition and reparation to victims subjected to unfair suffering because of the violation of their human rights between 1960 and 1978, in a context of the politically motivated violence in the Autonomous Community of the Basque Country.] https://noticias.juridicas.com/base_datos/CCAA/pv-d107-2012.html.

6   Ley 4/2014, de 27 de noviembre, de creación del Instituto de la Memoria, la Convivencia y los Derechos Humanos. BOPV, No. 230, diciembre 2, 2014. [Act 4/2014, of November 27, on the creation of the Institute for Remembrance, Coexistence and Human Rights. Official Gazette of the Basque Country (BOPV) n. 230, of December 2, 2014.] https://www.boe.es/buscar/pdf/2014/BOE-A-2014-13185-consolidado.pdf.

7   Ley 4/2014, de 27 de noviembre, de creación del Instituto de la Memoria, la Convivencia y los Derechos Humanos. BOPV, No. 230, diciembre 2, 2014. [Act 4/2014, of November 27, on the creation of the Institute for Remembrance, Coexistence and Human Rights. Official Gazette of the Basque Country (BOPV) n. 230, of December 2, 2014.] https://www.boe.es/buscar/pdf/2014/BOE-A-2014-13185-consolidado.pdf.

8   Ley 4/2014, de 27 de noviembre, de creación del Instituto de la Memoria, la Convivencia y los Derechos Humanos. BOPV, No. 230, diciembre 2, 2014. [Act 4/2014, of November 27, on the creation of the Institute for Remembrance, Coexistence and Human Rights. Official Gazette of the Basque Country (BOPV) n. 230, of December 2, 2014.] https://www.boe.es/buscar/pdf/2014/BOE-A-2014-13185-consolidado.pdf.

9   Official Gazette of the Spanish Parliament. Senate. 14th Legislature n. 386, of September 22, 2022. https://www.senado.es/legis14/publicaciones/pdf/senado/bocg/BOCG_D_14_386_3372.PDF.

10 González Egaña, Arantza, "Un informe para el Parlamento desaconseja crear una ley de Memoria Histórica en Euskadi," El Diario Vasco, Thursday, October 25, 2018. https://www.diariovasco.com/politica/informe-parlamento-desaconseja-20181025003836-ntvo.html.

11 Ferrándiz, Francisco; Hristova, Marije, "Valoración comparada de las políticas públicas de Memoria Histórica en Euskadi (2000–2018)," Gogora, 2019. https://digital.csic.es/handle/10261/237044.

12 "El Gobierno Vasco presenta el borrador del anteproyecto de Ley de Memoria Histórica de Euskadi," September 24, 2019. https://www.euskadi.eus/gobierno-vasco/-/noticia/2019/el-gobierno-vasco-presenta-el-borrador-del-anteproyecto-de-ley-de-memoria-historica-de-euskadi/.

13 "Memoria historikoaren lege proiektua defendatu du lehendakariak 'injustizia zuzentzeko,'" EITB Media, June 16, 2022. https://www.eitb.eus/eu/albisteak/politika/osoa/8880432/eztabaida-legebiltzarrean-memoria-historikoaren-lege-proiektuaren-harira-2022ko-ekainaren-16an/.

14 Decreto 36/2019, de 26 de noviembre, del Lehendakari, por el que se ordena el inicio del procedimiento de elaboración del Anteproyecto de Ley de Memoria Histórica y Democrática de

Euskadi. [Presidential Decree 36/2019, of November 26, which mandates the writing of the draft bill on the Democratic and Historical Memory of the BAC.] https://www.euskadi.eus/gobierno-vasco/-/proyecto-ley/ley-de-memoria-historica-y-democratica-de-euskadi/.

15 Decreto 4/2020, de 13 de febrero, del Lehendakari, por el que se aprueba con carácter previo el anteproyecto de Ley de Memoria Histórica y Democrática de Euskadi. [Presidential Decree 4/2020, of February 13, on the preliminary approval of the draft bill on the Democratic and Historical Memory of the BAC.] https://www.euskadi.eus/proyecto-ley/ley-de-memoria-historica-y-democratica-de-euskadi/web01-s2lehen/es/.

16 Decreto 4/2020, de 13 de febrero, del Lehendakari, por el que se aprueba con carácter previo el anteproyecto de Ley de Memoria Histórica y Democrática de Euskadi. [Presidential Decree 4/2020, of February 13, on the preliminary approval of the draft bill on the Democratic and Historical Memory of the BAC.] https://www.euskadi.eus/proyecto-ley/ley-de-memoria-historica-y-democratica-de-euskadi/web01-s2lehen/es/.

17 A/RES/60/147, Basic Principles and Guidelines on the Right to a Remedy and Reparation for Victims of Gross Violations of International Human Rights Law and Serious Violations of International Humanitarian Law. Resolution 60/147 adopted by the General Assembly, December 16 2,005. https://documents-dds-ny.un.org/doc/UNDOC/GEN/N05/496/42/PDF/N0549642.pdf?OpenElement.

18 "The rule of law and transitional justice in conflict and post-conflict societies," Report of the Secretary-General S/2004/616, August 23, 2004. https://documents-dds-ny.un.org/doc/UNDOC/GEN/N04/395/29/PDF/N0439529.pdf?OpenElement.

19 Decreto 4/2020, de 13 de febrero, del Lehendakari, por el que se aprueba con carácter previo el anteproyecto de Ley de Memoria Histórica y Democrática de Euskadi. [Presidential Decree 4/2020, of February 13, on the preliminary approval of the draft bill on the Democratic and Historical Memory of the BAC.] https://www.euskadi.eus/proyecto-ley/ley-de-memoria-historica-y-democratica-de-euskadi/web01-s2lehen/es/.

20 Lotina, Eriz, "Euskadik hobiak suntsitzea eta frankismoa goraipatzea isunekin zigortzeko asmoa du," EITB Media, July 27, 2021. https://www.eitb.eus/eu/albisteak/politika/osoa/8216054/euskadik-hobiak-suntsitzea-eta-frankismoa-goraipatzea-isunekin-zigortzeko-asmoa-du/.

21 Yurre, David, "Desactivado el intento de PP+Cs y VOX por frenar la ley de Memoria Histórica de Euskadi," SER, June 16, 2022. https://cadenaser.com/euskadi/2022/06/16/desactivado-el-intento-de-ppcs-y-vox-por-frenar-la-ley-de-memoria-historica-de-euskadi-ser-vitoria/.

22 Lotina, Eriz, "Euskadik hobiak suntsitzea eta frankismoa goraipatzea isunekin zigortzeko asmoa du," EITB Media, July 27, 2021. https://www.eitb.eus/eu/albisteak/politika/osoa/8216054/euskadik-hobiak-suntsitzea-eta-frankismoa-goraipatzea-isunekin-zigortzeko-asmoa-du/.

23 Yurre, David, "Desactivado el intento de PP+Cs y VOX por frenar la ley de Memoria Histórica de Euskadi," SER, June 16, 2022. https://cadenaser.com/euskadi/2022/06/16/desactivado-el-intento-de-ppcs-y-vox-por-frenar-la-ley-de-memoria-historica-de-euskadi-ser-vitoria/.

24 Lotina, Eriz, "Euskadik hobiak suntsitzea eta frankismoa goraipatzea isunekin zigortzeko asmoa du," EITB Media, July 27, 2021. https://www.eitb.eus/eu/albisteak/politika/osoa/8216054/euskadik-hobiak-suntsitzea-eta-frankismoa-goraipatzea-isunekin-zigortzeko-asmoa-du/.

25 Izarra, Joxean, "Euskadi castigará 'enaltecer el franquismo' con hasta 10.000 euros con su nueva Ley de Memoria Histórica," *El Mundo*, Vitoria-Gasteiz, Tuesday, July 27, 2021. https://www.elmundo.es/pais-vasco/2021/07/27/61000653fdddff5c378b4608.html.

26 "Memoria historikoaren lege proiektua defendatu du lehendakariak 'injustizia zuzentzeko'" (Basque president endorses historical memory law project to "mend injustices"), EITB Media,

June 16, 2022. https://www.eitb.eus/eu/albisteak/politika/osoa/8880432/eztabaida-lege-biltzarrean-memoria-historikoaren-lege-proiektuaren-harira-2022ko-ekainaren-16an/.

27 Justificación de la proposición no de ley sobre los instrumentos de las políticas públicas de memoria histórica en su proyección al futuro. [Explanatory statements for the non-legislative motion regarding the legal instruments to be used in the future for public policies related to historical memory] https://parlamentovasco.eaj-pnv.eus/es/adjuntos-documentos/18705/pdf/proposicion-no-de-ley-sobre-los-instrumentos-de-la.

three

Memory Policies In Navarre

THE INSTITUTE OF MEMORY OF NAVARRE

José Miguel Gastón Aguas and *César Layana Ilundain*

The 2015 political shift in Navarre inaugurated an era of memory legislation which finally institutionalized the long-standing demand to address historical memory. The ensuing set of measures was included, as an initial plan of action, in the 2015 government-plan agreement endorsed by several political groups. The agreement was reformed four years later, with profound changes in the subscribing political parties. Since the first government-plan agreement jump-started memory policymaking, a comprehensive memory-management program has grown wide and strong and received positive recognition.

The program aims at reclaiming a memory that enlightens and awakens the community from the amnesia under which it was deliberately put by the master culture, as Maurice Halbwachs contended. For almost a decade now, the Institute of Memory of Navarre, following in the footsteps of families and memory associations, has sought to recognize Franco-era victims as past and present bastions of the democratic project of the Second Republic of Spain.

However alive the memories of the victims may still be, the road to visibility has not been smooth. Walter Benjamin theorized this is likely because, after the physical death of the conquered, victors conjure up a plan to normalize their past actions until they cause the hermeneutical death of the victim.[1] It is Navarre's duty, as a democratic society, to rethink politics, ethics, aesthetics, and other aspects of social life, through the lens of the horror and brutality that erupted in the region in the aftermath of the military insurrection of 1936. This exercise will allow the community to familiarize itself with the right of victims to access truth, justice, and reparations, and to dispel, once and for all, the traditional belief that history is built upon victims and suffering. It is, therefore, crucial that victims of Navarre's recent past and their contexts of violence are at the center of society's critical retrospective debate.

The 2015 plan agreement established the creation of the General Directorate of Peace, Coexistence and Human Rights. From its inception, this agency has advocated primarily for just and real social harmony by casting light and educating the community on the injustices and abhorrent human rights violations that took place less than a century ago. The road to social harmony remains long, however, considering injustices have yet to see reparations, and discourses of hatred and intolerance still reverberate in certain spheres of society and in some political sectors. It is within this frame of democratic enhancement and respect for the memory of victims of human rights violations that the Institute of Memory of Navarre was born, to fulfill all tasks related to the memory legislation written by the government of Navarre.

A top priority in the pursuit of recovering historical memory was to develop and enforce Regional Act 33/2013, of November 26, which granted recognition and moral reparations to those Navarrese who lost their lives or were victims of repression because of the military coup of 1936. Unfortunately, the act saw little development, and none of its most substantial measures were adopted since its approval a year and a half earlier.

The Institute of Memory of Navarre is structured into six main courses of action for the development of specific memory policies and are interconnected through multifaceted projects. They are the location and identification of victims of the uprising of July 1936 who died or went missing; recognition and reparation acts for victims and their families; removal of Francoist symbols from public spaces; recognition and protection of sites of memory; the Escuelas con Memoria (Schools with Memory, EM) program; and the preservation and promotion of memory heritage through the institute's Documentary Center. This chapter will analyze the trajectory of each initiative.

The idea of memory in Navarre is often equated to the memory of the more than three thousand people killed in the political cleansing operation perpetrated by the insurrectionists. Efforts to reclaim their memory have generally revolved around locating and exhuming the bodies scattered throughout the region, although, in almost every instance, traditional anthropological guidelines have not been followed. Disinterring bodies from mass graves to rebury them in cemeteries has been a common practice since soon after the end of the war, but because it was done secretly and under cover, it is challenging to form a realistic picture of this phenomenon. Information on this subject can be found in *Lur Azpian—Bajo Tierra. Exhumaciones en Navarra,*

1939–2019 (Buried. Exhumations in Navarre, 1939–2019), published by the Institute of Memory of Navarre as part of a broader project to retrace the memory of the so-called early exhumations. The term "early exhumations" refers to the reburials carried out during the Transition by grassroots movements formed mostly of family members of victims killed in the Navarrese towns that faced the harshest forms of repression. Although the exact number of recovered bodies is unknown, it is estimated to be in the several hundreds.[2] While several towns managed to bring the process to completion, some others, where the movement was not as impactful, left a considerable number of graves unopened, failing to meet the expectations of many families. That is the striking case of Navarre's capital city; only an insignificant amount of remains were unearthed of the more than three hundred Pamplona-Iruñea residents killed after the uprising.

At the beginning of the twenty-first century, after a two-decade hiatus, family and historical memory associations got a new round of exhumations under way. Founded in 2002, the *Asociación de Familiares de Fusilados de Navarra AFFNA36NAFSE* (Navarre's Association of Family Members of Execution Victims) sponsored most of them, including those in Fustiñana, Urzante, Tutera (Tudela), Antxoritz, Erripa (Ripa), and Lecáun, and assisted in exhumations at the Urbasa Plains. Leading the effort was researcher Balbino García de Albizu, whose grandfather of the same name was killed there. Through the investigations performed by the *Memoriaren Bideak* (Paths of Memory) association, a prisoner killed in his escape from prison and buried at the cemetery of Erronkari (Roncal) was located and exhumed. Similarly, the *Txinparta-Fuerte de San Cristóbal* association conducted several campaigns at *Cementerio de las Botellas* (Cemetery of the Bottles) in the vicinity of Fort San Cristóbal on Mount Ezkaba, to recover the bodies of the political prisoners who died because of illness and disease. Family members of deceased prisoners at the fort residing in other provinces united to promote several exhumations. The *Los Cinco de la Nava* association sponsored the unburials in Añezcar, Berriogoiti (Berriosuso), and Oteitza Berriobeiti (Oteiza de Berrioplano). The exhumation efforts did not receive institutional support until the 2010s, when many municipal councils joined in the task. A new phase ensued: the cemetery of Bera underwent multiple exhumation attempts in search of the numerous people murdered at the quarry of Argaitz; the municipal council of Eguesibar Valley sponsored the exhumation in Elia, where the bodies of three runaway prisoners from San Cristóbal were recovered; the municipal council of Berriozar financed the exhumations in Esparceta, at the foothills of Mount Ezkaba, to find the remains of four prisoners who escaped during the jailbreak of May 22, 1938, and who were killed there.

A multidisciplinary team of experts sent by the scientific association *Sociedad de Ciencias Aranzadi* (hereinafter, Aranzadi) performed the exhumations. Aranzadi contributed its data from prior historical and anthropological research in addition to its archeological and forensic knowledge to carry out the tasks. The General Directorate of

Peace, Coexistence and Human Rights thrived after the 2015 agreement with Aranzadi as it gained instant access to the association's fifteen years of invaluable experience. The exhumation plans drafted yearly through this agreement, financed with €100,000 every tax year, used the data collected from and provided by several sources, including memory associations, private sources, and renowned researchers such as Fermín Ezkieta, an expert in the Fort San Cristóbal jailbreak.[3]

This mutual effort, which falls under the first action listed earlier, has already had some fruitful results. Although some were considered empty attempts, out of the 133 exhumations, thirty were successful, unearthing a total of 152 remains between 2015 and 2023. Many of these seemingly failed attempts often reawake the memory of the town or area where the burial site was supposedly located, bringing new accounts, information, and evidence to the surface. First-hand accounts become increasingly scarce as time goes by, and information becomes available only through people who heard the stories from family members, meaning third-person accounts of this kind cannot be verified by the original authors. Because of construction and infrastructure work, numerous grave locations have been compromised and the bodies buried there cannot be recovered. The rapid urban development of the metropolitan area of Pamplona-Iruñea, for instance, has hindered the exhumation efforts in that district. In Navarre, a good deal of *sacas* (unlawful mass executions of prisoners) from the Provincial Prison or Fort of San Cristóbal took place in the surrounding land of the capital city. Also known as the Cuenca, the area, once predominantly rural, dotted only with small towns, has grown quickly in the last few decades, destroying several of these burial sites. Many graves met a similar fate as roads were widened and highways built. To make things worse, inaccurate accounts and decades of silence have hindered the outcome of many efforts in the last four years. Many graves remain to be found. The Institute of Memory of Navarre is currently testing noninvasive techniques and tools to explore the underground, but little progress has been made so far.

In the second part of this path of action, the exhumed remains are genetically identified at the DNA bank of Navarre. Article 8 of Regional Act 33/2013, of November 26, called for the bank's creation in 2013, but it would not be launched until three years later, in September 2016. This is a clear example of how laws can flounder without the political will to put them into effect. As of mid-2023, 361 files had been opened and thirty-nine identifications certified. The genetics laboratory of Nasertic, a public company with an annual contract of €70,000, manages Navarre's DNA bank. At the lab, geneticists compare the genetic markers found in the exhumed remains against the samples provided by family members via one of these three methods: 1) Autosomal short tandem repeat (STR) marker testing. These markers are transmitted from parent to child. It is the preferred testing method for its high accuracy, but the shrinking number of offspring still alive and able to provide a sample poses a considerable challenge. 2) Y chromosome testing. The chromosome is transmitted only from father to son. 3) Mitochondrial DNA testing. Transmitted from mothers to children, both males and females can carry it. With these limited tests, when families have no eligible donor among their living members, genetic identification becomes a complicated task. Not all hope is lost, though. Considering how fast genetics and medical technology advance, it is reasonable to think that science will soon find a way to overcome current barriers by means of massive parallel sequencing. Additionally, future technology may help tackle identification issues from deteriorated bone remains. As it stands right now, the genetic matter extracted from deteriorated bones often does not provide enough quality material to obtain valid results.

A DNA bank offers the mid-term and long-term possibility to continue identifying victims, long after donors pass away—unfortunately, many relatives have already died. Taking DNA samples before the exhumation of the related victim even happens may soften the emotional impact of donors, who are usually seniors immersed in a race against time. Collecting genetic material ahead of time gives family members a sense of perdurability, since it is entirely possible that new identification methods will emerge in the future. While science may not guarantee successful identification results, the restorative effects of public institutions approaching families for the first time in eighty years, offering the means to address their situation and involving and accompanying them throughout every step of the process, should not be underestimated.

New digital tools of massive cross-referencing of genetic information have made it possible to identify some victims who would have remained unidentified with previous methods guided only by hypotheses of who the victim may have been. The case of the prisoners who were murdered after their failed attempt to escape Fort San Cristóbal on May 22, 1938, represents the strengths of these new methods. The 206 victims—of known identity, granted—were buried in dozens of graves, some of which have been located already. About a quarter of the bodies have been recovered. The DNA bank stores genetic samples from family members of a fifth of the killed prisoners. In this case, cross-referencing with no previous hypothesis was the only method applicable and it has already yielded some positive results, with almost ten identified bodies. Although progress is slow, without building this infrastructure, none of these cases would have had a favorable outcome. Thanks to genetic identification, some cases have even disproved popular historical hypotheses, pushing experts to reconsider the correctness of their sources. The remains of Claudio Doroteo Diéguez, thought to be buried in Sokozarreta, on the outskirts of Altsasu, were found in the chasm of Otsoportillo. Although the exact way it happened continues to be unknown, it is believed that the remains were secretly unburied and transferred to the chasm to protect them from an eventual road construction project. Agustín Joaquín Arroyo's remains were found in Etxalatz (Echálaz), in Eguesibar Valley, but he was thought to have been killed twelve miles away, in Etxauri (notice the phonetic similarity). Tomás Salinas, too, was found in Etxalatz, but his family believed he had been killed in Ororbia, as told by a priest.

Interviewing donors to complement genetic identification methods adds new information and allows for error correction. Delayed death certificates have proved to be a problematic source of information and should be used with caution. This is because families were required to file a death certificate for their killed relative to have them removed from the registry of missing citizens. The certificate granted surviving spouses and offspring legal widowed and orphaned status. As orphans, children received benefits, including exemption from military service. Filings skyrocketed after the end of the war. But, to obtain the certificate, requesters needed affidavits of people who had witnessed the death of the victim, so families had to reach out to their social network. They did so in a variety of ways. A few families obtained accounts of real witnesses, even of people who had been involved in the killing at some level. Other families had contacts in high positions of power within the Franco regime or the justice department who helped them fast-track the process. In some cases, families had to look for support within their closest circle. Some records list relatives of repression victims as witnesses for other families, suggesting that families supported each other through this difficult chapter. It follows from these observations that information cannot always be trusted, because accuracy may not have been the main goal at the time information was produced. Stating that a relative had died in a popular *saca* such as Valcardera or Tejería de Monreal, for example, was commonplace, because these sites were of public domain. As a result, such sources may have led to erroneous hypotheses on the location of certain victims and caused confusion on the identity of the victims buried at those places.

Interinstitutional collaboration is of essence to lessen the effects of this occurrence. Ramón Haro González, an escaped prisoner native of Salamanca (Castile-Leon), was identified through a DNA sample collected from his Barcelona-residing son. A collaboration agreement between the genetic identification program of the Catalan government and the government of Navarre enabled the DNA bank of Navarre to examine the sample and determine in 2020 that Haro's remains had been exhumed in Usetxi (Esteribar) in 2016. Aware of the benefits that collaboration among regions provided, the government of Navarre, bypassing the then uninvolved central government, organized in Pamplona-Iruñea the First Conference of the Inter-Regional Network Advocating for Historical Memory. Conducted in March 2018, the event welcomed representatives of thirteen autonomous communities and discussed the creation of a national DNA bank. Those who attended agreed it would facilitate the identification of human remains by establishing a communication network and standardizing laboratory and regional government criteria. Preliminary steps have already been taken toward this goal, and the project is stipulated in the Democratic and Historic Memory Bill, which is pending approval.

Once the body is exhumed and successfully identified, a formal ceremony to deliver the remains to their families closes the circle. This solemn ceremony is open to the public and is attended by government representatives and memory associations, symbolizing the support of the community. (During the COVID-19 pandemic, the number of people allowed in the ceremony considerably shrunk.) These are simple and emotional events where families have a platform to express what that moment means to them and reclaim the memory of their killed ancestor. Many ceremonies have been filmed as part of the efforts to document every aspect of the project. Summary videos can be accessed through the main menu of the General Directorate of Peace, Coexistence and Human Rights' website at https://pazyconvivencia.navarra.es.

The second course of action deals with recognition and reparation for victims and their families, including the public reparation ceremonies where families receive the remains of an identified relative. Ever since it took charge of memory policies in 2015, the government of Navarre has wanted to go a step further by deciding to send official representatives to all public acts celebrated within the autonomous community; and to organize a series of institutional events to honor victims of all forms of repression inflicted by the rebels after their victory in July 1936. Involving public institutions in the promotion of memory policies and acts of tribute finally settles a deep-rooted debt with the segment of society most committed to the recovery of memory. Memory acts multiplied across the region in 2016 with the eightieth anniversary of the 1936 coup and as a result of the sharp political shift Navarre underwent at all institutional levels, including at the municipal level. Government representatives have been invited to the stage on several occasions. Over the years, they have addressed relevant issues: they have condemned Francoism and the violence—exclusively of the rearguard, in the case of Navarre—that stemmed from the uprising; they have denounced the violence used against thousands of people for their ideas or their union or political affiliations; they have highlighted the value of critical memory in the construction of a democratic society that does not hide from its darkest passages of history and calls for collective reflection; and they have defined a culture of peace and nonviolence as the best environment to avoid similar events and violence from reoccurring.

In addition, different communities that were the target of repression have been recognized by the government in several events. In the fall of 2015, immediately after the General Directorate of Peace, Coexistence and Human Rights was structured, a ceremony to honor the killed civil servants of the provincial council of Navarre was conducted, during which organizers unveiled a plaque in the porches of the Royal Palace and General Archives of Navarre in their memory. A major ceremony in September of 2016 remembered teachers, thirty-three of whom were killed and more than three hundred of whom experienced some form of repression, ranging from purges to disciplinary action for civil or political allegations, prison time, or exile. The government immortalized in two events the memory of those who fled into exile. In September 2017 at the concentration camp of Gurs on the southwest of France, a monolith was erected in honor of the four hundred Navarrese people who ended up there, escaping the horrors of Francoism. The other event, in September 2021 in Elizondo, commemorated (following all COVID-19 guidelines) the people who left Navarre because of Francoist threats of violence and those who helped them cross the border through the solidarity networks created for that purpose. The ceremony ended with a wreath laid at the statue *Babesaren Muga* by sculptor Mikel Iriarte, which, in 2020, was designated a Historical Memory Site of Navarre. Sites of memory will be discussed in the coming section. Two additional ceremonies were held in 2019: On September 15, all victims of reprisals of Navarre and their families, who kept their memories alive, were honored at the Memory Park of Sartaguda. On October 27, a memorial opened at the cemetery of Torrero, Zaragoza (Aragón), in honor of the 225 Navarrese people enlisted in the Sanjurjo Regiment and killed at the San Gregorio military camp. Their families were recognized for exhuming the remains in 1979 from the mass grave into which the soldiers were thrown.

The organizers had two premises for these events: family engagement and community awareness. They wanted to encourage the active involvement of families and loved ones, and they did so, thanks to the invaluable help of memory and family associations and through public announcements of the ceremonies, which included preliminary lists and registries of people who were going to be recognized. Some lists were produced after extensive research. Open participation of the community has cast a positive, warm light on these events. And the relationships established with families have been surprising at times. For instance, weeks before the recognition ceremony for repressed teachers, several people contacted the General Directorate of Peace, Coexistence and Human Rights after learning through the list of honored people that one of their family members had been purged from their position. These cases were frequently related to teachers who, after a brief punishment period, had tried to erase what had happened from their past to avoid running into further problems with the Francoist regime. Suddenly, ample manifestations of memory and amnesia surfaced. It became apparent that while some families reclaimed and celebrated their ancestors' memories, other victims—of purges, usually—or families, who, for any given reason, did not acknowledge the violence faced by their relative, lived in a state of self-induced amnesia. Often, this behavior applied to victims, who, being in a vulnerable position within the dictatorship, chose to remain silent for the safety and well-being of their families, as a survival mechanism. And understandably so, because the Franco regime was fixated on ridding the country of the dissident ideas and cultures that predated the 1936 coup, subjecting its cruelest forms of violence against the citizens and communities that embodied them. As a result of this brutality, dissidence was effectively smothered and targeted citizens were coerced into consenting to the dictatorship.

In preparation for the 2017 ceremony, the government contacted the families of those who had died at the concentration camp of Gurs upon their crossing into France and extended an invitation to attend and participate in the event. This gesture revealed the eclipsed reality of the descendants of the unsung working-class activists who had gone into exile. Up until then, only the exiles of the leaders of the resistance and of renowned public figures had been investigated. But exiles with a lower profile, who had fled the coup and its aftermath and had eventually made their host country their forever home, had not attracted much attention. For the foreign national descendants of these activists, institutional recognition of the struggles withstood by their ancestors carried special meaning. A similar atmosphere pervaded the September 2021 ceremony in Elizondo in honor of the Republican exiles of Navarre and of the solidarity network that helped them cross the border. Both were popular events, but the crowd restrictions imposed by the pandemic reduced the size of the 2021 ceremony.

Equally interesting were the bonds formed in the weeks and months before the 2018 ceremonies of Sartaguda and the cemetery of Torrero in Zaragoza. Establishing contact proved easier because of the existing ties with the families from the towns where the early exhumation process was most consequential. It was during the body-recovery process of the Transition that the mass grave with the highest number of victims was exhumed: the grave of the men who were forcibly enlisted in the Sanjurjo Regiment and killed in October 1936, and whose remains were later transferred to Torrero. In addition to recovering their their bodies, the community worked hard to locate additional material in private collections and archives to digitize it and make it available to the public on the website of the Documentary Center of the Institute of Memory of Navarre.

Spreading the memory of honored communities was essential in these kind of ceremonies. Organizers have been true to this premise in many forms, although they have prioritized preserving the most ephemeral initiatives, namely, conferences and other oral presentations, such as the ones celebrated in honor of Navarrese teachers and the exile community who went through Gurs. In September 2016, three conferences were conducted as part of the agenda to honor repressed teachers: Emilio Majuelo introduced his research on the educational reform of the Spanish Republic, Reyes Berruezo spoke about the repression of the Republican educational project, and Marysa Navarro talked about exile. All three presentations with a focus on education are available to the public on the blog for Escuelas con Memoria at http://memoriahistorica.educacion.navarra.es.

Days before the act of tribute at Gurs in September 2017, professors Josu Chueca and Claude Laharie headed a conference about the history of the concentration camp and its initial use. Gurs was part of a network of camps created by the French government in February 1939 to house the flood of Republican exiles escaping the Francoist advance. At the start of World War II, Gurs was reconfigured as an internment camp for the mass killing of Jews and other minoritized ethnic groups, individuals considered politically dangerous, and maladapted or undesired people in general.

Lengthier projects to raise awareness of the memories of honored communities included relevant research around faculty who faced retaliation for their work or ideas and the documentary film *Camino a Gurs-Gurserako bidea* (Destination: Gurs), an audiovisual project consisting of several interviews about Gurs. The film premiered on February 5, 2019, within a series of commemorative events marking the eightieth anniversary of "La Retirada" (The Retreat), when thousands of Republicans fled a defeated Catalonia into France. The interviews can be watched at www.oroibidea.es.

Over time, these initiatives have been integrated into broader projects. An acclaimed exhibit about early exhumations complementing the double ceremony of 2018 in Sartaguda and Torrero opened in early 2019. The digital version of the exhibit has been available through Oroibidea's online portal since 2020. The institutional tribute to the exiled Navarrese, which the pandemic delayed until 2021, was a featured event in the "Exile, Art, and Memory" program introduced by the Institute of Memory of Navarre in 2020.

The next two courses of action tied to Navarre's memory policies deal with the presence and management of memory in public spaces. The third action addresses the removal of Francoist symbols. Negative memory, represented in Francoist plaques and street names, put into question the role of public spaces in the transmission of democratic values. This third approach dives deep into the reasons and manners in which, Francoism, like other fascist regimes, misappropriated public spaces for its vast ideological and symbolic display with street names paying tribute to Francoist leaders and fighters; fascist plaques displayed on public housing buildings; or through architectural works and urban planning. Only eclipsed in the Spanish state by the Valley of the Fallen, the monument to the fallen in Navarre honoring "the warriors lost in the crusade," is the ultimate expression of the regime's plan to perpetuate the division between victors and conquered: an enduring tribute to the victors for their contribution to the uprising and absolute silence and erasure of the conquered from public spaces. Pamplona-Iruñea's monument to the fallen has been long repudiated by a large segment of society. The future of the building is at stake as of some years ago; memory associations and the community have extensively debated what to do with it, but not even the international call for proposals set up by the City of Pamplona-Iruñea has brought any definitive answers and the resolution has been temporarily paralyzed. The issue of Francoist imagery in Navarre will not get closure until the fate of the monument is decided.

The complex and controversial nature of the matter, like any intervention of the public space, required prior conceptual and contextual knowledge. To that end, experts in different fields met to share and contrast the positive aspects and the downsides of the projects they had implemented in other regions. The bottom line was that Navarre's debate was not unique to the region, but rather, part of a greater debate framed in the context of fascist Europe. Their contributions materialized in the October 2016 conference *Fascismo y lugares de memoria* (Fascism and Sites of Memory), organized by the General Directorate of Peace, Coexistence, and Human Rights and led by prestigious scholars such as Ismael Saz, Reyes Mate, Ricard Vinyes, Lourenzo Fernández Prieto, Francisco Ferrándiz, and Jordi Guixé; and in the June 2017 conference *Simbología dictatorial. Arte y espacio público* (Symbols of Dictatorships. Art and Public Space), where symbols in public spaces were analyzed and interpreted as manifestations of a past that needs to be reformulated through modern values. How should society deal with these symbols? What is the role of history and memory in their treatment? How have neighboring countries approached this issue? A comparative view of the issue and the visionary proposals arising from the art world played substantial parts in the conference, which welcomed Jordi Guixé, Alberto de Bernardi, Marije Hristova, Fernando Sánchez Castillo, and Horst Hoheisel.

Taking detailed inventory of all public emblems and architecture honoring Francoism was the first step on the path to democratizing and removing imagery from public spaces during the initial stages of the program in 2016. Although memory associations had made determined attempts before,[4] the General Directorate of Peace, Coexistence and Human Rights requested a report in 2016 to the Historical Memory Archives of Navarre of the Public University of Navarre (UPNA) to determine the number of Francoist symbols still present in public spaces. Information relayed by local institutions swelled the report with additional more inconspicuous imagery. With the resulting data, the Technical Commission Responsible for the Coordination of Historical Memory Affairs drafted a tentative inventory of existing Francoist symbols in Navarre.

Because emblem removal and replacement are within the responsibility of municipal authorities, the commission reached out to the Federation of Local Councils of Navarre, which agreed to follow the commission's removal guidelines. Especially encouraging was that councils from across the political spectrum committed to the removal process. At present, 292 Francoist symbols of the 350 listed, and 95 honorary mentions of the 112 identified, have been or are being removed. Additional research based on municipal records and other sources suggests that the geographic scope of the honorary mentions to Francoist leaders and to dictator Franco in particular went well beyond the bounds of major urban areas, reaching places unimaginable even for current generations.

Although the symbol-removal process will remain open indefinitely because of the occasional find of unsuspected marks and the challenging aspect of symbol removal in private spaces, where current legislation has no jurisdiction, most of the work was finished by 2019. With the intent to bring these projects to a close and showcase the achievements of local entities in their effort to strengthen Navarre's democratic memory and move toward a culture of peace and respect for human rights, the institute, inspired by a similar event in Barcelona, organized the exhibit *Deconstruir el franquismo—Frankismoaren dekonstruzioa egiten* (Deconstructing Francoism) in partnership with EUROM, the European Observatory on Memories. Through an interactive map of Navarre, visitors had the chance to learn about the process by tapping on the spots where Francoist emblems had been taken down by municipal and local councils and the regional government since 2016. The highest priority of the exhibit was, however, to lay out the reasons behind the removal of Francoist symbols and to stress the substantial role of the project in the construction of a more just and ethical democracy.

The fourth course of action counterpoints its predecessor; it seeks to reclaim the memory of places once sentenced to oblivion. It brings forth a set of constructive policies aimed at spreading and giving visibility to the memory of victims and the resisting margins, and at recognizing the communities that were silenced, punished, and defeated in the wake of the military coup of 1936 and the victory of the Francoist dictatorship. The term *lieux de memoire* (sites of memory), coined by French historian Pierre Nora,[5] originally did not refer, exclusively nor primarily, to traumatizing pasts. But, in the last two decades, sites of memory have evolved to represent spaces where serious human rights violations happened, placing the focus on fascist Europe, the dictatorships of Latin America's Southern Cone and their history of horror and disappearances, and the South African apartheid, to mention some of the most infamous examples of human rights violations of the twentieth century.[6]

Undeniably, it was the community who first reclaimed Navarre's sites of memory. Even during the dark ages of Francoism, places where people knew that victims of the 1936 political purge had been buried would often receive flowers in their memory on special dates such as All Saints' Day. More durable gestures include what is likely the oldest mark of memory in the state,[7] the commemorative plaque placed in the 1960s at the chasm of the Urbasa Plains in memory of the three Amescoans killed there. Starting in the Transition, with the beginning of the early exhumation period, several towns built Republican pantheons to house the remains recovered from mass graves and honor local victims of repression. A sculpture by José Ramón Anda was placed at the chasm of Otsoportillo in Urbasa in 1980 to remember the murdered victims thrown into the karstic cavity. A monolith was installed on Mount Ezkaba in 1988 in remembrance of the gruesome episode of the jailbreak of Fort San Cristóbal on May 22, 1938, and of the prisoners who took part in it. At the turn of the century, as the memory movement caught a second wind in Navarre, plaques, sculptures, and monoliths of all sizes started populating the region to raise awareness of the many episodes of the vast history of Francoist violence that took place in the autonomous community. The *Txinparta Fuerte de San Cristóbal* association sponsored a number of plaques to commemorate the prisoners of Fort San Cristóbal who died from disease and were buried in several cemeteries on the foothills of Mount Ezkaba; the *Ahaztuak* association installed interpretive signs showing the location of mass graves; and the *Memoriaren Bideak* association erected a monolith remembering the thousands of prisoners sentenced to forced labor who built the road between Igari (Igal) and Bidankoze (Vidangoz), between the valleys of Zaraitzu (Salazar) and Erronkari (Roncal). Most importantly, in 2008, the *Pueblo de Viudas* association and Navarre's Association of Family Members of Execution Victims opened the Memory Park of Sartaguda, one of the main sites of memory in southwestern Europe.

The concept of memory sites was first legally referenced in Regional Act 33/2013, concerning the recognition and moral reparations of killed victims and victims of repression in Navarre because of the military coup of 1936. It recognized Sartaguda's Memory Park and Fort San Cristóbal as sites of memory. Unfortunately, because the law failed to appropriately regulate these spaces with protective measures and awareness strategies, only five years later, Parliament had to pass Regional Act 29/2018, of December 26, of Historical Memory Sites of Navarre, to create a legal framework for the regulation of memory sites. According to this law, memory sites are spaces where tragic instances of Francoist violence took place. Mass graves containing thousands of bodies of murdered and kidnapped victims; internment and repression spaces where thousands of people were incarcerated and repressed; and the public construction projects forcibly carried out by political prisoners punished for their support of the legitimate Republican government are considered Historical Memory Sites of Navarre. So, too, are the memorials placed and built by relatives, memory associations, and local and institutional entities mentioned earlier. These spaces were built in memory of the thousands of victims who endured unlawful and unjust violence, to preserve their memory, provide reparations to their families, and present history to future generations as the most effective way to avoid the reoccurrence of similar events.

The registry of Historical Memory Sites of Navarre was created through Regional Act 29/2018, which also introduced a preservation and protection framework, and enforced awareness of these spaces by use of display maps and interpretive signage informing about the historical value of each area and the values it represents. In the immediate stages following the approval of the act, the government of Navarre added thirteen Historical Memory Sites of Navarre to the registry. The Institute of Memory of Navarre and the General Directorate of Peace, Coexistence and Human Rights requested the inclusion of some of these sites, which were listed in the tentative inventory drafted by the Technical Commission Responsible for the Coordination of Historical Memory Affairs. Local agencies and memory associations advocated to add the remaining places. This first batch was formed by sites known for having left a deep mark in Navarre's memory: Sartaguda's Memory Park;[8] the graves in Valcardera, la Tejería de Monreal and Olabe; Otsoportillo's chasm; the memorials built in recent years in Etxauri's Memory Park, Ibero's Tres Cruces Hill, Argaitz's quarry in Bera and by the mass graves of Mount Erreniega; the sculpture erected in Peralta to condemn repression against women; Mount Ezkaba's GR225 long-distance trail re-creating the route taken by prisoners of Fort San Cristóbal after the May 22, 1938, jailbreak; and a well-protected replica of the barracks where captives lived huddled together, which was based off a picture of a prisoner and built by the road between Igari and Bidankoze, close to a monolith placed years earlier by the *Memoriaren Bideak* association. New memory sites such as Pamplona-Iruñea's old provincial prison, the sculpture by the mass graves of Loiti Hill and the memorial in Elizondo commemorating the Navarrese gone into exile and the solidarity networks that helped them in their undertaking have been gradually added to the registry. Until the summer of 2022, official procedures have been carried out to recognize the memorials for the detention centers of Pamplona-Iruñea as Historical Memory Sites of Navarre: an area in the vicinity of the bullfighting arena covered in cement blocks simulating tombs; a plaque remembering the inhabitants of Pamplona-Iruñea killed in the wake of the 1936 military coup placed at the Vuelta de Castillo park; the sculpture "For memory" in Larraga's Memory Park; Oroibidea, the digital archive; the Uroz memorial park and the memorial space of Plazuela de Lodosa. Steadily, the preliminary inventory brought forward in 2017 by the Technical Commission Responsible for the Coordination of Historical Memory Affairs is steps closer to completion.

Both the commission and memory associations have been considering adopting new approaches to the matter. With the extensive collection of burial sites, detention centers, forced labor spaces and memorials spread throughout the region, the registry of Historical Memory Sites of Navarre would struggle to reach full completion. To steer clear of that scenario, they determined it would be best to narrow the registry's focus down to iconic and symbolic places that either are of particular importance to the memory movement or represent other places through their own recognition. The memorial commemorating the burial sites of Loiti recognizes, for instance, all irregular inhumations that took place on both gradients of Loiti Hill, including the undiscovered graves. Nonetheless, the Institute of Memory of Navarre is determined to increase visibility of all sites of memory, listed or not on the registry, through a comprehensive awareness campaign. The project *Espacios de memoria—Memoria Guneak* (Memory Sites) was conceived under this campaign to afford local and out-of-region visitors quick and easy access to Navarre's traumatizing history by means of interpretive signs and displays placed along several itineraries and on sites of memory that are and are not included in the official registry. Thirteen itineraries, available on espaciosdememoria.com, were designed to cover the miscellany of memory spaces across Navarre's geography. Thousands of brochures with maps featuring these routes have been distributed and are available to the public at tourist offices, country guest houses, educational institutions, and memory associations. Together, the itineraries make up a wide network of two hundred sites with the prospect of incorporating at least that many more.

These efforts emanate from the firm conviction that memory sites and spaces serve as perpetual witnesses to a terrible past and inform future generations and society at large of the multiple forms of violence that the rebels unleashed after July 1936 and during the Francoist dictatorship.

The Escuelas con Memoria (EM) school program is the fifth course of action of the Institute of Memory of Navarre. Innovative and interdisciplinary, the project aims to establish a dialogue between the areas of education and of public policy, specifically of policies related to exhumations, places of memory and research on human rights violations and on the political violence perpetrated by the victors of the 1936 uprising. It paves the way for a novel teaching methodology of the social sciences, one which gives precedence to education in democratic values, problematizes the school curriculum, and encourages faculty to help students navigate complex social issues.[9] Several research outcomes suggest that schools repeatedly fail to accurately portray the military uprising of July 1936, the Civil War, and the Francoist dictatorship.[10] It is, therefore, essential that students are exposed to the widely supported historiography produced in recent decades on Francoist repression, which challenges traditional views of the past so deeply ingrained in Spanish society. The program does not boil down to new historiographic findings only. It makes sure that knowledge of this research does not happen in an isolated, self-contained environment; students simultaneously get acquainted with the enduring legacy of these historical processes, which, still today, bear palpable consequences and are a source of heated debate in Navarrese society. Critical thinking is at the basis of the current education reform, along with the commitment to instill a sense of duty to respect human rights and defend democracy, as opposed to teaching philosophies imposed by fascist regimes and similar ideologies.

The EM program has three main points. The first one relates to faculty training. Teachers receive periodical training on scientific advances and new teaching methods, and they are encouraged to work with one another to create new material and experiences. The second point outlines activities related to memory. Schools have access to activities that expose students to the places and people involved in the historical events of their recent past. The third point introduces the network of Escuelas con Memoria. This network will be open to those educational institutions that incorporate memory projects into their school curriculums.

The faculty training program is offered in the Annual Faculty Training Plan managed by the Department of Education's Faculty Support Center. This package of courses and seminars promotes the professional development of teachers by introducing them to the latest teaching strategies to work with memory in the classroom. Despite their variations in content and structure, these courses are united by five defining goals: to value memory as a meaningful learning tool; to learn about memory-related public policies and projects of other regions; to integrate memory sites into the students' learning journey; to analyze cases in which historical memory became the backbone of the teaching experience; and to create customized teaching materials from audiovisual sources. Occasionally, these trainings have led to public conferences such as *Fascismo y Lugares de memoria* (Fascism and Memory Sites) in October 2016 or *Gerardo Lizarraga*. In *Pintor en el exilio* (Gerardo Lizarraga. Painter in Exile) in January 2021, scholars in a range of fields shared their perspectives and expertise on the matter. Most courses combine an overview of the leading projects carried out in other regions and a theoretical approach to the role of memory in the school setting. Many tools and resources, initially not intended for school use, are available to faculty to enhance their student's research projects, including the database of Navarre's Historical Memory Archives (https://memoria-oroimena.unavarra.es) or the series of interview compilations, virtual exhibits, and digital archives preserved at the Institute of Memory of Navarre, which will eventually also be accessible through the Oroibidea online portal.[11] Likewise, seminars tailored to the requests of the teachers attending the courses have produced encouraging results. In the multidisciplinary seminar *La Gran Fuga* (The Great Escape), faculty from multiple trade schools came together to create an escape room themed around the jailbreak of Fort San Cristóbal for their students.

Escuelas con Memoria is most known for the activities it offers students. The program adds improved and more varied activities every year, and for the last few, it has distributed handouts with the list of activities scheduled for the school year. The scope of the catalog is too broad to analyze in detail here, but we invite readers to browse its digital version through the link provided on the list of online resources.[12] The conferences, documentaries, and exhibits within the catalog aim to help teachers successfully use memory in the classroom. They are also devised to reinforce school projects, but since demands are usually unique to each school, the Memory Section of the government of Navarre provides more effective and personalized solutions for these demands. Based on a local-to-global methodology, the program goes against uniform approaches to memory in the school setting, and, instead, favors memory strategies that fit localized expressions of Francoist violence and that ultimately lead to conversations on the global phenomenon of fascist violence against humanity.

The two school projects designed by the Institute of Memory of Navarre follow this line of thinking. The first one, *Memoria de Libertad—Libertaden Memoria*[13] (Libertad's

Memory) is a high school learning unit developed by teachers Oskia Ramírez Barace and Cristina Palacios Belloso from Iturrama High School. Originally conceived as a school project focusing on the play *Donde el bosque se espesa*[14] (Where the Woods Thicken), the project proved valuable enough to be tested at other schools with promising results. In view of this, the institute adapted it into a learning unit. Through it, students embark on an investigative project to learn about the life of Libertad Uriz—the project's only fictional character. Libertad takes students on a somber tour of the repression exerted in Navarre, the military coup, the Civil War, exile, World War II, the fight against Francoism, the extermination camps, and the lack of recognition upon the end of the war. Guided by their teacher, students work on their research in collaborative teams and, at the end of the project, present their results to the rest of the class. The process does not constrain students to fixed narratives and discourses, but rather, encourages them to examine the primary sources with critical thinking and creativity.

The second learning unit, titled *Amonarenean kea—Humo en casa de la abuela*[15] (Smoke at Grandma's House), targets children in elementary school, and it stems from a story of the same name written by journalist Dani Martirena and illustrated by Ana Ibáñez. This auspicious project, drafted by elementary teachers Eneko Gamarra and Irantzu Rodríguez Senosiain, focuses on shared reading and dialectical thinking strategies and seeks to engage students in the active analysis of sources.

The meetings set up to get the younger generations acquainted with the families of victims are among the most tantalizing events of the program's broad catalog of activities. Places that once witnessed the repression practices and the political cleansing of the 1936 coup now host these gatherings. The intergenerational critical discussions that ensue there have the potential to reclaim the meaning of these spaces of terror and they touch on current examples of human rights violations, which younger generations may find more relatable. Contexts of armed conflict, massacre, mass graves, refugee crises, and exile provide key insights into how human interactions could become more just and democratic, and, as a result, more respectful of human rights.

These intergenerational gatherings have happened across a spectrum of activities and contexts. The perfect example are the school trips planned to burial sites; students from schools participating in the EM program visit a mass grave that the team of experts from Aranzadi is prospecting and exhuming. There, they learn about and understand first-hand the tragedy of the disappeared, listen to witness accounts or to residents retelling the memories of their family members, and converse with members of the associations present at the exhumation. Additionally, they have direct access to the intricacies and methodology behind the multidisciplinary work performed by Aranzadi. Teachers agree that the visit leaves a powerful and unforgettable impression on students, who can usually form a more realistic picture of the impact of Francoist repression on human lives, as remains emerge from the grave. On more than one occasion, students born in Latin America have connected these violent deaths to the deaths occurred in their home countries. Although the most frequent visitors are high schoolers, they are not the only participants. Trade school students, students with a nonformal education background, and elementary school students visit these sites from time to time. The outing of a group of sixth graders from Ezkaba Public School to the grave where the remains of two runaway prisoners from Fort San Cristóbal were being exhumed on May 22, 2018, exactly eighty years after the jailbreak, may have been the most memorable visit to date. Certainly, prior work in the classroom was key to an enriching experience and proof that a historical memory curriculum can be appropriate for all school grades.

The hike *Las Botellas de la Libertad* (Bottles of Freedom), centered on the jailbreak of Fort San Cristóbal, is another excellent school experience. Students from different schools gather to walk two of the four sections of Trail GR225. The trail, recognized as a Historical Memory Site of Navarre, is highlighted with interpretive signs and sponsored by the Institute of Memory of Navarre. It retraces the most popular route taken by prisoners in their mostly failed attempt to find freedom; the last section of the trail follows the steps of Jovino Fernández, one of the only three runaways—out of 795—who managed to cross into France, in Máximo's case, into the French Basque town of Urepele (Urepel). Experience shows that schools spend varying amounts of time preparing their students for the event. In view of this, the project provides a transdisciplinary package of material to all schools. Students learn the basics of hiking in physical education class; as a science project, they explore and analyze the trail's ecosystems with the invaluable help of the Forestry Unit of the government of Navarre, which always joins the hikes and has shown great interest in the project; and they understand the fundamental purpose behind the trail and the hike— to remember the tragic feat of a group of starving, shoeless men who tried to flee the fort through unknown terrain but were ultimately hunted down by merciless armed men. Most of them were captured and 206 of them arbitrarily killed and buried in a string of graves spread along the trail. Throughout the hike, the students, no more than two hundred per section at a time for capacity reasons, listen to the explanations of researchers and forest rangers. At the end of each section of the trail, a brief act of tribute in memory of the runaways takes place with music, poetry, prose, and dance pieces performed and prepared by students. The first section of the trail surrounds Olabe's burial site, where, in 2016, sixteen bodies of prisoners not much older than the visiting students were exhumed. For the 2022 edition, students attended the delivery ceremony of the recently identified remains of Máximo Sainz Plaza, the youngest prisoner, who was killed not long after his eighteenth birthday. Máximo's family was also able to attend the deeply emotional ceremony. The second section ends in Urepele, whose municipal council has offered great support from the beginning. Bottles filled with the pictures, letters, and other documents provided by the families to commemorate the escaped prisoners are then delivered in an act which families can attend in person or telephonically. These bottles symbolize the original ones used at the *Cementerio de las Botellas* in the surrounding area of Fort San Cristóbal to identify the prisoners buried there. The bottles have become the centerpiece of the hike. Distributed at the beginning of the hike at Mount Ezkaba and delivered in Urepele, the bottles are meant to symbolically guide the prisoners to the freedom that was taken from them. All the bottles delivered since the hike's first edition in 2018 will be exhibited at the new Interpretation Center of Urepele set to open in the summer of 2022.

Sometimes, the hikes resonate deep within certain participants who go on to design inspiring projects such as the *kamishibai* Japanese-style play and the documentary film created by the Ochoa de Olza secondary school students,[16] which received an honorable mention in the Eustory history contest open to young researchers of twenty-five European countries.

The Memory Park of Sartaguda, Navarre's renowned site of memory and one of the most important in southwestern Europe, welcomes young students and families of Franco-era victims during its famous yearly gatherings. Following the opening speech, the meeting splits into smaller groups formed by forty to fifty youths and a relative of a victim of Francoist violence. Scattered around the park, family members tell their stories to their groups. The jovial and loud atmosphere typically present at a park filled with teenagers gradually gives way to a respectful silence as the emotional accounts of the guest speakers enthrall their audiences. After the small-group activity, attendees can join an art or literary workshop or take a guided tour of the park. The final act features music, dance, and other art forms commonly performed by students. Some artists, such as Navarrese singer Enrique Villarreal "El Drogas," a big memory advocate, have also taken part in the closing act.

The first edition, in 2019, had a turnout of three hundred students, and the art created at the workshop was included in a chapter of an art and memory journal.[17] The 2020 edition was canceled because of the COVID-19 pandemic, and the 2021 edition was hosted online. The 2022 edition returned to Sartaguda amid eager anticipation; the gathering had to be held on two consecutive days to accommodate the thousand students who had signed up for the event.

As mentioned, the EM program offers flexibility and support to adequately serve the proposals of the participating schools. The program sponsored visits to the prison of Bustarviejo in Madrid, as requested by two Navarrese high schools. It endorsed the initiative by the City of Erronkari (Roncal), its local school, and the *Memoriaren Bideak* association to install a plaque and an interpretive panel about the building's history as the first stop for prisoners sentenced to forced labor where they stayed while building the road between Igari and Bidankoze. Along with these initiatives, Escuelas con Memoria gives students the chance to visit the concentration camp in Gurs, which housed more than four hundred Navarrese people running away from Francoist terror, through the student exchange programs developed by several Navarrese schools in partnership with other foreign schools such as the Lycée Jules Supervielle in the French town of Oloron Ste Marie. When French students come to Navarre, they visit popular sites of memory such as Fort San Cristóbal, Mount Ezkaba, or the Memory Park of Sartaguda.

The Institute of Memory of Navarre has supported a variety of school-specific projects through Escuelas con Memoria. Several school institutions have requested the institute's assistance in managing and financing school plays themed around memory. Theater companies from Navarre and elsewhere have shared their ideas with the institute on how to collaborate in these art projects. The 2021 trailblazing project *Teatro con Memoria* (Theater with Memory), launched through Escuelas con Memoria, establishes a symbiotic relationship between theater companies and schools. In this elevating experience, thousands of students have the chance to watch plays about local and European memories in their many expressions and to talk to the actors afterward.

Other forms of collaboration between the Institute of Memory of Navarre and school institutions involve the international and I+ high school programs. The first collaborative agreement was signed with IES Valle del Ebro High School in Tutera (Tudela) to promote two student-led research projects. One was about the concentration camp of Gurs, which housed several interns from Tutera, and the other was about the early exhumations in the Erribera (Rivera) region of Tutera. For this last project, students were able to obtain rare written and graphic records from private collections which have helped cast new light on a hardly explored subject. Over time, the institute has established collaborative ties with three high schools: IES Plaza de la Cruz, IES Navarro Villoslada, and IES Barañain.

The book *Escuelas con Memoria*, with three core chapters, elaborates on a large selection of these experiences. The first chapter details the key aspects of the program and outlines the accompanying educational resources, including the two learning units mentioned earlier. The second chapter revolves around fifteen elementary and secondary school experiences. Some of them have already been addressed here, but the chapter includes many others particular to each school. The third chapter showcases several senior theses from UPNA's Social Sciences Education Department featuring research data and teaching methodologies on how to integrate memory in the school setting. These experiences were set to be presented at the *I Historia con Memoria en la Educación* (History and Memory in the Classroom) international conference in Pamplona-Iruñea in 2022, co-sponsored by the Institute of Memory of Navarre and research groups and institutions specializing in teaching methodologies. It received at least 160 paper proposals and has sparked the interest of the entire country.

The international volunteer work program launched in 2017 belongs to the section of general collaboration projects with the youth and the nonformal education field. Through this program, young volunteers have had the chance to work at *Cementerio de las Botellas*, where more than a hundred prisoners from Fort San Cristóbal who died from disease and hardship were buried; at the Pyrenean fortifications of Auritz (Burguete), Erratzu, Bera, Eugi and Erronkari; and on the construction of a replica of one of Igari's barracks, where Francoist prisoners were crammed while they were forced to build the road mentioned earlier.

This trailblazing program ultimately strives to establish a network of schools with memory. At present, because of an agreement between the two agencies, the General Directorate of Peace, Coexistence and Human Rights and the Department of Education are shaping the network's administrative side. Once the network is in place, schools will be able to collaborate with each other and form a reciprocal relationship with their social environment, working together and sharing experiences, nurturing from their community's accounts of a common devastating past, and contributing through projects of diverse formats as a way of giving back.

Lastly, the sixth course of action pertains to all initiatives involving the transmission and spreading of memory. The Institute of Memory of Navarre is predominantly concerned with the preservation of the heritage of memory through written records, testimonies, pictures, and audiovisual content; the writing of reports focused on victims' right to truth; and the awareness and spreading of memory by use of exhibits, documentary films, and conferences.

Preserving the heritage of memory is one of the main duties of the Documentary Center of the Institute of Memory of Navarre, which has a Memory and Human Rights special library, part of Navarre's public library network. As of June 2023, the library held a collection of more than six thousand cataloged titles accessible to the public. The center is working on ways to make the collection more accessible to the community, including through a newsletter that informs readers about new titles and themed reading guides. The other major feature is the center's digital archive, a project for the preservation and promotion of memory built on the Oroibidea-Camino de memoria online portal (https://oroibidea.es), through the document-management platform Dédalo.[18] All materials, no matter their format or origin, are first funneled through Dédalo, before they undergo a standard record-management process and are indexed through a common thesaurus centered on the victims of rebel repression and the Francoist dictatorship. Materials are also indexed by name, place, theme, and chronological criteria.

Because of its complexity, the Oroibidea-Camino de memoria project had to be developed in multiple phases. During the first phase, 161 interviews amounting to 108 hours of recorded content from fourteen different projects were published. With this material, the center indexed more than twelve hundred clips that can be accessed using individual or combined search criteria. Full interviews are available, too. In the coming months, this archive of oral memories of Navarre will incorporate new sets of interviews.

During the second phase, under development, the center is set to transfer to the portal much of the archival collections digitized by the Institute of Memory of Navarre or given by other institutions and foundations to be included in the portal. The phase is expected to be completed by the end of 2023. There are two types of collections. The first type consists of digitized collections from public archives. The second type comprises private documents provided by their owners or custodians to the Institute of Memory of Navarre for their digitalization and archival arrangement following ISAD guidelines. After their digitalization, the physical documents go back to their custodians, while the digitized copies are sent to Dédalo where they are registered, indexed, and published following parameters like those for oral collections. This way, the institute makes all the material related to specific towns or victims, regardless of its format, easily accessible to the public. To give an idea of the archive's volume, the Institute of Memory of Navarre currently preserves about thirty collections comprising more than sixty thousand digital artifacts, including pictures, images, brochures, and other written material.

In addition to the digital archive, Oroibidea offers a search box to find places and people in the forty most relevant research works on Francoist repression in Navarre, and it also offers several virtual exhibits meant to introduce the collections to visitors through brief explanatory texts and digitized materials particular to each exhibit's theme. Exhibits include *Lur Azpian-Bajo Tierra. Exhumaciones tempranas en Navarra* (Buried. Early Exhumations in Navarre); *Memorias de la objeción de conciencia y la insumisión en Navarra* (Memories of Conscientious Objectors and Draft Dodgers in Navarre); and *La ciudad de los cautivos. Centros de detención en Pamplona, 1936–1945* (The Captive City. Detention Centers in Pamplona-Iruñea, 1936–1945).

Over the last years, the Institute of Memory of Navarre has conducted major investigative work to elucidate and conceptualize the repression exerted in Navarre and to contribute to the victims' right to truth. The institute furthers the activities of the Historical Memory Archives of Navarre, located at the UPNA and financed by the government and Navarre Parliament. Their synergy has produced remarkable outcomes. A few of their most relevant publications include registries listing Navarrese people in exile and articles on economic repression, deportations to Nazi concentration camps, Franco-era repression of the LGBTQ+ community, border repression, and the detention centers of Pamplona-Iruñea. The Institute has promoted additional publications and has contributed in the addition of other research works on repression.

Promoting memory heritage and general investigative work on Francoist repression constitutes the central mission of the Institute of Memory of Navarre. Part of this mission is to identify the media and platforms that ensure easy access for the whole of the community, not just memory advocates and specialists. Documentary festivals such as *Imágenes con Memoria* (Images with Memory), on its fourth edition, are a shining example of this effort.[19] Additionally, all events and ceremonies are recorded and shared whenever possible. Short clips of the events are uploaded to social media platforms, mainly, to the YouTube channel of the General Directorate of Peace, Coexistence and Human Rights.

Awareness and spreading efforts are project-based. These projects act as binding agents that bring initiatives from multiple courses of action together, effectively hindering isolation and fostering collaboration in the development of youth and school projects, plans for the recognition of places of memory, exhumation programs, institutional tribute ceremonies, and awareness activities. The plan is to launch a project every year to coordinate all the institute's awareness initiatives. The 2018 project "Ezkaba 1938–2018," marking the eightieth anniversary of the jailbreak of Fort San Cristóbal, encompassed the still unfinished exhumation works of the runaways' graves; the opening of the GR225 trail following the steps of the escaped prisoners; the opening edition of the *Las Botellas de la Libertad* hike within the EM program; and the youth volunteer work program at the *Cementerio de las Botellas*. Within the same project, the famous *Ezkaba, 1938–2018* exhibit, which has welcomed thousands of visitors from all corners of Navarre since its opening, along with a catalog and Amaia Kowasch's book *Tejiendo redes-Sareak ehortzen. Mujeres solidarias con los presos del Fuerte de San Cristóbal (1934–1945)* (Weaving Nets. Women in Solidarity with the Runaways of Fort San Cristóbal) were presented. In the book, Kowasch rebuilds the solidarity networks established to help the prisoners of Fort San Cristóbal through a hand-woven lacework of direct and indirect testimonies of dozens of women. The 2019 exhibit *Lur Azpian-Bajo Tierra* showcased the early exhumation period, of exceptional relevance in Navarre between 1978 and 1980. In September and October 2018, the above-mentioned institutional ceremonies in Sartaguda and Torrero took place. The gestation of the physical and virtual versions of *Bajo Tierra-Lur Azpian* drove the launch of the Documentary Center's digital archive to assist in the digitalization of thousands of pictures and written records and in the recording of the accounts of the people involved in the movement. The 2020–2021 project featured the lives of those Navarrese who went into exile and remembered them through a number of activities and projects: registries of exiled and deported citizens, as previously mentioned; research projects; an institutional recognition ceremony and a commemorative sculpture, recognized as a Historical Memory Site of Navarre, in Elizondo; and a major exhibit about Gerardo Lizarraga, an artist from Pamplona-Iruñea exiled in Mexico.[20] The public exhibit was first held at the Museum of Navarre and later at Fundación Lázaro Galdiano in Madrid along with the presentation of a catalog with his works and a conference on art and memory. This exhibit catalyzed the ongoing project *Fronteras de Hormigón* (Concrete Borders) headlining a major traveling exhibit presented at venues on both sides of the Pyrenees displaying the fortifications of the Pyrenees and along the Atlantic Wall with a focus on the forced labor performed by the prisoners, and a youth volunteering program to restore the fortifications in northern Navarre.

Within the scope of these courses of action, the Institute of Memory of Navarre strives to restore the right of Franco-era victims to truth and reparations and to remind the community at large that its present and future, as a society based on human rights and democratic values, largely depend on its critical memory.

BIBLIOGRAPHY

Ares, Berta. "Entrevista a Reyes Mate, filósofo de la memoria." *Revistas de Letras. Periodismo, Cultura, Pensamiento*, https://revistadeletras.net/reyes-mate-existe-un-deber-de-memoria-porque-al-conocimiento-se-le-escapa-mucha-realidad/ (Accessed July 19, 2022).

Autobús de la Memoria/Oroimenaren Autobusa. Simbología golpista en Navarra. Memoria y presencia del franquismo, 1936–2014. Pamplona-Iruñea: Pamiela, 2014.

Díez Gutiérrez, Enrique Javier, and Alberto Garzón. La asignatura pendiente: la memoria histórica democrática en los libros de texto escolares. Madrid: Plaza y Valdés, 2020.

Ezkieta, Fermín. *Los fugados del Fuerte de Ezkaba*. Pamplona-Iruñea: Pamiela, 2013.

García de Albizu, Balbino. ¿Qué hicimos aquí con el 36? La represión de civiles en retaguardia por su ideología en las Améscoas y Urbasa. Pamplona-Iruñea: Lamiñarra, 2017.

Gastón, José Miguel, César Layana, Nuria Ricart, and Jordi Guixé. " 'Se lo llevaron. Nunca más lo hemos visto.' Sartaguda. Transmisiones de la memoria." *Arte, memoria y espacio público*, edited by Carme Barbanys, Iratxe Momoitio and Jordi Guixé, 191–205. Granollers: Ayuntamiento, 2020.

González de Oleaga, Marisa, Carolina Meloni González (eds). "Topografías de la memoria: de usos y costumbres en los espacios de violencia en el nuevo milenio." *Kamchatka: revista de análisis cultural* 13 (2019).

Mainer, Juan (ed.). Pensar críticamente la educación escolar. Perspectivas y controversias historiográficas. Zaragoza: Prensas Universitarias, 2008.

Nora, Pierre. *Les Lieux de mémoire*. Paris: Gallimard (Bibliothèque ilustrée des histoires), three volumes, 1984–1992.

Pagès, Joan, Antoni Santisteban. "Una mirada del pasado al futuro en la Didáctica de las Ciencias Sociales." In *Una mirada al pasado y un proyecto de futuro. Investigación e innovación en didáctica de las Ciencias Sociales*. Barcelona: Universitat Autònoma de Barcelona, 2014.

NOTES

1 References to Halbwachs and Benjamin can be found in Berta Ares's "Entrevista a Reyes Mate, filósofo de la memoria," *Revistas de Letras. Periodismo, Cultura, Pensamiento*, https://revistadeletras.net/reyes-mate-existe-un-deber-de-memoria-porque-al-conocimiento-se-le-escapa-mucha-realidad/.

2 The priest Victorino Aranguren estimated 2,168 bodies were recovered, although he probably included both Navarre and La Rioja's exhumations in his calculations.

3 Fermín Ezkieta, *Los fugados del Fuerte de Ezkaba* (Pamplona-Iruñea: Pamiela, 2013).

4 Autobús de la Memoria/Oroimenaren Autobusa, *Simbología golpista en Navarra. Memoria y presencia del franquismo, 193—2014* (Pamplona-Iruñea: Pamiela, 2014).

5 Pierre Nora, *Les Lieux de mémoire* (Paris: Gallimard Bibliothèque ilustrée des histoires, three volumes., 1984–1992).

6 A recent compilation: Marisa González de Oleaga and Carolina Meloni González (eds),

"Topografías de la memoria: de usos y costumbres en los espacios de violencia en el nuevo milenio," *Kamchatka: revista de análisis cultural* 13 (2019).

7 The hypothesis that this may be the oldest memory symbol in the state remembering the violence of 1936 is formulated by historian Roldán Jimeno in Balbino García de Albizu's *¿Qué hicimos aquí con el 36? La represión de civiles en retaguardia por su ideología en las Améscoas y Urbasa* (Pamplona-Iruñea: Lamiñarra, 2017), 270.

8 Soon after they were added, the *Pueblo de las Viudas* association and Navarre's Association of Family Members of Execution Victims signed an agreement with the government of Navarre to hand over the sculptures at Sartaguda's Memory Park to the government for their management.

9 Joan Pagès and Antoni Santisteban, "Una mirada del pasado al futuro en la Didáctica de las Ciencias Sociales," in *Una mirada al pasado y un proyecto de futuro. Investigación e innovación en didáctica de las Ciencias Sociales.* (Barcelona: Universitat Autònoma de Barcelona, 2014), 17–41; Juan Mainer (ed.), *Pensar críticamente la educación escolar. Perspectivas y controversias historiográficas* (Zaragoza: Prensas Universitarias, 2008).

10 Enrique Javier Díez Gutiérrez and Alberto Garzón, La asignatura pendiente: la memoria histórica democrática en los libros de texto escolares (Madrid: Plaza y Valdés, 2020).

11 The blog *Memoria Histórica y Educación* comprises the bulk of resources and materials used in these trainings and some of the projects developed within the program. Memoria Histórica y Educación: https://memoriahistorica.educacion.navarra.es.

12 See https://memoriahistorica.educacion.navarra.es/escuelas-con-memoria/ and https://pazyconvivencia.navarra.es/escuelas-con-memoria.

13 https://pazyconvivencia.navarra.es/ud-memoria-de-libertad.

14 The play, directed by Laila Ripoll and Mariano Llorente and performed by the Micomicón acting company, was created within the Unsettling Remembering and Social Cohesion in Transnational Europe (UNREST) European project, in partnership with the Spanish National Research Council (CSIC) and several European universities. It premiered in Pamplona-Iruñea on December 13 and 14, 2018, with an audience short of two thousand tenth and eleventh graders.

15 https://pazyconvivencia.navarra.es/ud-amonarenean-kea.

16 https://www.youtube.com/watch?v=hTwChAGQ4iI.

17 José Miguel Gastón et al., "'Se lo llevaron. Nunca más lo hemos visto.' Sartaguda. Transmisiones de la memoria" in *Arte, memoria y espacio público*, eds. Carme Barbanys, Iratxe Momoitio and Jordi Guixé (Granollers: Ayuntamiento, 2020), 191–205.

18 Dédalo (https://dedalo.dev/) is a tangible and intangible heritage management platform developed by Render, a company specialized in the management of heritage and memory.

19 https://pazyconvivencia.navarra.es/imagenes-con-memoria.

20 Information of the physical exhibit and the conference here: https://pazyconvivencia.navarra.es/es/gerardo-lizarraga. Readers can visit the permanent online exhibit here: https://pazyconvivencia.navarra.es/es/gerardo-lizarraga-virtual.

four

Heritagization of Sites Associated with Conflicts

An Analysis of UNESCO's Current Debate*

Maider Maraña

INTRODUCTION

For decades now, several institutions, wanting to broaden the scope of cultural heritage, have been granting heritage status and protection to properties where human rights violations were committed or that were witness to some kind of conflict. Known, among other terms, as *dark heritage, sites of memory*, or *spaces for peace*, these sites are not free from controversy. They still fuel intense debates because of the political and legal implications—and even identity implications for some groups—that they carry.

As one of the leading intergovernmental forums in heritage matters, UNESCO's World Heritage Committee is one of the agents involved in the controversy surrounding heritage associated with conflicts. When, in 2018, France and Belgium nominated Funerary and Memorial Sites of the First World War for inscription on the World Heritage List, ICOMOS, as UNESCO's advisory body, suggested that UNESCO's 1972 World Heritage Convention was not equipped with the appropriate tools to assess the nominations associated with the recent past and conflicts.

Their nomination reignited a long-standing discussion within the World Heritage Convention, which has experienced a notable resurgence in recent times. In response to the French-Belgian case, the World Heritage Committee established, during the same 2018 session, a working group to evaluate and address the needs of properties defined as sites of memory associated with recent conflicts. In the discussion paper presented during the 2021 session, the working group recommended that it remain open considering no consensus had been reached on the matter because of the committee's internal debates.

The chapter's aim is to analyze the reality behind the nominations of post-conflict sites for heritage, with a special focus on UNESCO and other United Nations bodies.

HERITAGIZATION OF SITES ASSOCIATED WITH CONFLICTS
EVOLUTION OF THE DISCOURSE OF HERITAGE

New understandings and angles on cultural heritage have pushed the concept of heritage forward within the academic discourse and the "authorized heritage discourse,"[1] through the accumulation of data alone and through the process of data reshaping existing notions. Over the decades, more elements previously considered "unworthy" of receiving heritage status and protection have made the Heritage List.

Heritage is a subjective concept constructed by institutional, political, and "authorized" voices, defined by our own structures and based on choice and selection processes. The power relations within our society influence the heritage elements we choose to preserve at a specific time and place.[2] As an artifact of memory, heritage represents a power struggle, or, to quote professor" is "a mediation process where a variety of actors negotiate positions of value and interest to determine what is worth preserving and studying."[3]

Heritagization is a process that begins with society wanting to understand its past from a different point of view and crystallizes when institutions respond to that need with programs and legislation. Sometimes, this process can happen from the top down, when public institutions trigger the community's sense of heritage toward certain elements of its past by elevating and celebrating them.

On this basis, while academia and field-heritage practice explore ways to accommodate new perspectives, representatives of the authorized heritage discourse work to formally give shape to a static definition of heritage through political, legal, and administrative instruments.[4] In an evolving society, with ever-changing notions of heritage, legislation becomes a pliable and adaptable mechanism. As a result, heritage properties receive a legal treatment that directly stems "from the social, economic and symbolic interests attributed to them by the systems of power" as professor Javier García Fernández asserts.[5] UNESCO and the European Union are two high-standing promoters of this authorized discourse, as evinced in national and local legislations.

It is widely known that, throughout history, political powers have frequently misused cultural heritage to achieve mostly political and ideological ends. Heritage was, and still is, used to legitimize power and for political propaganda purposes, prized for its national identity-building power and its efficacy at conveying specific narratives. For García Fernández, using heritage to justify political ideals "entails a rigorous legal dimension."[6] The legal aspect of heritage plays a pivotal role in formulating the regulatory measures to effectively tackle the distinct challenges arising from heritage associated with conflicts, as this chapter explains.

Since the mid-twentieth century, because of the extensive development of international law brought about by the creation of the United Nations System and other regional systems, international agents have toiled to promote, protect, and build a legal framework for cultural reality, and cultural heritage, in particular. Regulatory measures and conventions are a few of the intergovernmental tools that have come out of the efforts to protect heritage in all its forms. Never in history "has there been such a heightened international awareness nor have nation states been so strongly committed to the international community" in relation to heritage.[7] It should be noted that international law does not go by one general concept of heritage;[8] multiple conventions and regulations, and even the organization's internal bodies, embrace different categories and definitions of it.

Regarding conflict, all societies throughout history and across the world have suffered some manifestation of it, whether it be war, social divisions, ethnic clashes, oppression and discrimination, or structural violence. In its aftermath, "the scars left by a painful past may show in a multiplicity of shapes"[9] and may inhabit public and private spaces, as well as objects. Today, the past is playing an increasingly relevant role in issues that concern the present, and historical injustices are gaining traction in contemporary debates on justice and human rights.[10]

The polymorphic nature of conflict and memory makes it impossible to produce an exhaustive list that would accurately represent what sites of conflict stand for. An absence of a common agreement to identify the dimensions of such conflicts obscures their definition even further. Violence, war, and conflict are most frequently the focus, whereas other perspectives tend to highlight resilience and the fight for human rights. Time is also an obstacle in this context: heritagization of sites where wars, battles, and clashes of the historical past happened is undisputedly accepted, but any element tied to conflict and human rights violations of the past hundred years seems to face strong opposition when it comes to heritage recognition and protection.

Sites of recent conflicts usually refer to spaces where killings, genocide, and massacres occurred. These places include cemeteries, prisons, battlefields, military complexes, symbolic buildings, murals, and even spaces where artifacts and testimonies of victims are preserved, including museums and archives. Because in part to lack of consensus, many of these sites lie abandoned and neglected and have transformed into private spaces of grief, excluded from the inventory of sites that are seemingly crucial for the identity and cohesion of societies.

Sara McDowell, a lecturer in human geography at University of Ulster, proposes an alternative reading of these spaces when she suggests that sites associated with conflicts are, in fact, originally ordinary spaces where people go about their lives, which, after a traumatizing event, acquire emotional significance and evolve into heritage sites.[11]

In recent decades, ideas of heritage have been evolving away from nation-state narratives that glorify fallen soldiers and moving resolutely toward a more victim-centered culture.

The lack of a concrete typology clearly hints at the complexity of the issue. In 2017, the World Tourism Organization (UNWTO), a UN Specialized Agency, launched a project to explore the implications of tourism in post-conflict areas. The goal of this research project involved identifying best practices that would benefit peace-building processes worldwide. In their search, the investigative team embarked in a painstaking selection process of ten iconic places around the world. After several discussions over the nature and scope of post-conflict sites, the team finally agreed to study sites and landscapes with the following characteristics:

a) The site or landscape offers a first-hand account of the conditions and circumstances under which the conflict happened.
b) The site or landscape contains architectural and archeological evidence—physical points of reference—that help explain the historical events.
c) Citizens are able to approach the conflict with mature and objective judgment, even if they still suffer from its consequences. If this approach is unfeasible, the site should be a potential catalyst for mutual reconciliation.
d) Historical evidence is verifiable, and the conflict in case had a significant impact on the nation or nations at play.
e) The site or landscape may become accessible by the public with the appropriate funding.
f) Youth and adults, locals with a connection to the site or related to the victims who died there, and people simply interested in history will benefit and learn from visiting the site or landscape.
g) Sites or landscapes associated with conflicts that occurred in the historical past may also be studied if they meet the eligibility criteria listed above.[12]

These criteria establish the importance of preserving material traces of memory that attest to historical events, suggesting that materiality still plays a relevant role in heritagization processes. It can be inferred from the word "objective" in point C that the significance of the site can only be guaranteed through prior diligent research and investigation. The World Tourism Organization shows awareness of the pain that inhabits these spaces when it establishes that the site should be either subject to objective and mature judgment or a space for reconciliation. In fact, conflicts too close to the present were initially excluded from the property-selection process because society may still be living with their consequences, but the proposal was soon dismissed as an-almost-impossible-to- meet metric. The investigative team concluded that, because of their scale, most of these conflicts still cast a long shadow over contemporary societies with repercussions, contexts of discrimination, and wounds that are not always properly addressed.

The several terms used to refer to post-conflict sites add to the difficulty of handling the matter. While some authors relate them to *dark heritage* or *dark tourism*, others such as William Logan and Keir Reeves consider them a form of *difficult heritage*.[13] They are also known as *sites associated with conflict, post-conflict sites* (emphasizing the successful aspect of it), *sites of memory*,[14] *sites of pain and shame*,[15] *sites of traumatic memory*,[16] and *sites of negative memory*. This non-exhaustive list of terms illustrates the lack of general agreement on how the issue should be approached.

Perhaps, one of the only unifying ideas may be that sites associated with suffering and conflicts are loaded with emotional and political meanings. Memory scholars forewarn that the discourses attached to these properties need to be carefully crafted, given societies emerging from contexts of pain and division might have a difficult time confronting the reality of these sites.[17] Eugenia Allier Montaño poetically refers to "the plaques, [and] the names of streets [as] political dilemmas,"[18] denoting in *dilemma* the complexities of memory-making processes and the myriad of turns they can take.

As it happens, the fields of memory and interpretation of heritage have firmly focused on and produced the richest literature on the needs of such heritage sites. In sharp contrast, few documents are designed for their legal protection or touch on the need for institutional protection and management. The vast range of typologies coupled with chronological and thematic impreciseness set additional hurdles on the road toward the creation of a category that would confer protection to post-conflict heritage.

Disregarding heritage protection in post-conflict contexts bears major consequences. "Implementing heritage policies in the immediate aftermath of a conflict carries unforeseeable consequences for the community in the long-run, affecting the discourses and definitions surrounding victims and perpetrators, and winners and losers."[19]

This is why it is critical that "heritage is deprived of its ability to continue inflicting violence through other means."[20]

THE DEBATE WITHIN UNESCO'S WORLD HERITAGE CONVENTION
FOUNDATIONS OF THE CURRENT DEBATE WITHIN THE CONVENTION
UNESCO's 1972 World Heritage Convention is the center of a current debate regarding the status of memory sites. The outcomes of these discussions hold significant importance because of the substantial impact of the convention on the development of national policies and regulations.

Protecting heritage has been a commitment of UNESCO since its establishment. In 1972, the agency took a decisive step forward with the adoption of the Convention Concerning the Protection of the World Cultural and Natural Heritage.

It is considered a unique document because it was the first tool to protect heritage at an international level; before this convention, countries could only protect heritage within their own borders.[21] The convention established an international cooperation system for the protection of heritage with a solid legal foundation that bound countries to several legal commitments. The World Heritage Convention, currently ratified by 193 countries, is one of the great successes of the United Nations, both in terms of international diplomacy, as well as in disseminating and raising awareness of the value of heritage. Its well-known World Heritage List, which already integrates 1,154 properties in 167 states parties, is likely responsible for much of the convention's achievements.

In its five-decade-long trajectory, the convention has become an authoritative agent in heritage protection matters around the world. Gradual changes in its implementation have inspired new heritage conceptions, and national legislations have evolved to accommodate them.

Since the convention abides by the principle of evolutionary interpretation,[22] its operational guidelines—establishing the principles for the implementation of the convention—undergo continuous updates and integrate any new development in international law.[23] In essence, the convention has proven to be a living instrument with great adaptability to the new understandings and preservation formulas operating under this international standard.

The convention's most momentous facets help illustrate the scope of the current debate on memory sites. First, the convention only allows site nominations for the World Heritage List from states parties. What is problematic about this is that the list may lean toward national identities that are representative of specific values and sociopolitically dominant groups, consequently rendering other communities invisible and denying their cultural rights.[24] The World Heritage List often echoes the agendas of states parties[25] and the narratives they wish to convey to the international community.

Especially impactful in this context is the World Heritage Committee, the convention's highest decision-making body. Composed of twenty-one states parties, the committee oversees political decisions, and its resolutions determine the fate of the demands of specific groups. But the committee has received unprecedented backlash for its extremely politicized decisions in recent years.[26] The discussions on post-conflict sites are surely to be affected by this politicization.

Simultaneously, the convention requires state parties to justify a site's outstanding universal value to be inscribed on the list. To meet this criterion, countries often overlook local community values in favor of more international ones. The assumption that certain properties are so exceptional to all humanity that their inclusion in the list would be undisputable is what makes the outstanding universal value be perceived as an objective metric. Following this line of reasoning, all individuals, regardless of their socioeconomic status, national origin, or cultural background, would come to interpret properties of outstanding universal value from a similar angle. But, rather than objectivity, this criterion reveals a Eurocentric bias and shows little understanding of the cultural diversity of the world, ignoring controversial perspectives and the different histories linked to one same place.[27] As a way to prove the outstanding universal value of their nominated property, states generally stick to the positive values associated with it, steering even further from objectivity.

Today, countries continue to nominate properties based on their own interpretations of the convention's outstanding universal value, frequently understanding it in relation to the country's national identity and collective memory, which are not necessarily inclusive of all worldviews. Far from the positive and optimistic rhetoric generally attributed to a World Heritage property, this kind of designation may actually either mitigate or intensify existing local conflicts and dynamics.[28]

The World Heritage List already includes some sites associated with conflicts or struggles for freedom, mainly those connected to key historical human rights events. Þingvellir National Park (Iceland) was recognized for its significance as the predecessor of parliamentary democracy, and Robben Island (South Africa) as a symbol not only of South Africa's right to self-determination, but also of tolerance and human dignity. The island of Gorée (Senegal) was inscribed because of its direct ties to slavery, and the Silk Road entered the list as an example of integration and dialogue between nations. Other properties such as Auschwitz and Hiroshima are on the list for their history of human rights violations. Arguing that these international recognition processes are really a form of memorialization, some scholars are trying to grasp why human rights are not given their due weight as inscription eligibility criteria.[29]

Bibliography on the World Heritage Convention along with the committee's decisions over the decades point to the fact that the latter has always been reluctant to inscribe property of such characteristics. Overall, the convention and its surrounding bodies struggle to accept the spiritual and community values attached to the tangible properties nominated for inscription. While the approved set of inscription criteria technically includes one that pertains strictly to community or spiritual values—criterion (vi)—a series of heated discussions drove the committee to increasingly restrict it, and even to recommend against its use. The committee currently only accepts its application in conjunction with other criteria that justify a property's inscription. The final decision was captured in paragraph seventy-seven of the convention's operational guidelines: "the Committee considers that this criterion should preferably be used in conjunction with other criteria."[30]

The challenging aspect of candidacies associated with conflicts emerged after cases such as Auschwitz and Hiroshima. When the Polish concentration camp was inscribed in 1979, it was specifically noted in the decision that "the Committee decided to enter Auschwitz concentration camp on the List as a unique site and to restrict the inscription of other sites of a similar nature."[31] This decision followed a recommendation by Michel Parent, who, as the committee's rapporteur, presented a study that same year suggesting that "in order to preserve its symbolic status as a monument to all the victims, Auschwitz should, it seems, remain in isolation. In other words, we recommend that it should stand alone among cultural properties as bearing witness to the depth of horror and of suffering, and the height of heroism, and that all other sites of the same nature be symbolized through it."[32]

Something similar happened with Hiroshima, which was inscribed in 1996 in an exceptional decision, with the rejection of the US delegation.[33] These decisions set a precedence and greatly complicated the subsequent nominations of many sites, including Robben Island, and the candidacy of World War I sites, nominated by France and Belgium in 2018, that sparked the current debate. Indigenous peoples and other communities have also seen their efforts to support their worldviews and relationships with the environment hampered by the restriction of criterion (vi).

Despite its older origins, the debate took center stage again during the forty-second session of the World Heritage Committee in Manama, Bahrain, in 2018. The committee discussed how the convention should address the requests of some states to inscribe properties associated with recent conflicts. Two decisions follow these conversations. The most significant one concerned the nomination by Belgium and France of the property Funerary and Memorial sites of the First World War, which ICOMOS, as an advisory body of the committee, assessed between 2017 and 2018.

Picture 1: Forty-second session of the World Heritage Committee in Manama, Bahrain, in 2018.

https://www.flickr.com/photos/159678548@N03/. Taken on June, 24, 2021.

In its evaluation of the candidacy, ICOMOS warned that the convention did not have the appropriate tools to assess such properties. The advisory body defined the candidacy as a *transnational serial property*[34] of 139 sites, comprising large-scale necropolises housing tens of thousands of graves of soldiers of different nationalities and some memorials. The properties are, for the most part, publicly owned, either by the state or by municipal councils.

The report identified some of the key factors driving the debate: it contended that cemeteries of the recent past are not old enough to meet the eligibility criteria[35] and that proving the outstanding value of a property knowing that other sites in the world have the same or similar relevance was challenging. This is yet another instance of how difficult it is to interpret, define, and convey the meaning of *outstanding universal value*.

ICOMOS made a brief reference to a controversial topic in the last few decades: Auschwitz and the application of criterion (vi). With the sentence "questions arise again in the current nomination,"[36] the evaluation suggested that the World Heritage Convention never clarified, after the inscription of Auschwitz, if such inscriptions lose their value when other properties of similar characteristics are inscribed under the same category. As for France and Belgium's candidacy, ICOMOS was unable to identify a clear reason as to why the states parties wished to memorialize this property and raised objections to the lack of broader references linking burial traditions to the history of the First World War and its impact.

Equally significant, and related to this study, were ICOMOS's remarks on the legal protection of nominated sites: "Although many sites are covered by forms of protection as public properties and war cemeteries, the measures that derive from this type of protection do not guarantee that the heritage dimensions and attributes relevant for the present nomination are taken care of adequately."[37]

This is a common reality in many countries. Even Spain integrates properties associated with conflicts into memory laws and other kinds of legislation, but it fails to protect them through legal frameworks of heritage.

Given the changing nature of the issue, the evaluation of the committee's advisory body contained a more technical assessment of the sites, covering, among other aspects, non-specific categorization and state of conservation, and reflections on the challenges posed by properties associated with recent conflicts. ICOMOS concluded that "this nomination raises some fundamental issues with regard to the purpose and scope of the World Heritage Convention and its appropriateness to celebrate properties that commemorate aspects of wars and conflicts."[38] It went on to say that "even when sites are proposed as a call for peace and reconciliation, ultimately their value is related to the conflict which generated them."

In addition, ICOMOS reminded the committee that having to prove the outstanding value of a property against other similar sites through a comparative analysis carries serious implications, as ICOMOS does not consider itself able to judge juxtapositions of suffering, human loss, memories, or scope of conflicts.

Again, this emphasizes the limitations of the concept of *outstanding* within the World Heritage List.

ICOMOS called for a deeper reflection on the matter, considering this candidacy could set a precedence for how future nominations are processed[39] and proposed to leave the decision on the nomination open, and even to postpone it, until this reflection took place.

The nomination and its evaluation were presented to the committee on June 30, 2018. In its draft decision, the World Heritage Center endorsed ICOMOS's recommendation to request a postponement on the decision. The nomination triggered a debate among the members of the committee, only revealing how sensitive and complex the issue is. Most members were in favor of deliberating in detail about memory sites before reaching a decision on France and Belgium's candidacy.

During their discussion, Norway shared its skepticism about the possibility of arriving at an objective decision when it came to this kind of property. We believe, however, that Norway erroneously assumed that all decisions beyond the boundaries of sites of memory are objective, when, in fact, any decision concerning heritage is, in effect, a choice. It was also Norway that stated that properties associated with memory would alter the "universality of the Convention."[40] Tunisia stressed the unique nature of the case. All in all, these interventions imply that the committee members are aware of the attention this issue requires from them and of the changes it may bring to future guidelines. India's intervention to denounce the inadequate memorialization of the death of thousands of Indian soldiers during World War I exemplifies the concern that exists among states parties to give a voice to divergent stories.[41]

After convening several times with the committee's legal adviser, the World Heritage Committee ultimately decided to postpone the consideration on the nomination.[42] The plan was substantiated in the committee's general decision related to nominations,[43] which stated that a thorough reflection on the subject was imperative before any decision could be reached.

In the case of France and Belgium's nomination, the committee had its reservations about the inscription of properties associated with "negative memories."[44] The term *negative* is not generally accepted or used in the field of memory studies, because what is understood to be negative are the events and the violations of rights that occurred in a given place, and not memory itself. The language used in paragraph four of the committee's decision is slightly different, as it mentions "sites associated with recent conflicts and other negative and divisive memories." Again, we cannot help but feel that the terminology chosen for this decision—*negative, divisive*—reveals a bias against memory.

The World Heritage Committee had already held a discussion on sites of memory a few days earlier. As we noted, the World Heritage Center had requested various reports in anticipation of an increase in nominations of sites associated with conflicts. After the reports were presented before the committee, paragraph seven of "Decision 42 COM 5A" was edited to include a request to convene an expert meeting that would "allow for both philosophical and practical reflections on the nature of memorialization, the value of evolving memories, the inter-relationship between material and immaterial attributes in relation to memory."[45]

The first expert meeting was held in December 2019. The conclusions were presented at the January 2021 information meeting, where the expert group detailed[46] the ways in which a static (not changing or evolving) definition of *outstanding universal value* may hinder ongoing reconciliation processes and explained that UNESCO acting as an arbitrator and having to choose and side with one specific narrative of a given conflict could result in a hierarchical view of victims and create barriers.

For all this—and based on two other studies we analyze below—the expert group concluded that this category of properties "does not relate to the purpose and scope of the World Heritage Convention and its Operational Guidelines," and called for further research to clarify the issue.

The committee embraced the group's viewpoint at its July 2021 meeting; a section in "Decision 44 COM 8" gives account of the work performed by the expert group and endorses its conclusions.[47] In the decision, UNESCO used the same language: "sites associated with memories of recent conflicts and other negative and divisive memories," casting a negative light on this kind of property. The decision captures the mixture of opinions surrounding this topic, as the interventions of several government representatives made plain when the decision was presented to the World Heritage Committee. UNESCO committed to keeping the expert group open until at least 2023, when it is scheduled to present the committee with new data.

Meanwhile, countries have continued to nominate properties for the World Heritage List, including properties associated with recent conflicts.

POSSIBLE ACTION PLANS AND EXPERT VIEWS ON THE MATTER

In response to the debates mentioned earlier, UNESCO commissioned a series of reports to study how the World Heritage Convention addressed memory sites. In the reports, memory sites were referred to by a wide range of terms including *sites associated with memories of recent conflicts, sites of memory*,[48] or *sensitive cultural sites related to memory*,[49] indicating yet again a lack of consensus in their designation.

The discussion paper proposed by ICOMOS[50] listed properties associated with recent conflicts drawn from the Tentative Lists of States Parties for possible near-future nominations. These include the beaches of the Normandy landings in France and Argentina's Museo Sitio de Memoria ESMA (Ex ESMA Museum and Site of Memory).

Picture 2: Ex ESMA Museum and Site of Memory (Author: Maider Maraña)

Like ICOMOS, we believe that evaluating these sites puts into question the mission and scope of the World Heritage Convention and that this probe is precisely what lies at the core of the debate and what makes the agents working in the world heritage field feel uneasy. According to ICOMOS, "the scope and scale of these potential nominations (...) reflect a growing interest in sites associated with memories of recent conflicts and the high profile given to some of them at the national level."[51] As it would assert later in the evaluation of France and Belgium's candidacy, the advisory body stated that the convention did not offer the appropriate tools to assess this kind of property.

ICOMOS gathered from this situation that "there are difficulties with evaluating memories which inherently are still evolving or partisan in one way or another, or where memory is re-invested with retrospective 'truths.'"[52] This statement indicates that the controversy really revolves around the most recent conflicts, and that what sparks debates, concerns, and discrepancies has little to do with the legal aspect of heritage categorization or material heritage, but rather with whether these sites should be considered and interpreted as heritage, considering the political and ideological interests that processes of heritagization potentially mask.

The advisory body believed that inscribing a property whose justification is still under development may lead to inconsistencies between what was initially considered to be a property of outstanding universal value and the meanings it may acquire in the future. One might argue this is not new in the history of the convention: Auschwitz was inscribed in 1979 because of the pain and suffering inflicted to the Polish people, but, later, the site was reinterpreted to adopt a more Holocaust-centered approach focusing on the extermination of the Jewish population. This revision led to a name change in 2007.[53]

Another sign of the list's expansion over the years is the approval of a cultural landscape category. This new category made it possible for properties that were initially inscribed following natural criteria to be renominated and inscribed under cultural parameters. This was the case for the cultural and spiritual landscapes of Indigenous peoples, including Uluru-Kata Tjuta National Park in Australia, which was inscribed in 1987 under natural criteria, and reinscribed in 1994 following parameters more in line with the wishes and demands of the local Aboriginal communities. A similar initiative was that of New Zealand's Tongariro National Park, which was reinscribed as a cultural landscape in 1993.

As these examples confirm, it is a widespread occurrence that the understanding and interpretation of a property evolves over time. This, however, should not be sufficient grounds for excluding properties associated with recent conflicts and memory from the protection of existing regulations.

To ICOMOS, the term conflict encompasses wars, battles, massacres, genocide, and other negative events involving opposing factions, but not sites linked to slavery or liberation movements. The word *recent*, on the other hand, refers to any conflict which occurred during the twentieth and twenty-first centuries.[54]

The report emphasized how Auschwitz was once inscribed as a distinct example and symbol of sites of a similar nature. But the uniqueness of Auschwitz is a subjective perception, and it is not shared by all the convention's states parties. Hiroshima's nomination also faced sound opposition.

ICOMOS wanted to determine how long communities need to adequately develop a memory; it explored how societies confront their truths and the fact that these truths may sometimes deepen divisions; and it considered the dilemma of required comparative analyses of sites, which consist of contrasting and comparing traumatic events. To conclude the report, ICOMOS outlined a number of challenges these sites might pose under the 1972 convention, including under what circumstances may the history of humanity and the global community integrate local or regional histories; the universality of partial memories or political memories; the link between such memories and their physical space; how an outstanding site can represent all similar sites associated with the same conflict; which agents should be sought for advice; or how the outstanding universal value, seemingly immutable, can reflect the dynamic and evolving nature of memories.[55]

The International Coalition of Sites of Conscience geared its study toward the interpretations of "sensitive" sites—to use ICSC's terminology—paying special attention to the moral dimensions of such interpretations.[56] The study reviewed the evolution of the concept of heritage over the last seventy years, especially after the Second World War, and how it increasingly became an integral part of national identities. The coalition concluded that because heritage is a construct that acquires meaning only through society, different groups may have different conflicting perspectives. The study stressed the importance of factoring in all possible approaches[57] and of welcoming multiple narratives in relation to these properties.[58]

According to the ICSC study, memory sites should not be required to fulfill the waiting period criterion associated with the historical event, because, unlike other properties, these sites are inherently meant to educate the community on the events that happened there.[59] It also makes a strong case for interpreting these sites from a moral perspective,[60] similar to what the study about the potential benefits of tourism for these places suggested.[61]

The ICSC study dealt with a fundamental issue: legal designations. It contended that the legal designation of a site determines the protection category under which it will be placed, which, in turn, will inform the subsequent interpretation of the site. In other words, the interpretation of a property vastly depends on its legal designation.[62] This explains why some of the properties nominated by France and Belgium were not protected by a heritage legal framework, but rather by memory and other kinds of legislation. The ICSC claims that "if the value of a heritage place as a Site of Memory is not adequately recognized by the designation, there is risk that the memorial aspects will not be treated sufficiently in the place's interpretation."[63]

Additionally, the study warned of the great consequences international recognition of the property may have on its ensuing interpretation.[64] The Old Bridge Area of the Old City of Mostar is a prime example of this. The international community is believed to have promoted new interpretations of the bridge's reconstruction that differ from the memories of the communities involved in the conflict.[65]

To gain more insights into the issue, ICOMOS published a new report in 2020[66] based on probes carried out in different regions of the world. The outcomes pointed to what we believe is one of the key elements of this debate: the role of the World Heritage Convention in the peace-building policies promoted by UNESCO. In the report, ICOMOS asked for clarification on this point. This new document established that the inscription of these properties may come with its own set of consequences; it may trigger moral dilemmas, or the need for mediation, and it may cause some to ignore parts of the human suffering experienced by some communities. ICOMOS argued that "sites associated with recent conflicts cannot be accommodated by the key concepts of the World Heritage Convention."[67] Of the potential creation of a special subgroup within the World Heritage List, which could better represent this category, ICOMOS thinks that it would be contrary to the very values of the convention and advocates for integrating these properties under other umbrellas.

Performed in 2020 and presented by UNESCO during its 2021 committee, a new study by Olwen Beazley and Christina Cameron examined how this kind of site influence reconciliation processes, how transitional justice interacts with these spaces, and the United Nations' standpoint on this relationship. It also looked into the postulation that activities related to world heritage are considered part of the so-called public history. Beazley and Cameron claimed that inscribing this kind of property on the World Heritage List may be detrimental to reconciliation: "By taking sides and giving official approval to one version of a conflict, inscription of sites may have the opposite effect to the desired one, by creating barriers among people."[68] The study concluded that these properties do not align with the principles of the World Heritage Convention and encouraged the creation of specific programs for their recognition.

PRACTICES AND METHODOLOGIES OF OTHER INTERNATIONAL INSTITUTIONS
Like UNESCO, several other international institutions have tackled the issue of memory sites. Because of the high volume of literature and the broad range of methodologies and research, we decided to examine two of the most institutionally significant and consequential bodies: the United Nations Human Rights Council, through the special rapporteur's research on cultural rights, and the European Commission. In addition, we analyzed a UNESCO program, created within its communication sector, meant to address memory and documentary heritage.

With the 2009 special mandate in the field of cultural rights established by the Human Rights Council, the United Nations took a definite step toward clarifying and expanding the scope of these rights. Since then, the rapporteurs' annual themed reports have featured promising human rights-based approaches to culture.

In 2013 and 2014, the then-rapporteur, Farida Shaheed, promoted two reports related to memory processes. The first one focused on history-teaching and on the importance of historical narratives as cultural heritage. The 2014 report examined memorials and museums. Shaheed firmly defended the cultural heritage value of historical accounts before the United Nations General Assembly in 2013. Two years earlier, in her thorough 2011 report for the General Assembly, she had claimed that cultural heritage belonged to the human rights field. During her years as special rapporteur, Shaheed elucidated a connection between the construction of memory, cultural heritage, and human rights.

Some of the topics explored in these reports deal with the issues discussed in connection to the World Heritage Convention. Shaheed justified the need to focus on the protection of memory sites when she established that "the rising trend of memorialization processes today makes discussing these issues both urgent and necessary."[69]

These polarizing processes have transitioned from private initiatives driven by family members and conflict survivors to the public sphere with active policies promoted by nations and institutions.[70]

In this vein, her 2014 report indicated that the United Nations had yet to perform "a global study to examine memorial practices" grounded in the principles of reparation and justice.[71] Her observations may be equally applicable to the debate within the World Heritage Committee, which has yet to identify an approach based on the principles of reparation.

In the report, the special rapporteur stressed that "history is always subject to differing interpretations"[72] and that "memory (. . .) is never immune from political influence and debate,"[73] meaning that even when facts can be proved, their interpretation is always subjective. Following this thought, Shaheed argued that the problem does not lie in the continual reinterpretation of history; "the [actual] challenge is to distinguish the legitimate continuous reinterpretation of the past from manipulations of history for political ends."[74]

Clearly, "memorials address issues that can be very divisive"[75] and resolving these situations requires a specific case-by-case plan.[76] Perhaps, this methodology should also be applied to the inscription process of the World Heritage List.

About the concern that ICOMOS voiced—that the properties nominated by Belgium and France could not be evaluated because their memory had not yet fully settled—the special rapporteur noted at the Human Rights Council that these monuments are constantly acquiring new meanings, "interposing layers of stories and complexity."[77]

In the 2013 report, she exposed a common pattern in international cultural heritage lists. She believed that "darker" historical episodes, ranging from crimes against humanity to genocide, colonization, slavery, civil strife, and occupation, tend to be omitted.[78] Regarding the typology of the sites, Shaheed recommended that the Human Rights Council included:

- Original sites: concentration camps, former torture and detention centers, sites of massacres, and mass graves or landmarks of repressive regimes, among other locations.
- Symbolic sites: permanent or ephemeral monuments, monuments with names of victims, or renamed streets and buildings.[79]

The monuments and sites of past oppressive regimes, whose architectural legacy with strong symbolic connotations should be managed, should also be part of this typology. The decision to preserve a space of such features should be made on a case-by-case basis. Among the examples cited in the report to the Human Rights Council were the Valley of the Fallen in Spain, the mausoleum of former communist leader Georgy Dimitrov in Bulgaria, and Hitler's bunker in Berlin.[80]

History is generally told and remembered through wars and conflicts, while periods of peace are usually downplayed.[81] Similar to what we noted about World Heritage,

Shaheed contended that "constructed monuments do not always correspond to the wishes or culture of the communities concerned,"[82] mainly, because "too frequently [governments] initiate top-down projects resulting in the imposition of unilateral or partial visions of history."[83]

The special rapporteur indicated that while memorial practices have historically centered on deceased soldiers, current approaches tend to focus more on the victims and reconciliation efforts.[84] In an attempt to justify the presence of cultural heritage associated with conflicts in international conventions, the United Nations report stated that, like legal reparations, symbolic reparations by means of memorials and open access to the original sites are of particular importance in successful national reconciliation processes.[85]

Likewise, Shaheed addressed "temporal distance," one of the requirements of the World Heritage. She explained before the United Nations that societies sometimes need some temporal distance—usually a full generational period—to understand the past.[86]

These reports are particularly relevant to this chapter because, coming from within the United Nations, they suggest courses of action that could be useful for the current debate around world heritage. They evince that sites associated with conflicts are, in fact, cultural heritage, and part of reparation and justice policies, and they exhort United Nations' agencies to act on the growing demand for the promotion of memorialization processes. In short, they remind us that, although "memorial dynamics are always political processes,"[87] they are not incompatible with human rights approaches, especially, when they follow the guidelines laid out by the United Nations.

Separate from UNESCO, the European Commission has designed several tools to promote cultural heritage, including the European Heritage Label (EHL). Created in 2013, the EHL was designed to recognize sites for their symbolic value, for the role they played in European history, and for the activities they offer to promote cohesion among European Union citizens. Unlike UNESCO's World Heritage List, which focuses on the material preservation of properties, the EHL considers heritage a medium to educate the community. Another way in which the EHL diverts from other international heritage agents is that sites must have played a specific role in recent European history, opening the door to the recognition of sites of the recent past.

In contrast to the World Heritage List, this heritage initiative is more clearly incorporating sites associated with peace (or with old conflicts), even though it also shows a clear bias toward certain narratives, including a tendency again to use cultural heritage as founding sources for dominant national identities of countries.

We noticed that, when describing and justifying the historical relevance of a site nominated for the European Label, nations often reshape national narratives to highlight elements of peace and democracy.[88] Places such as the Peace Palace in The Hague, the Cities of Peace of Westphalia in Germany, and several others related to the First and Second World War are some of the sites that have followed this formula. It is also common to feature events related to human rights, such as the Charter of Law of Abolition of the Death Penalty Act of 1867, approved in Portugal; and to solidarity, such as Poland's European Solidarity Center.[89]

However popular this pattern may be, the ties connecting these narratives to values of democracy and human rights often remain vague. The European narrative, which is embodied in the European Heritage Label, posits, for instance, that European nations overcame their common past of world wars and totalitarian regimes through a common project of unity and integration. But this discourse leaves other difficult pasts, like colonialism, which lay the foundation of Europe as we know it today, out of the conversation.[90] This case draws attention to how international institutions choose to ignore the dark areas of our past when they decide to incorporate properties associated with conflicts in heritage initiatives.

Back to UNESCO, the Memory of the World Program[91] has promoted the preservation of documentary heritage since 1992 with three main goals: to advance the preservation of documentary heritage worldwide to minimize the risk of loss and deterioration, to promote universal access to this kind of heritage, and to enhance public awareness of the substantial role of documentary heritage in the world. The fact that the right to truth is the bedrock of the program suggests how important documents are to understanding our histories. According to Memory of the World, "memory institutions may include but are not limited to archives, libraries, museums and other educational, cultural and research organizations."[92]

The general guidelines are perhaps the most relevant element of the program.[93] In particular, point 5.4 interconnects the mission of Memory of the World and the international days proclaimed by the United Nations. A good share of the international days related to documentary heritage concern values of peace and human rights: along with the World Radio Day, the World Book Day, the World Press Freedom Day, and the World Day for Audiovisual Heritage, the program specifically underscores the importance of Human Rights Day.[94]

This is also captured in the register created by the Program, the International Memory of the World Register. Rather than emphasizing the outstanding universal value of a property, the register values the role and historical weight of the property in the community and refers to it as *of world significance*. The program claims that the property's evaluation must always be comparative and relative, because "there is no absolute measure of cultural significance."[95]

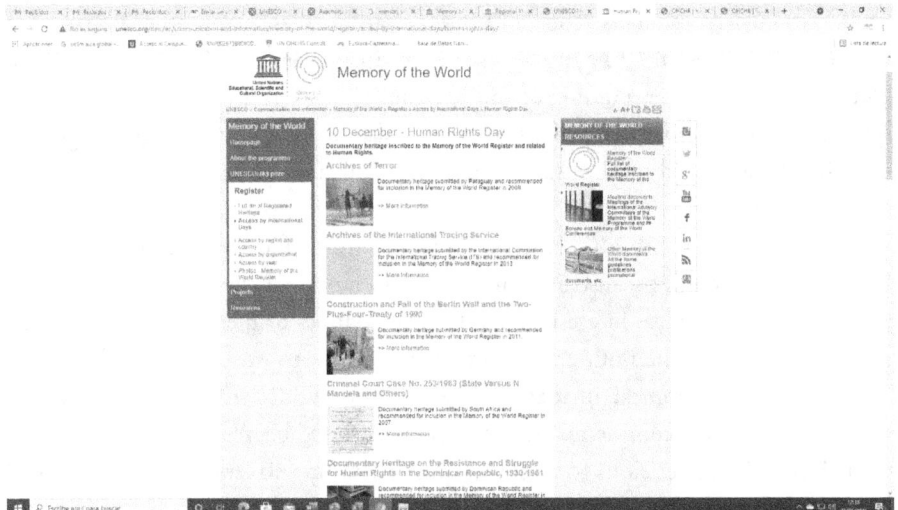

Picture 3: Screenshot of UNESCO's website. International Memory of the World Register associated with Human Rights. http://www.unesco.org/new/en/communication-and-information/memory-of-the-world/register/access-by-international-days/human-rights-day/ Taken on May 31, 2021.

The diaries of Anne Frank and the Warsaw Ghetto Archives are some of the documents listed on the Memory of the World Register as part of the documentary heritage related to the victims of the Holocaust. The International Day for the Elimination of Racial Discrimination includes critical documents such as the Criminal Court documents surrounding Nelson Mandela and several records linked to slavery. Those archived under the Human Rights Day include documents on the Latin American dictatorships, documents on the Resistance and Struggle for Human Rights in the Dominican Republic during the twentieth century, the 1893 Women's Suffrage Petition, the Tuol Sleng Genocide Museum Archives in Cambodia, and recent photos of Palestinian refugees.

In its own way, the Memory of the World Program, which focused on documentary heritage and aimed at the protection of books and historical documents, brings attention and blazes a trail within UNESCO to the heritagization of memories associated with conflicts and struggles for freedom. This has led to disagreements within the program, with some nations insisting on the need "to comply with the principles of dialog, mutual understanding and respect and avoid new political tensions related to the Program."[96]

CONCLUSIONS

The main subject of this chapter—the role of memory sites within the UNESCO World Heritage Convention—raises fundamental questions about the convention itself, particularly about its scope and interpretation. Like many other debates (on Indigenous peoples and on cultural landscapes, for instance), this one, too, informs and obscures our understanding of the outstanding universal value and how certain types of properties measure against it. An analysis of the debate brings to light the complex decisions and administrative matters the convention's decision-making bodies need to handle.

Sites associated with human rights violations or conflicts are certainly meant to be sources of discord, because of their enormous emotional charge and the potential political and ideological interests behind them. Matters of memory and the heritagization of memory are nothing new and will continue to exist well into the future. The debate remains topical; in 2020 many Americans decided to topple, in the spur of the moment, statues commemorating owners of enslaved people, and some museums made institutional decisions to remove works celebrating slavery. These events could be understood as new processes of "demonumentalization."[97]

No less urgent is the need to reflect on other "traditional" or popular elements of cultural heritage whose ideological and political load is deliberately suppressed and silenced. Attitudes and actions such as the countless inscriptions of Christian churches on the World Heritage List, the fixation on the conservation of historic cities, the conservationist approach to the rural world, and the celebration of colonial values over Indigenous cultures contribute to a particular ideology and worldview that gives preference to one-sided heritage interpretations.

Post-conflict places around the world have demonstrated that human rights-based narratives that are respectful of human dignity and victim's rights, and supportive of difference and alternative voices, radically alter how visitors experience the sites. Besides the impact of curated narratives, the legal framework protecting the sites inevitably molds the way society interprets them, too. The legal articulation of a site will depend on its initial designation as an element of cultural heritage or of memory, among other designations. This is why it is critical to continue researching and designing practical solutions for post-conflict properties.

Overall, the areas engaged in the interpretation of memory sites have advanced quicker than the fields committed to their legal protection. Legal systems for the protection of cultural heritage often fail to meet society's changing needs, interests, and values in relation to heritage. Although existing regulations make some room for new inscriptions and expanded concepts, they set—often invisible—obstacles that make alternative perspectives, which were disregarded at the time of drafting and approving the standard, hard to accept and integrate.

We seem to forget that culture can have a great impact on reconciliation processes. In this sense, although, in theory, the creation and further development of the World Heritage Convention is underpinned on a narrative of reconciliation, this does not always carry over well in practice. The reality is that while both the United Nations and national legislations consider post-conflict properties elements of reparation, these are not always acknowledged for their heritage value and for the contributions they may make to society in the mid- and long-terms.

On the other hand, it is unsurprising that the World Heritage Committee tends to err on the side of caution: any change or step forward within the framework of the World Heritage Convention has a domino effect on national and international legislations. Not only because it is considered a hard law instrument of international law, but because, over the decades, it has had a clear effect on heritage regulations and has established legitimacy on the matter. Countries have adopted many widespread initiatives including cultural landscapes, community engagement, and heritage awareness campaigns that are the product of the discussions, programs, and decisions originating within the world heritage field.

Certainly, the line between the heritagization of sites associated with struggles for rights and social justice and the misuse of such sites to revalue and promote national narratives in the international arena is extremely fine.[98]

In view of this, because the convention was not designed with adequate mechanisms to resolve the abovementioned controversies and state parties and other actors involved generally resort to dialogue and diplomatic tools to solve them, institutions should create spaces that provide an opportunity to settle these kinds of discussions and differences.

Throughout this chapter, we saw how other United Nations agencies, including through the special rapporteur's reports, point to avenues of work that could benefit the World Heritage Convention and the current debates. The special rapporteur noted that candidacies for the World Heritage List should be evaluated from a human rights perspective to ensure a plurality of stories and avoid exclusive discourses told through a single voice. Likewise, the rapporteur calls for community engagement in a way that it focuses not only on victim-centered narratives but on critical reflections that enable society to advance its understanding of human rights violations.

In short, heritage linked to peace will always trigger a counterreaction,[99] as happens with many other heritage categories. In embracing new perspectives and approaches, the World Heritage Convention has shown that heritage properties are conflictive in essence, insofar as they are the result of processes of contention, discussion, and consensus.

Heritage associated with recent conflicts, although thornier, can (and should) be resolved through the traditional strategies of dialogue and discussion used by the agents that make up the "authorized discourse of heritage." In this context, UNESCO and its World Heritage Committee must cater to the international community's growing interest in sites of memory.

BIBLIOGRAPHY

Allier Montaño, E. "Lugar de memoria: ¿un concepto para el análisis de las luchas memoriales? El caso de Uruguay y su pasado reciente," Cuadernos del CLAEH, no.96–97 (year 31, 2008/1-2): 87–109.

Arrieta Urtizberea, I. (ed). *Lugares de memoria traumática*. Bilbao: Universidad del País Vasco, 2016.

Beazley, O. and Christina Cameron. Study on Sites Associated with Recent Conflicts and other Negative and Divisive Memories. https://whc.unesco.org/archive/2021/whc21-44com-inf8.2-en.pdf (Accessed November 10, 2022).

Bertacchini, E., Claudia Liuzza, Lynn Meskell, et al. "The Politicization of UNESCO World Heritage Decision Making." *Public Choice* 167, (2016): 95–129.

Cameron, C. And Judith Hermann (eds). Guidance and Capacity Building for the Recognition of Associative Values using World Heritage Criterion (vi). January 2018. http://whc.unesco.org/document/167760.pdf (Accessed May 27, 2021).

CESCR. Observación general Nº 21 Derecho de toda persona a participar en la vida cultural (Art. 15 para. 1a), del PIDESC. https://www2.ohchr.org/english/bodies/cescr/docs/E.C.12.GC.21.Rev.1-SPA.doc (Accessed May 27, 2021).

European Commission, *Directorate-General for Education, Youth, Sport and Culture. European heritage label: Guidelines for Candidate Sites*, Publications Office of the European Union, 2022, https://data.europa.eu/doi/10.2766/835742 https://ec.europa.eu/programmes/creative-europe/sites/creative-europe/files/files/ehl-guidelines-for-candidate-sites_es.pdf (Accessed Spanish version May 27, 2021).

Constitución Española (1978). https://www.boe.es/buscar/act.php?id=BOE-A-1978-31229 (Accessed May 27, 2021).

Cruces, F. "Problemas en torno a la restitución del patrimonio. Una visión desde la antropología." *Política y Sociedad* 27, (1998): 77–87.

Deegan, N. "The Local-Global Nexus in the Politics of World Heritage: Space for Community Development?" *Community Development through World Heritage*, World Heritage Papers 31, (2012): 77–83.

Ekern, S., William Logan, Birgitte Sauge, and Amund Sinding-Larsen. *World Heritage Management and Human Rights*. Nueva York: Routledge, 2015.

Fernández Liesa, Carlos R. *Cultura y Derecho Internacional*. Madrid: Universidad de Alcalá—Cuadernos Democracia y Derechos Humanos, 2012.

Francioni, F. "Treinta años después: ¿está la Convención sobre el Patrimonio Mundial preparada para el siglo XXI?" Patrimonio Cultural y Derecho 7, (2003): 11–38.

Franco, L. G. and Pablo Alonso. "Nuevas memorias para nuevos futuros: reflexiones sobre el patrimonio cultural en contextos de conflicto." OPCA 09, (2015).

García Fernández, J. "Presupuestos jurídico-constitucionales de la Legislación sobre Patrimonio Histórico." *Revista de Derecho Político* 27–28, (1988): 181–212.

García Fernández, J. "La protección jurídica del patrimonio cultural. Nuevas cuestiones y nuevos sujetos a los diez años de la Ley del Patrimonio Histórico Español." *Boletín de la Facultad de Derecho* 8–9, (2nd season 1995): 369–391.

García Fernández, J. "Los retos actuales a la Protección del Patrimonio Histórico." *Revista Patrimonio Cultural y Derecho* 15, (2011): 217–236.

Gómez Isa, F. "El derecho de los pueblos indígenas a la reparación por injusticias históricas." In *Declaración sobre los Derechos de los Pueblos Indígenas. Hacia un mundo intercultural y sostenible*, edited by Álvarez, Oliva, García-Falces. 157–191. Madrid: Catarata, 2009.

ICOMOS. discussion paper. Evaluations of World Heritage Nominations Related to Sites Associated with Memories of Recent Conflicts. 2018a. https://whc.unesco.org/document/167810 (Accessed May 27, 2021).

ICOMOS. Evaluations of Nominations of Cultural and Mixed Properties. ICOMOS Report for the World Heritage Committee. 2018b. http://whc.unesco.org/archive/2018/whc18-42com-inf8B1-en.pdf (Accessed May 27, 2021).

ICOMOS. "Our Common Dignity Initiative"—Rights-Based Approaches. 2019. https://www.icomos.org/en/focus/our-common-dignity-initiative-rights-based-approach (Accessed June 23, 2021).

ICOMOS. Sites Associated with Memories of Recent Conflicts and the World Heritage Convention —ICOMOS Second discussion paper. 2020. https://www.icomos.org/en/documentation-center/75913-sites-associated-with-memories-of-recent-conflicts-and-the-wh (Accessed November 10, 2021).

International Coalition of Sites of Conscience. Interpretation of Sites of Memory. 2018. https://whc.unesco.org/en/activities/933/ (Accessed May 27, 2021).

Jelin, E. La lucha por el pasado. *Cómo construimos la memoria social.* Buenos Aires: Siglo Veintiuno Editores, 2017.

Labadi, S. UNESCO, Cultural Heritage, and Outstanding Universal Value. Plymouth: Altamira Press, 2013.

Lähdesmäki, T. et al. *Dissonant Heritages and Memories in Contemporary Europe.* Cambridge: Palgrave MacMillan, 2019.

Larsen, P. (ed). World Heritage and Human Rights. *Lessons from the Asia-Pacific and Global Arena.* New York: Earthscan, 2018.

Logan, W. et al. Places of Pain and Shame. Dealing with "Difficult Heritage." London: Routledge, 2009.

Logan, W. et al. Cultural Diversity, Heritage and Human Rights. Intersections in Theory and Practice. London: Routledge, 2010.

Mäkinen, K. "Interconceptualizing Europe and Peace: Identity Building Under the European Heritage Label." In *Dissonant Heritages and Memories in Contemporary Europe*, edited by Lähdesmäki et al., 51–78. Cambridge: Palgrave MacMillan, 2019.

Maraña, M. "Patrimonio y Derechos Humanos." Una Mirada desde la participación y el género en el trabajo de Naciones Unidas en patrimonio cultural. Bilbao: UNESCO Etxea, 2015.

Maraña, M., Maire Braniff, Peter Doak and Sara McDowell. Harnessing the Potential of Tourism in Post Conflict Sites in Advancing Peace: Reflecting on the Past and Inspiring the Future. http://www.flandersintheuk.be/sites/default/files/atoms/files/Harnessing%20Tourism%20Peace_report.pdf (Accessed May 27, 2021).

Maraña, M. (ed). Aprovechar el potencial del turismo en lugares de conflicto histórico para promover la paz: una reflexión sobre el pasado y una fuente de inspiración para el futuro. Vitoria: Gobierno Vasco, 2020.

Meskell, L. "UNESCO's World Heritage Convention at 40: Challenging the Economic and Political Order of International Heritage Conservation." *Current Anthropology* 54(4), (August 2013): 483–494.

Meskell, L. (ed). *Global Heritage: a reader.* West Sussex: Blackwell, 2015.

Naef, P. "Memorial entrepreneurs and dissonance in post-conflict tourism." In *Tourism and Hospitality in Conflict-Ridden Destinations,* edited by Rami. Abingdon-on-Thames: Routledge, 2019.

Nora, P. *Les lieux de mémoire.* Montevideo: Trilce, Montevideo, 1992.

Shaheed, F. Report of the Independent Expert in the Field of Cultural Rights, Farida Shaheed, A/HRC/17/38, Human Rights Council of the United Nations. March 2011. https://digitallibrary.un.org/record/706502?ln=en (Accessed May 27, 2021).

Shaheed, F. Report of the Special Rapporteur in the Field of Cultural Rights, A/68/296, General Assembly of the United Nations. August 2013. https://digitallibrary.un.org/record/756373?ln=en (Accessed May 27, 2021).

Shaheed, F. Report of the Special Rapporteur in the Field of Cultural Rights, Farida Shaheed, A/HRC/25/49, Human Rights Council of the United Nations. January 2014. Memorialization processes. https://digitallibrary.un.org/record/766862?ln=en (Accessed May 27, 2021).

Smith, L. *Uses of Heritage*. London: Routledge, 2006.

Turunen, J. "A Geography of Coloniality: Re-narrating European Integration." In *Dissonant Heritages and Memories in Contemporary Europe*, edited by Lähdesmäki et al., 185–214. Cambridge: Palgrave MacMillan, 2019.

UNESCO. Convention Concerning the Protection of the World Cultural and Natural Heritage. https://whc.unesco.org/en/documents/170665/ (Accessed May 27, 2021).

UNESCO. Convention for the Safeguarding of the Intangible Cultural Heritage. 2003. http://portal.unesco.org/es/ev.php-URL_ID=17716&URL_DO=DO_TOPIC&URL_SECTION=201.htm (Accessed May 27, 2021).

UNESCO. UNESCO Memory of the World Programme—General Guidelines. 2017. https://en.unesco.org/sites/default/files/mow_draft_guidelines_approved_1217.pdf (Accessed May 27, 2021).

UNESCO. The Operational Guidelines for the Implementation of the World Heritage Convention. 2019. https://whc.unesco.org/en/guidelines/ (Accessed May 27, 2021).

Van Huis, I. et al. "Introduction: Europe, Heritage and Memory—Dissonant Encounters and Explorations." In *Dissonant Heritages and Memories in Contemporary Europe*, edited by Lähdesmäki et al., 1–21. Cambridge: Palgrave MacMillan, 2019.

Von Droste, B. "World Heritage and globalization: UNESCO's contribution to the development of global ethics." *Community Development through World Heritage*, World Heritage Papers 31, (2012): 10–15.

WHC. CC-79/CONF.003/11. 1979. http://whc.unesco.org/archive/1979/cc-79-conf003-11e.pdf (Accessed May 27, 2021).

WHC. Decision CONF 003 XII.46. Consideration of Nominations to the World Heritage List. 1979. https://whc.unesco.org/en/decisions/2203/ (Accessed May 27, 2021).

WHC. CONF 201 VIII.C. 1996. https://whc.unesco.org/en/decisions/2997 (Accessed May 27, 2021).

WHC. Decision 31 COM 8B.8. Changes to Names—Auschwitz Birkenau as Title and German Nazi Concentration and Extermination Camp (1940-1945). 2007. https://whc.unesco.org/en/decisions/1306 (Accessed May 27, 2021).

WHC. Decision 39 COM 8B.14. Sites of Japan's Meiji Industrial Revolution: Iron and Steel, Shipbuilding and Coal Mining, Japan. 2015. https://whc.unesco.org/en/decisions/6364/ (Accessed May 27, 2021).

WHC. Summary Record of the 42 COM. Document WHC/18/42 COM/INF.18. 2018. https://whc.unesco.org/archive/2018/whc18-42com-inf18-Final.pdf (Accessed May 27, 2021).

WHC. Decision 42 COM 5A. Report of the World Heritage Centre on its Activities and the Implementation of the World Heritage Committee's Decisions. 2018. https://whc.unesco.org/en/decisions/7109/ (Accessed May 27, 2021).

WHC. Decision 42 COM 8. Nominations—General Discussion. 2018. https://whc.unesco.org/en/decisions/7165/ (Accessed May 27, 2021).

WHC. Decision 42 COM 8B.24. Funerary and Memorial Sites of the First World War (Western Front) (Belgium, France). 2018. https://whc.unesco.org/en/decisions/7137/ (Accessed May 27, 2021).

WHC. Decision 44 COM 8. Nomination Process. 2021. https://whc.unesco.org/en/decisions/7918/ (Accessed May 27, 2021).

NOTES

* This chapter was completed in November 2022, and it does not include information on the latest developments that occurred during the eighteenth extraordinary session of the World Heritage Committee on January 24–25, 2023.

1. Smith, *Uses of Heritage*.
2. Maraña, *Patrimonio y Derechos Humanos*.
3. Cruces, "Problemas en torno a la restitución del patrimonio," 77–87.
4. Van Huis, "Introduction: Europe, Heritage and Memory—Dissonant Encounters and Explorations," 1–21.
5. García Fernández, "Presupuestos jurídico-constitucionales de la Legislación sobre Patrimonio Histórico," 187.
6. García Fernández, "Presupuestos jurídico-constitucionales de la Legislación sobre Patrimonio Histórico," 184.
7. García Fernández, "Los retos actuales a la Protección del Patrimonio Histórico," 221.
8. Fernández Liesa, *Cultura y Derecho Internacional*, 135.
9. Williams and Reives, 2008. In Maraña, Aprovechar el potencial del turismo en lugares de conflicto histórico para promover la paz: una reflexión sobre el pasado y una fuente de inspiración para el futuro, 8.
10. Gómez Isa, "El derecho de los pueblos indígenas a la reparación por injusticias históricas," 217–236.
11. McDowell, 2008. In Maraña, Aprovechar el potencial del turismo en lugares de conflicto histórico para promover la paz: una reflexión sobre el pasado y una fuente de inspiración para el futuro, 9.
12. Maraña, Aprovechar el potencial del turismo en lugares de conflicto histórico para promover la paz: una reflexión sobre el pasado y una fuente de inspiración para el futuro, 11–12.
13. Logan, *Places of Pain and Shame*.
14. Nora, *Les lieux de mémoire*.
15. Logan, *Places of Pain and Shame*.
16. Arrieta, *Lugares de memoria traumática*.
17. Maraña, Aprovechar el potencial del turismo en lugares de conflicto histórico para promover la paz: una reflexión sobre el pasado y una fuente de inspiración para el futuro, 9.
18. Allier Montaño, "Lugar de memoria: ¿un concepto para el análisis de las luchas memoriales? El caso de Uruguay y su pasado reciente," 100.
19. Franco, "Nuevas memorias para nuevos futuros: reflexiones sobre el patrimonio cultural en contextos de conflicto," 42.
20. Franco, "Nuevas memorias para nuevos futuros: reflexiones sobre el patrimonio cultural en contextos de conflicto," 45.

21 Maraña, *Patrimonio y Derechos Humanos*.
22 Labadi, *UNESCO, Cultural Heritage, and Outstanding Universal Value*.
23 Francioni, "Treinta años después: ¿está la Convención sobre el Patrimonio Mundial preparada para el siglo XXI?," 11–38.
24 Maraña, *Patrimonio y Derechos Humanos*.
25 Labadi, *UNESCO, Cultural Heritage, and Outstanding Universal Value*.
26 Bertacchini, "The Politicization of UNESCO World Heritage Decision Making," 95–129.
27 Labadi, *UNESCO, Cultural Heritage, and Outstanding Universal Value*.
28 Larsen, *World Heritage and Human Rights*.
29 Logan, *Cultural Diversity, Heritage and Human Rights*; Maraña, *Patrimonio y Derechos Humanos*; Von Droste, "World Heritage and Globalization: UNESCO's Contribution to the Development of Global Ethics," 10–15.
30 UNESCO, *The Operational Guidelines for the Implementation of the World Heritage Convention*.
31 WHC, Decision CONF 003 XII.46.
32 WHC, CC-79/CONF.003/11.
33 WHC, CONF 201 VIII.C.
34 This World Heritage List category accepts candidacies of properties related to each other by theme or historical event, but that are not necessarily physically or geographically bound.
35 ICOMOS, *Evaluations of Nominations of Cultural and Mixed Properties*, 143.
36 ICOMOS, *Evaluations of Nominations of Cultural and Mixed Properties*, 144.
37 ICOMOS, *Evaluations of Nominations of Cultural and Mixed Properties*, 148.
38 ICOMOS, *Evaluations of Nominations of Cultural and Mixed Properties*, 153.
39 ICOMOS, *Evaluations of Nominations of Cultural and Mixed Properties*, 153.
40 WH 2018, Session record, 468–469.
41 WH 2018, Session record, 473.
42 WHC, Decision 42 COM 8B.24, para. 4.
43 WHC, Decision 42 COM 8.
44 WHC, Decision 42 COM 8B.24, para. 2.
45 WHC, Decision 42 COM 5A.
46 More information available on this PowerPoint presentation: https://whc.unesco.org/en/memoryreflection.
47 WHC, Decision 44 COM 8.
48 ICOMOS, discussion paper, 4.
49 International Coalition of Sites of Conscience, Interpretation of Sites of Memory, 3.
50 ICOMOS, discussion paper.
51 ICOMOS, discussion paper, 4.
52 ICOMOS, discussion paper, 4.
53 WHC, Decision 31 COM 8B.8.
54 ICOMOS, discussion paper, 5.
55 ICOMOS, discussion paper, 9.
56 International Coalition of Sites of Conscience, Interpretation of Sites of Memory, para. 2.
57 International Coalition of Sites of Conscience, Interpretation of Sites of Memory, para. 28.
58 International Coalition of Sites of Conscience, Interpretation of Sites of Memory, para. 39.
59 International Coalition of Sites of Conscience, Interpretation of Sites of Memory, para. 37.
60 International Coalition of Sites of Conscience, Interpretation of Sites of Memory, para. 42.
61 Maraña, Harnessing the Potential of Tourism in Post Conflict Sites in Advancing Peace:

Reflecting on the Past and Inspiring the Future; Maraña, Aprovechar el potencial del turismo en lugares de conflicto histórico para promover la paz: una reflexión sobre el pasado y una fuente de inspiración para el futuro.

62 International Coalition of Sites of Conscience, Interpretation of Sites of Memory, para. 40, 79.
63 International Coalition of Sites of Conscience, Interpretation of Sites of Memory, para. 80.
64 International Coalition of Sites of Conscience, Interpretation of Sites of Memory, para. 83.
65 Maraña, Harnessing the Potential of Tourism in Post Conflict Sites in Advancing Peace: Reflecting on the Past and Inspiring the Future; Maraña, Aprovechar el potencial del turismo en lugares de conflicto histórico para promover la paz: una reflexión sobre el pasado y una fuente de inspiración para el futuro; Naef, "Memorial Entrepreneurs and Dissonance in Post-Conflict Tourism."
66 ICOMOS, Sites Associated with Memories of Recent Conflicts and the World Heritage Convention.
67 ICOMOS, Sites Associated with Memories of Recent Conflicts and the World Heritage Convention, 22.
68 Beazly, Study on Sites Associated with Recent Conflicts and Other Negative and Divisive Memories, 27.
69 Shaheed, Report of the Special Rapporteur in the Field of Cultural Rights A/HRC/25/49, para. 3.
70 Shaheed, Report of the Special Rapporteur in the Field of Cultural Rights A/HRC/25/49, para. 24.
71 Shaheed, Report of the Special Rapporteur in the Field of Cultural Rights A/HRC/25/49, para. 32.
72 Shaheed, Report of the Special Rapporteur in the Field of Cultural Rights A/68/296, para. 6.
73 Shaheed, Report of the Special Rapporteur in the Field of Cultural Rights A/HRC/25/49, para. 3.
74 Shaheed, Report of the Special Rapporteur in the Field of Cultural Rights A/68/296, para. 7.
75 Shaheed, Report of the Special Rapporteur in the Field of Cultural Rights A/HRC/25/49, para. 19.
76 Shaheed, Report of the Special Rapporteur in the Field of Cultural Rights A/HRC/25/49, para. 20.
77 Shaheed, Report of the Special Rapporteur in the Field of Cultural Rights A/HRC/25/49, para. 58.
78 Shaheed, Report of the Special Rapporteur in the Field of Cultural Rights A/68/296, para. 20.
79 Shaheed, Report of the Special Rapporteur in the Field of Cultural Rights A/HRC/25/49, para. 6.
80 Shaheed, Report of the Special Rapporteur in the Field of Cultural Rights A/HRC/25/49, para. 62.
81 Shaheed, Report of the Special Rapporteur in the Field of Cultural Rights A/68/296, para. 62.
82 Shaheed, Report of the Special Rapporteur in the Field of Cultural Rights A/HRC/25/49, para. 7.
83 Shaheed, Report of the Special Rapporteur in the Field of Cultural Rights A/HRC/25/49, para. 49.
84 Shaheed, Report of the Special Rapporteur in the Field of Cultural Rights A/HRC/25/49, para. 9.

85 Shaheed, Report of the Special Rapporteur in the Field of Cultural Rights A/HRC/25/49, para. 9.
86 Shaheed, Report of the Special Rapporteur in the Field of Cultural Rights A/68/296, para. 26.
87 Shaheed, Report of the Special Rapporteur in the Field of Cultural Rights A/HRC/25/49, para. 99.
88 Turunen, "A Geography of Coloniality: Re-Narrating European Integration," 185–214.
89 Turunen, "A Geography of Coloniality: Re-Narrating European Integration," 185–214.
90 Mäkinen, "Interconceptualizing Europe and Peace: Identity Building Under the European Heritage Label," 51-78.
91 UNESCO, UNESCO Memory of the World Programme.
92 UNESCO, UNESCO Memory of the World Programme, 11.
93 UNESCO, UNESCO Memory of the World Programme.
94 UNESCO, UNESCO Memory of the World Programme, 23.
95 UNESCO, UNESCO Memory of the World Programme, para. 6.3.3.
96 UNESCO, Memory of the World Nominations 2016–2017.
97 Dogliani, 2008. In *Arrieta, Lugares de memoria traumática.*
98 Larsen, *World Heritage and Human Rights.*
99 Mäkinen, "Interconceptualizing Europe and Peace: Identity Building Under the European Heritage Label," 57.

five

Mass Grave Exhumations: a Testament to Repression in the Spanish State

An Overview of the Exhumations Conducted between the Years 2000 and 2021

Lourdes Herrasti

Exhumations have uncovered the hidden reality of the hundreds of clandestine mass graves that had been doomed to oblivion

INTRODUCTION

Exhumations are not a new phenomenon. The first grave-exhumation campaigns—launched by the Franco regime—began as early as the Spanish Civil War (1936–1939). According to Mariano Maroto García,[1] the Francoist government made sure that its sympathizers received a decent burial, their deaths properly recorded, and their family members financially compensated. These campaigns sought to locate Francoist deaths; exhume, transfer, and rebury combatants who had died in the battlefield; locate disappeared Francoists; and lodge the deaths and disappearances in the Registry of Vital Records. In addition, surviving family members of dead Francoist fighters received pensions, and those mutilated in war were able to collect benefits and secure employment.

The remains of the insurrected were recovered and interred in cemeteries, and, once the bodies were identified, their full names were entered in the Registry of Vital Records. Only three months into the Civil War, the Francoist government set up a plan to transfer the fallen members of "our Glorious army" from their places of death or provisional burial to the local cemeteries of their hometowns.

Immediately after the war, the dictatorial regime demanded that every town in Spain submit a tally of the victims and reports of the violent acts and events perpetrated against the rebels. The May 6, 1939, order mandated: "Those who wish to exhume the remains of a relative dead at the hands of the Marxist mob and to rebury them in the cemetery may file a request with their provincial civil governor."[2]

The Francoist exhumation and reburial campaign peaked in 1958 and 1959 with a massive number of bodies being moved to the Valley of the Fallen in Cuelgamuros (Madrid). The government decree of April 1, 1940, signed by Francisco Franco, ordered the construction of a basilica in Cuelgamuros to perpetuate the memory of those fallen for the Francoist cause. That was the initial purpose, but, after 1958, the site began taking in remains from any mass grave of the wartime period, regardless of "the side the dead soldier had fought for." Thousands of bodies taken from the cemeteries of Grinón, Getafe, and Ciempozuelos, which housed combatants from the Madrid front, ended in Cuelgamuros as a result.[3] The entry book of the Valley of the Fallen, keeping record of the remains inhumed there, puts the official figure at 33,847 people.

Spain's conversion to democracy began with Franco's death in 1975 and the approval of the constitution in 1978. During this transitional period, families and neighbors volunteered their time and energy to exhume a slew of graves. They would show up to the location on the agreed date and time, and, equipped with picks, shovels, and hoes, would buckle down to unburying and collecting bones on bed sheets. Although the identities of the people underground had always been common knowledge, fear had deterred the community from recovering their bodies until then. In a way, the memories of the disappeared resurfaced as victims were exposed in their graves.

Families were fully aware of the relatives who had gone missing, who had been arrested, taken out of their homes, and had never come back. Families also knew the approximate date they had been killed and buried from the accounts of the neighbors who had been involved in the secret burials.

The exhumation efforts of the Transition, known as the early exhumation period, had a great impact on regions such as Navarre, La Rioja, and Palencia. In Navarre they had the staunch support of many clergymen, either because they knew the families of the victims, or because they espoused the teachings of the Second Vatican Council and were members of the HOAC—a brotherhood of Catholic workers—or other religious associations firmly committed to social causes. Priests could obtain valuable information without drawing attention to themselves. Several town mayors, too, allied with the families and helped organize local exhumations.

Some efforts rested on the shoulders of individuals such as Esperanza Pérez, a member of the Communist Party, who, on returning from her exile in Brussels after the death of the dictator, took it upon herself to organize and perform the unburials of more than 150 victims of Palencia's repressive practices, including some of her direct relatives. Her dad, a day laborer in Cevico de la Torre (Palencia), and her grandfather were the first two of Esperanza's eight male relatives to be arrested. None of them were ever seen again. When her exile was over, Esperanza was resolute in her decision to locate and exhume the mass graves of her relatives. And, while she had no one rooting for her, Esperanza, like the brave woman that she was, persevered, and gathered information and used up her resources until she finally accomplished her mission.

Community-driven exhumations came to an abrupt halt on February 23, 1981, when a general of the Guardia Civil—the national police force of Spain—staged a coup in which he gained control of the Parliament and the Spanish government, albeit for a few short hours. Despite its brevity, the insurgency fueled fears of renewed times of repression and a new civil war. Works to recover the missing dead stopped as a consequence.

The first technical exhumation following archeological methods would not happen until the year 2000. The place was Priaranza del Bierzo in the autonomous community of Castile and León. There, a scientific team of archeologists, anthropologists, and a forensic pathologist unearthed a mass grave containing the remains of thirteen people. Families and local authorities, including the town's mayor, assisted by identifying the location of the burial site. In the grave was the grandfather of Emilio Silva, who, after coming to the realization that repression was a phenomenon of nationwide consequences affecting not only his family or region, but the whole of Spain, decided to create the *Asociación para la Recuperación de la Memoria Histórica* (Association for the Recovery of Historical Memory, ARMH).

These events exposed the long-hidden reality of the hundreds of unidentified, clandestine mass graves that had been lost to oblivion.

Only then did society start to talk, as media coverage of the exhumations helped people shed their fears and voice their experiences and memories. On one occasion, moved by a radio piece on the discovery of a mass grave in León by the scientific association *Sociedad de Ciencias Aranzadi*, a Zaldibia (Zaldivia) resident called the station to talk about a grave located in his property that his own father had to dig up. His was one of the many accounts that followed Priaranza del Bierzo's exhumations, as people's memories awakened and they began to tell stories, and more broadly, to overcome their fears.

THE EVENTS

> In a civil war, a systematic occupation of the territory reinforced with the necessary [social] cleansing, is always preferable to a quick defeat of the enemy armies, which would leave the country infested with adversaries.
>
> *Francisco Franco*

The Spanish Civil War was the outcome of the foiled military coup of July 1936, which was launched against the Republican regime it was legally elected in February 1936. The war pitted the supporters of the lawfully constituted government of the Second Republic, also known as Loyalists, against the military and the army, and the conservative and anti-reform groups. The insurgents ultimately succeeded in imposing a four-decade-long dictatorship by means of brutal violence and later secured the continuity of the regime with a successor for dictator Franco.

In their interventions, the insurrected generals did not shy away from commenting on the destructive aspect of their force, frequently echoing the orders of one of the conspirators of the military coup, General Emilio Mola: "Our actions must be extremely violent." For his part, General Jesús Yagüe stressed the ultraconservative and reactionary nature of the operation: "We must eliminate all leftist elements," eradicate extremists, and proponents of leftist revolutionary ideas. Their plan entailed a military victory over the Republican forces in the battlefield and the systematic control of civil society and the rear guard by means of utter terror. In words of the press officer of the Francoist army, Gonzalo Aguilera: "To inspire dominance, we ought to spread terror and eliminate those who don't think like us." That meant exterminating a third of the male population in Spain. It was a ruthless three-step system of occupation, domination, and simultaneous extermination of potential opponents. "We are purging the rear guard" is the quote that best portrayed the Francoist frame of mind. These terror strategies were an unequivocal holdover of the military training and career years the Francoist generals spent in the Moroccan Rif, where they applied colonialist policies of military imposition and dominance.

After hundreds of people were murdered in Badajoz, in an interview to *The New York Herald*'s John Whitaker and *Chicago Tribune*'s Jay Allen, Yagüe stated:

> "... You know what to do with those who resist us: send them to prison, or execute them, whichever. (. . .) We set our minds to redeem you, and that is what we will do, whether you want to or not. (. . .) We won't be needing you, at all. There will be no more elections, ever! Your vote is worthless to us! We will first redeem the opposing side, and seeing as they won't embrace our civilization willingly, we will have to impose it on them. (. . .) Of course, we killed them," he told me. "What did you think? That I was going to drag 4,000 *rojos* (liberals) with me, while my column advanced against the clock? That I was going to set them free for them to win Badajoz back?"[4]

The message captured by Whitaker in another interview with Aguilera left little to the imagination:

> We need to kill, kill, kill (. . .) Commoners are no better than beasts in that they may infect us with the virus of Bolshevism, just as rats and lice do with the plague. Do you see now what we mean by regenerating the Spanish state? We needed to eradicate and exterminate the carriers of leftist revolutionary ideas, and eliminate leftist elements: communists, anarchists, trade unions, masons.

All Francoist forces operated under these premises and orders since the beginning of the Civil War, subjecting Republican Loyalists and civil detractors of the coup to extreme repression.

The actual death toll and number of people who disappeared within the historical context of the war has been a dominant topic for discussion among historiographers. Figures have varied widely. Today, the number of repression victims is estimated to have been between 114,000 and 130,000. During the Civil War, repression not only emerged in the battlefield as a military strife between two armies, but it was also used in a social, ideological, and class purge to get rid of all who rejected the coup. This atmosphere of terror was the breeding ground for more localized forms of violence motivated by hatred, envies, and other small-scale conflicts.

CHRONOLOGY OF THE REPRESSION

Repression began on the same day the coup was staged. The first months of the war, from July to December 1936—July to October being the cruelest—came to be known as the Hot Terror period. The expression is credited to historian Julián Casanova, who used it to define the repression, killings, and forced disappearances of people whose deaths went unrecorded. Violence instigated by military and social powers quickly devolved into unrestrained repression, with the consent and knowledge of the insurgent military and political authorities.

Francisco Espinosa, a scholar of repression, noticed that many people from the regions who endorsed the insurrection fell victim to the repression rather than the war.[5] As a matter of fact, repression was brutal in these areas, because the insurgent Nationalists did not need to justify their actions; they were free to do as they pleased. As cases of repression mounted and the local population was forced into silence, terror and submission pervaded every aspect of life. That is what happened in Castile and León, Navarre, La Rioja, and Galicia.

Arrests of large groups of people, and the death squads—raiding towns daily and without hindrance to detain people on lists crafted by the authorities or the victims' own neighbors—became infallible terror tools in the Francoist faction's quest to achieve the total submission of society. Witnessing how their neighbors were arrested, thrown into a truck, and driven away to their sure deaths must have paralyzed town residents with fear, unable and unwilling to believe what was happening before their very eyes. Stumbling upon dead bodies on the side of the road, piled by the walls of cemeteries or lying in the middle of a field filled locals with terror and kept them from speaking up.

The effects of the planned and premeditated repressive campaign designed by the insurrected authorities and military figures were strengthened from the bottom with the collaboration of locals and other citizens. Many neighbors informed on other members of the community. These anonymous tips were precious for the groups of the Falange fascist party, which often came from other towns in the region. Through this cross-hierarchical collaboration, repression grew larger and more generalized, and the new social and political order lodged itself firmly in the state.

On October 5, 1938, the Ministry of Public Order (the Central Office of the National Security Service) issued a request to all the provincial delegations of Public Order to provide a detailed town-by-town report on "the count of victims who were executed, arrested, sent to forced labor battalions, exiled, sanctioned, murdered, or who disappeared or escaped from their municipalities since the beginning of the Nationalist Movement until the end of September 1938."[6] To bring the request to fruition, the Guardia Civil was to exert total control over the population. This meant that, even before the war was over, Francoist authorities already had comprehensive data about the repression practices that occurred in the areas under the insurgents' control since 1936, and the areas they occupied as the war progressed.

The period from July to December 1936 was the most pugnacious, with the highest number of disappearances and murders. About 70 percent of the victims recovered from exhumed graves date back to those months.

After December 1936, repression acquired legal status. The *paseos* (rides to summary executions) and *sacas* (unlawful mass executions of prisoners) gradually decreased. The rebels sought to pass as a legitimate regime, putting victims on sham summary trials with predetermined verdicts. On the plus side, they were forced to keep records of the names of the executed victims.

Once the war was over, repression was institutionalized and "justice was turned on its head." As trials became increasingly prevalent and death sentences soared, thousands of people were imprisoned and many of them executed. Valencia and Madrid—the last territories to be occupied by Francoist troops—were particularly vulnerable to these practices.

THE PERPETRATORS

Conversations about wartime executions generally center on victims and leave out the perpetrators. Be it for fear, shame, collusion, or a collective sense of guilt, the criminals are rarely mentioned. While the children and descendants are not guilty for their parents or ancestors' actions, we should not abstain from exposing the identities of the perpetrators just out of respect for their families. They were often members of the Guardia Civil and the Falange party, and they did not waste time in joining the rebel army as soon as the war broke out. Members of other armed conservative groups such as the *requetés*, of Carlist ideology, or the right-wing Catholic group *Acción Ciudadana*, too, fought with fervor for the insurrected side.

EXHUMATION AND ANALYSIS OF THE GRAVES

Collecting information and data surrounding the moments before the death is a critical preliminary phase of the exhumation process. Researching the area's history and the stories of eyewitnesses, family members, and neighbors provides key insights about the location of the graves, the number of victims, the victims' identities, and how they died.

The burial site in Larrasoaña is a prime example. A mass grave containing the remains of four escaped prisoners from Fort San Cristóbal, at the top of Mount Ezkaba, in Pamplona-Iruñea, was found thanks to Paulina Linzoain's account. The runaways were caught less than two miles away from the prison. Linzoain recalled a day in May 1938 when, on her way back from school, she heard a commotion and saw a crowd of people, the Guardia Civil, and some vehicles close to Larrasoaña's cemetery. Walking closer to see what was happening, she and her group of friends found her dad along with other neighbors burying the bodies of four people on the outside corner of the cemetery. Her memories of the event offered invaluable help in finding the grave.

In the town of Barcones (Soria), the local association *Recuerdo y Dignidad* obtained the testimony of a witness who had watched several executions. One day, he saw six people with their hands bound being taken to the outskirts of town. The inquisitive young man decided to follow the group from a distance. He settled right in front of the men, where he had a clear view of the killings. His information helped locate a grave with six neighbors of Berlanga de Duero (Burgos) of leftist union affiliation.

But these are only exceptional cases. The whereabouts of most of the graves remained secret or were forgotten as citizens felt fearful of sharing their experiences. To find the emplacement of a grave, a preliminary manual or mechanical survey of the area is needed. Lack of accurate information of the location and/or decades of land alterations exacerbate the task and sometimes make it impossible to locate the burial sites.

1. MORPHOLOGY OF THE GRAVES

To indicate the location of a grave, people occasionally left marks or signs in the surrounding area by carving out a cross on a nearby tree, piling rocks or soil on top of the grave, erecting makeshift wooden crosses—later made in iron—delineating the site with stones, or resting plastic flowers on it. Other times, trees, tree stumps, roads, and similar environmental elements served as geographical markers of the location of the site.

Mass graves are holes excavated for burial purposes. They are commonly dug in a rectangular shape to accommodate the greatest number of bodies possible, sometimes stacked next to each other in a horizontal position. The corpses were buried by the murderers themselves, volunteer neighbors, or neighbors forced by the military or the authorities; they grabbed the bodies by their upper and lower extremities and placed them in the grave. To maximize the space, the distribution of the victims varied in accordance with the frame of the site. Bodies were frequently deposited on the corners, parallel to each other or alternating head and feet, although many times bodies were just swung into the grave landing on heaps of other bodies.

For graves excavated within longitudinal ditches, victims were laid in line, one after the other. Ditches were easier to dig when the gravedigger was forced to do so and wanted to be done quickly. When an area became the scene of repeated executions and burials, broad ditches were used to deposit the bodies perpendicular to the grave and in an alternating pattern, head touching feet. Excellent examples of this practice are the sites in La Pedraja (Villafranca Montes de Oca, Burgos) and Fregenal (Cáceres). In La Pedraja, archeologists found the remains of 105 victims that had been buried in a chain of eleven graves in a ditch that was seventy-nine feet long and seven feet wide. In Frenegal, forty-seven bodies were recovered from seven contiguous graves.

In reality, any cavity, water well, or mine was good enough to swiftly get rid of and hide murdered victims. In Extremadura, León, Asturias, and Navarre, some bodies were thrown off cliffs.

When researchers form an approximate idea of where the burial site may be, they request appropriate permits for the exhumation, namely, a signed authorization of the owner of the property where the site is located, and an authorization for the archeological intervention. Notice to the local and regional authorities is also a prerequisite.

Once the first layer of soil is removed from the area, a second mottled layer reveals the surface of the grave. Usually, the fill of the grave is darker because of the organic products it contained. After the site is marked out, archeologists move on to extract the soil covering the remains. The soil-removal process is typically done with extreme care until the bones of the piled bodies become visible.

Documentation of the position of each individual and their associated artifacts is conducted in a systematic manner in a way that will allow for the reconstruction of the grave later. Researchers ideally must know the position of every element in the grave—bone or other artifacts.

2. RECOVERY OF AND INFORMATION PROVIDED BY ASSOCIATED ARTIFACTS

Associated artifacts are all elements of non-osseous and non-biological origin that are buried alongside their owners. Each body is recorded with its associated artifacts, and their description and position in the grave. Most of the time, the objects are related to the clothes the victim was wearing at the time of their murder, including shirt buttons at the chest level or on the wrists, belts and belt buckles, button flies and the belt loops of the back side of pants. Fabric elements are harder to ascertain, but scraps of shirts, pants, corduroy jackets, pockets, and handkerchiefs have been recovered from time to time. Exhumed footwear usually consists of good-quality leather shoes, the rubber bottoms of espadrilles, or simple farmer shoes called *abarcas* made of reused pneumatic tires.

Besides clothing, articles of personal care such as combs, mirrors, lice combs, and toothbrushes are also common. Just as personal, and even unique to the owner, are watches, cuff links, and rings. Some of these associated artifacts have led to the identification of their owners.

A gold wedding band bearing the inscription "Benita 20-12-1931" and found on the finger of a body buried in Burgos's La Andaya IV grave initiated the identification process—which was later genetically confirmed—of Tomás Requejo Requejo, a parliamentarian and council member in the municipal council of Aranda de Duero (Burgos). The ring was essential to learn what group of victims shared the grave with him.

Another gold wedding band found in grave #3 in Estépar (Burgos), inscribed with two initials—P. and E.—and the wedding date, pointed to Plácido Pérez Barriuso, a teacher murdered on September 9, 1936, and buried with a *saca* of twenty-five prisoners taken from Burgos's Central Prison.

Other artifacts indicate the habits and customs of the victims. We know smoking was an extended habit among the deceased because of the lighters, matchboxes, rolling paper, cigarette filters, and pipes found with them. Games and entertainment elements, including dice, cards, knucklebones, are game tiles, used to kill time during their long prison stays, have also been recovered from these graves.

Contrary to the common belief that all victims of repression and murder were anti-religious, devotional medals representing various saints and the Virgin Mary are frequently found. Although the bulk of them are Virgin Mary medals, others symbolize the patron saint of the owner's hometown or region.

Objects related to health and sickness include inguinal hernia support belts; partial and complete dentures, implants, and other dental prostheses; ocular prostheses such as glass eyes; artificial limbs; and capsules, vials, and pill boxes.

The prisoners inhumed in the cemetery of Porreres in Majorca (Illes Balears) had been taken from the prisons of Can Mir or the Bellver Castle in Palma and transferred to Porreres to be killed and buried in the graves that had been dug for them. Some of the 114 exhumed bodies were found with pill boxes containing sore throat and cough lozenges—inseparable companions through the long harsh winters spent in the freezing prisons.

Exhumations conducted in the cemeteries of battlefield hospitals have unearthed remains with back and/or limb braces typically used in medical treatments. The cemeteries of Pernafeites de Miravet and Mas de Santa Magdalena (Tarragona), exhumed by the Catalan group *Iltirta*, are famous examples.

Some associated artifacts such as combs or hair pins, and even earrings, thimbles, bobby pins, heeled shoes, and corset boning—although men's orthopedic corsets resembled them, too—suggest a tie between the victim and a female. Sometimes, these kind of objects reveal the presence of female bodies in the grave. The remains discovered in one of La Pedraja's (Villafranca Montes de Oca, Burgos) graves were too deteriorated to determine the sex of some of the bodies, but thanks to a hair pin found on one of them, archeologists were able to conclude that at least one of the 105 exhumed victims was female.

Other artifacts from the same graves included the bullets with which the victims were killed. Rounds used with Mauser rifles—a popular firearm especially among the Guardia Civil and the army—and 9 mm long and short rounds used with Astra or Star service pistols are the two most frequently found types of ammunition.

3. ANTHROPOLOGICAL ANALYSIS AND BIOLOGICAL PROFILE

The human remains of each unburied victim are individually packed in boxes together with their associated artifacts before they are transferred to the anthropological laboratory. There, remains are analyzed following a standardized methodology to determine their sex, age, specific pathological characteristics, dental morphology, and the injuries leading to death.

According to the most recent data, as of December 2021, more than 870 graves and the remains of more than 11,800 people had been exhumed, over a twenty-year span. The analysis of their remains helped estimate an anthropological profile. Most of the victims recovered from Civil War graves are male. The overall analysis of the results points to only 3 percent of the victims being female.

Almost half of the male victims are young adults between the ages of twenty and forty; about 30 percent were middle-aged men over 40; a third group were senior men older than fifty; and a fourth group was composed of men younger than twenty. On many occasions, it is not possible to give an accurate estimate of the age of the victims because of the poor state of conservation of the bones, and they are grouped under the general category of adult remains.

4. CAUSE OF DEATH

The remains of the individuals recovered from the graves show clear signs of fatal gunshot wounds. An analysis of the location of the wounds indicates that most of them were at head level. This means shots were not fired at their bodies, but straight to the head and in proximity. Entry wounds are commonly found in the posterior aspect of the skull with a forward trajectory, meaning victims were shot in the back of the head. These are, by definition, summary executions.

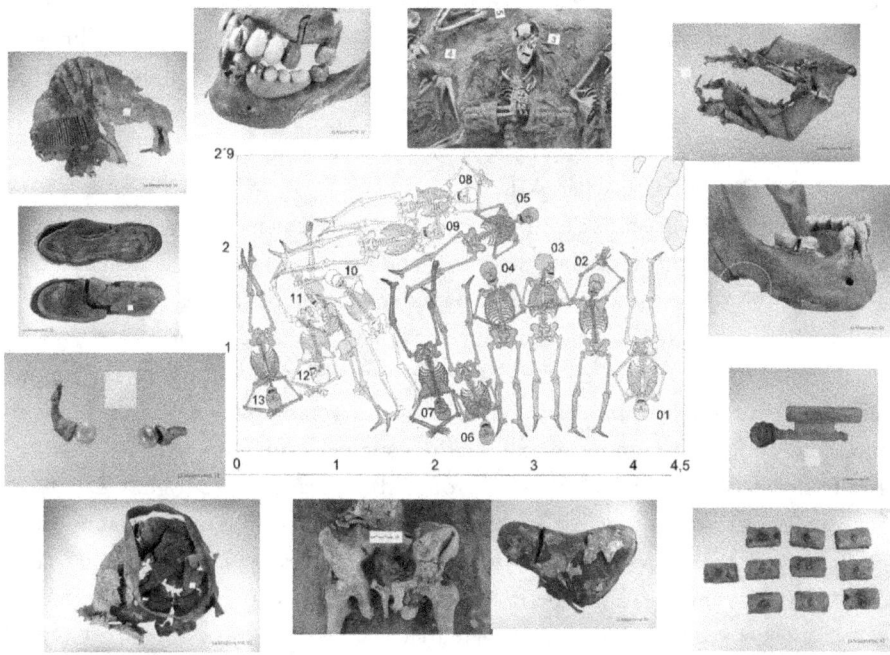

Artifacts recovered from the La Mazorra grave in Burgos. Note on the schematic re-creation that the hands of the victims were tied at the time of their murder and burial.

Clockwise from the top left: female hat and comb, dental prosthesis, clothes of the victim, zipper of a sweater, mandibular gunshot entry wound, flint wheel lighter, hinges of a wooden carpenter's tape, inguinal hernia support belt over left hip, beret, earrings, and shoes.

5. INTEGRATED REPORT

Historical research and a compilation of witness accounts help put together the puzzle of repressive events that took place in the area. Research involves gathering as much information as possible concerning the identity of the victims, their origin and biography, the context in which repression happened, and the story of the events.

The report, meant to assist in the genetic identification of the victim, compiles the data resulting from the survey and localization of the grave; the exhumation works, which require detailed documentation of the arrangement of the bodies and their associated artifacts in the grave; the anthropological analysis that will determine the biological profile of the victims regarding their sex and age; the dental analysis and identification of possible pathological signs; and the identification of fatal injuries. When a victim is genetically identified, the genetic information is added to the integrated report, before it is delivered to the family along with their relative's remains and associated artifacts. The government of the autonomous community also receives a copy of the report for public access.

CHRONOLOGY OF THE EXHUMATIONS

The exhumation in Priaranza del Bierzo in 2000 is considered to be the first one to have followed an archeological methodology and been conducted by a team of archeologists, anthropologists, and a forensic pathologist. Others, such as the exhumation of Bishop Irurita in the Cathedral of Barcelona, may have predated it.

Despite a slow start in 2001 and 2002, exhumations had an uptick the following year with forty-two unburials, many of which were individual graves. Between 2004 and 2006, the number of exhumations ranged from twenty-seven to thirty. The Historical Memory Act[7] of 2007 proposed by José Luis Rodríguez Zapatero's Socialist government propelled exhumation actions, providing enough support to unearth more than three hundred victims and many graves. Data show that 2008 to 2012 was the most fruitful period, totaling between sixty and ninety unburied graves and between 385 and 630 recovered victims every year. In 2011, the Council of Ministers approved and published a protocol for exhumations, which established the requirements and methodology to be followed. That year, sixty-six graves were opened and more than four hundred people recovered. In 2012, the number of victims rose to five hundred from a total of sixty-five graves. After it took over the government following a victory in the general elections, the conservative party Partido Popular (PP) stopped subsidizing exhumations, and in 2013, totals plummeted to fourteen graves and fifty-five bodies.

When autonomous communities took up the baton for all initiatives related to the recovery of historical memory—a few taking control in 2014, but most in 2016—the number of graves and victims that were exhumed yearly climbed dramatically, sometimes exceeding six hundred a year and reaching up to one thousand in 2021. The secretary of state renewed the budget plan for initiatives of Democratic Memory in 2020, with direct financial help, and through the *Federación Española de Municipios y Provincias* (Spanish Federation of Towns and Provinces, FEMP).[8]

Cemeteries were heavily exhumed during this last period, and scores of victims reclaimed: two thousand in Paterna (Valencia) and three thousand in Pico Reja (Sevilla)—fifteen hundred of whom died because of repression acts. A similar number of bodies was found in Nerva (Huelva) and in the San José cemetery (Cádiz).

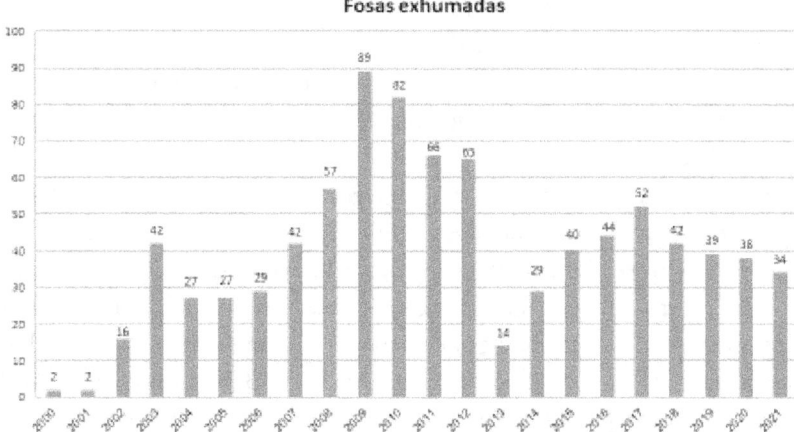

Timeline of the number of exhumed graves and recovered victims.

(Own creation)

TYPOLOGY OF MASS GRAVES

The type of victim and the cause and manner of their death may be used to classify graves into different categories.
- a) Extrajudicial executions
- b) Summary executions
- c) Combatants and noncombatants fallen in the battlefield
- d) Imprisoned victims
- e) Repression acts against *maquis* and guerrillas

A) EXTRAJUDICIAL EXECUTIONS:
These were mass killings committed during the first months of the war after arbitrary arrests and conducted without any legal protection. These executions went unrecorded, and the bodies were buried in a clandestine fashion. Families were never notified of their relative's death.

Many of the graves found on the side of the roads, in remote areas, and in the mountains contain victims of extrajudicial executions. Because of their characteristics, these killings are an example of the absolute impunity with which repression was inflicted.

At La Mazorra Hill (El Alminé, Burgos), thirteen neighbors from Las Merindades (Burgos) were murdered, including two women. Their bodies were abandoned by the side of the road, and the passengers on the bus headed to Burgos saw them. A shepherd and a group of locals picked up the bodies and took them to an elevated plain near the chapel, where they dug up a rectangular grave to bury them. The victims had their hands bound when they were killed, and their buriers never untied them. Although some families were notified of the location of the grave—which was excavated in haste and fear—many of them decided to erase the events from their memories, and with their decision, the grave's very existence was forgotten.

The grave in Picón de Valdeabejas (Rabanera del Pinar, Burgos) was found thanks to a cross carved on the trunk of a nearby pine tree to indicate its location. Upon the exhumation, archeologists found the remains of five residents of Salas de Los Infantes (Burgos). They were taken from the local prison and executed in the mountains. They were five men ranging from the ages of eighteen to sixty-five. Their hands were also tied, and the ligatures were still present at the time of the exhumation.

A relatively small grave containing the skeletons of a wedded couple and an additional male victim was found in La Tejera Hill (Erriberagoitia, Araba). They had been killed by a group of Falangistas who had apprehended the victims in their hometown of northern Burgos, only to murder them in the neighboring province. When they went to arrest the husband, the wife decided to go with him, even when she correctly assumed that she would be killed.

Many prisoners were taken out of prisons in massive *sacas* to be shot to death in remote areas. A *saca* with more than three hundred prisoners from the Central Prison of Burgos was driven to the Estépar mountains (Burgos) to be executed. The remains of ninety-six victims distributed among four graves were recovered during the exhumation process. The systematic manner in which the graves were excavated establishes a pattern and a *modus operandi* that makes us believe they were part of a premeditated plan devised by the insurgent Francoist government headquartered in Burgos.

The four cases cited within this category happened during the first months of the war, where repression was unleashed in the most violent, uncontrolled, and disproportionate way.

B) SUMMARY EXECUTIONS:

After 1937, to confer legitimacy to Francoist-forced submission and violence, the rebels held manipulated summary trials charging leftist detainees who were loyal to the Republic and opposed the military insurgence with "military rebellion." Francoist minister Ramón Súñer referred to this as "justice turned on its head," because the insurgents who rose up in arms against the lawful government of the Republic now accused Loyalists of rebelling against Francoist rule.

Massive groups of victims were usually executed against the walls of cemeteries. Thousands of Valencian detainees were killed against the wall of Paterna's cemetery, with most of them dying between 1939 and 1940. Groups of varying numbers were executed and buried in graves excavated for them in the cemetery. A total of 2,238 people died mostly from April 1939 until the end of 1942, according to the data collected by historian Vicente Gabarda.

C) FALLEN IN THE BATTLEFIELD:

These were combatants fallen in the battlefront, mostly in the northern front, in the Ebro region, in the surrounding area of Madrid, and in the Levante front. The disparities between the Republican and the rebel forces soon materialized in the battlefield. As Francoist troops advanced into territory previously held by the Republican government, they recovered the dead members of their own battalions, but abandoned the corpses of many who fought and died for the Republic. As a result, the bodies of hundreds of fighters remain missing.

War actions such as town raids, planned or unintended explosions of ammunition, and bombings, especially, had an enormous impact on civilian life, leaving many casualties behind. Known worldwide for the infamous bombings that leveled it in 1937, Gernika (Bizkaia) has become a symbol of the many towns that were terrorized during wartime Spain. Women, children, and senior citizens were killed indiscriminately.

A number of dead fighters have been recovered in the Ebro Valley, in the Basque Autonomous Community, in Catalonia, in Cantabria, and in Asturias. Some of the bodies unearthed in the Bizkaian mountains belonged to soldiers of the so-called Iron Ring, a defensive line composed of bunkers and fortifications built to shield Bilbao-Bilbo from the rebels. Among their personal belongings, a few of the bodies still carried some ammunition and most importantly, their dog tags, which helped identify the remains thanks to the identification numbers engraved on them.[9] The exhumation of a trench in La Fatarella (Zaragoza) revealed the body of a soldier who probably died of the injuries caused by a grenade that went off in his hand.[10]

As troops moved from one combat zone to the next, dead soldiers lay abandoned in the middle of fields or in the mountain. In populated areas, locals removed and inhumed the corpses to either hide them from sight or avoid health risks or the presence of vermin. An easy way to get rid of the bodies was to bury them in the ditches that had been used as war trenches. In Zeanuri's Altun Mountain (Bizkaia), five guerrilla men still equipped with cartridge belts, helmets, boots, and ammunition, and carrying spoons and combs, among other gear, were recovered from a trench dug in a zigzag pattern. Again, their dog tags provided the names of the victims, and posterior genetic analysis confirmed their identities. Also, in El Rellán (Asturias), thirty-eight civilian victims were exhumed from war trenches used as improvised graves.

D) IMPRISONED VICTIMS:

Not all deaths were gun related. The countless factories, schools, and estates that were refashioned into prisons and detention centers to accommodate the exorbitant number of people who were sent to prison between 1938 and 1942—a popular expression portrayed the Spain of that era as an *enormous prison*—were behind the high mortality rate among the prison population. The terrible living conditions resulting from overcrowded spaces, freezing temperatures, humidity, starvation, parasites, poor hygiene, and the spread of disease caused the deaths of thousands of neglected and unattended prisoners.

The *Cementerio de las Botellas* (Cemetery of the Bottles), a graveyard exclusively used between 1942 and 1945 to bury the prisoners of Fort San Cristóbal, on Mount Ezkaba, is an illuminating example of this deplorable treatment. The cemetery held individual graves with the coffins of 131 male prisoners, most of whom died from tuberculosis or a similar respiratory illness they developed while living in a dreadful environment of bitterly cold temperatures and humidity. All men were inhumed with a bottle between their legs containing an official document bearing the prison's seal and stating the personal information, cause of death, and prison sentence of the prisoner. A sketch map drawn by the prison's chaplain identified the victims and located their spot in the cemetery. His rendering is compatible with the information found in the bottled documents that have been recovered.

Breakout attempts produce a special category of imprisoned victims. Navarre lived through the dire consequences of escape attempts like no other region; it was involved in what has probably been the largest prison break in Europe to date. On May 22, 1938, 795 prisoners of Fort San Cristóbal escaped the prison and attempted to reach the French border some thirty miles away. Francoist authorities swiftly gave the order to all troops in the territory to arrest the runaways and stationed guards on trails, roads, and river crossings. Civilians were ordered to remain alert and inform authorities of any stranger or foreigner they may have seen. Their plan proved effective: Francoist forces arrested and reimprisoned 586 of the escaped prisoners. More than two hundred of the runaways were shot to death where they had been captured, and they were buried secretly. Some of the clandestine graves were located thanks to Fermin Ezkieta's research work,[11] and they were exhumed by a team of experts. So far, fifty-four bodies of the escaped prisoners have been found buried in thirteen different graves.

E) REPRESSION AGAINST MAQUIS AND GUERRILLAS:

As mentioned, repression continued throughout the Franco regime. In the 1940s, particularly after 1944, guerrilla fighters, also known as *maquis* (*Aristotelia chilensis*), because they fled to the woods, organized in groups to fight against Francoism. *Maquis* carried out surprise attacks as part of their plan to destabilize the dictatorial regime. The Guardia Civil received orders to wage a relentless fight against the *maquis* and had carte blanche to engage in conflict with them, and to arrest, capture, and kill them. The Spanish police force pressured family members, liaisons, and members of their support network; relied on locals reporting on their neighbors; and employed interrogation tactics that included abuse and torture practices. They also engaged in counterguerrilla warfare and infiltrated the various groups. With the Spanish Communist Party's decision of 1947 to dissolve the guerrilla fight, many of the groups, most of Communist ideology, dispersed. The remainder of *maquis* continued fighting until the end of the 1950s.

In 2010 a team of experts from *Grupo Paleolab*, specialized in funerary archeology and bioanthropology, conducted the exhumation of a mass grave where nine guerrilla men, members of the AGLA group (Guerrilla Group from Levante and Aragón), were buried in 1947 after the Guardia Civil executed them. This exhumation is exemplary because of all the determining factors that contributed to the identification of the victims and the events, including an eyewitness of the murders, records from the Registry of Vital Records, autopsy reports, proper documentation of the exhumation process, and successful genetic identification of six of the nine individuals.

DELIVERY OF THE REMAINS

A combination of historical documentation, witness accounts, evidence found in the grave, and the approximate anthropological profile of the victim provides a hypothesis of who the individual or the group of individuals may be. Genetic sampling of the potential relatives of the victims is taken to the genetic lab to be contrasted against the samples extracted from the remains. If the results come back positive, the identification is successful. Unfortunately, negative results are also possible for a variety of reasons.

Families then decide if they would like to receive the remains in an intimate ceremony or in a public or institutional event, to which local or regional authorities attend to show their support. The undeniable symbolic aspect of such ceremonies resides in the community showing support and participating in the restitution of the family's memory. After all, the families are the true leading figures of and the driving force behind the recovery of historical memory.

THE CONSTRUCTION OF EVIDENCE WITHIN THE HUMAN RIGHTS CONTEXT

Opening and exposing graves offers tangible evidence of the human rights violations that were perpetrated against the victims, who were murdered and their bodies hidden away, and against their relatives, who were robbed of their right to know what happened to their family members and condemned to perpetually mourn their disappearance.

A disappeared person is one who is arrested in an unlawful manner by state authorities, or affiliated groups on their behalf, and murdered, and whose body is placed out of sight. The practice of disappearing people seeks to instill fear in the community of the victim. A disappeared person, Uruguayan sociologist Gabriel Gatti argues, is "a body separated from its name, a conscience excised from its physical support, it is a timeless and spaceless identity."[12] The purpose of locating, exhuming, and analyzing the remains buried in mass graves is to reunite body and name, body, and identity. Mass graves are where the disappeared can be found.

Among the reasons listed on the explanatory statements of the Democratic Memory Bill, which has already received congressional approval and will be discussed and reportedly confirmed by the Senate in 2022, was the 2014 visit and report of the special rapporteur of the Working Group on Enforced or Involuntary Disappearances.

The application of the new law will open the door to the institutionalization of exhumations, which, as established in this chapter, give credence to the small but crucial local stories that help write a more complete history of the repression inflicted in the Spanish state during the Civil War, the postwar period. and the Francoist regime.

BIBLIOGRAPHY

Babiano, José, Gutmaro Gómez, Antonio Míguez, and Javier Tébar. *Verdugos impunes. El Franquismo y la violación sistemática de los Derechos Humanos*. Barcelona: Ediciones Pasado y Presente, 2018.

Espinosa, Francisco, Concepción Mir Curcó and Francisco Moreno Gómez. *Morir, matar, sobrevivir: La violencia en la dictadura de Franco*, edited by Julián Casanova. Barcelona: Crítica, 2002.

Espinosa, Francisco. "La memoria de la represión y la lucha por su reconocimiento." Dossier: Generaciones y memoria de la represión franquista: un balance de los movimientos por la memoria. Hispania Nova. Revista de Historia Contemporánea, no. 6, 2006.

———. *Violencia roja y azul. España 1936–1950*. Barcelona: Ed. Crítica, 2010.

———. "La represión franquista. Las circunstancias de la muerte." In Antropología forense de la Guerra Civil Española. In *Boletín Galego de Medicina Legal e Forense*, Santiago de Compostela, no. 18 (2012): 47–54.

———. "Antropología y patología forense como elementos de prueba en las fosas de la Guerra Civil y dictadura franquista." *Actes de la II Jornada d`Arqueología y Patrimoni de la Guerra Civil al Front de l`Ebre*. Tortosa, 2017 79–107.

Etxeberria Francisco ed. *Las exhumaciones de la Guerra Civil y la dictadura franquista 2000–2019. Estado actual y recomendaciones de futuro*. Madrid: Ministerio de Presidencia, Relaciones con las Cortes y Memoria Democrática, 2020.

Etxeberria, Francisco, Almudena García-Rubio, Lourdes Herrasti, Jimi Jiménez, and Nicholas

Márquez-Grant. "Mass Graves from the Spanish Civil War: Exhumations, Current Status and Protocols." *Archaeological Review from Cambridge* 31(2016): 83–103.

Etxeberria, Francisco, Lourdes Herrasti, Fernando Serrulla, and Nicholas Márquez-Grant. "Contemporary Exhumations in Spain: Recovering the Missing from the Spanish Civil War." In *Forensic Archaeology. A Global Perspective*, edited by Mike Groen, W. J. M., Nicholas Márquez-Grant and Robert Janaway, 489_497. Wiley Blackwell, 2015.

Etxeberria, Francisco, and Koldo Pla. El Fuerte de San Cristóbal en la memoria: de prisión a sanatorio penitenciario. El cementerio de las botellas. Pamplona-Iruñea: Pamiela, 2014.

Etxeberria, Francisco, Fernando Serrulla, and Lourdes Herrasti. "Simas, cavernas y pozos para ocultar cadáveres en la Guerra Civil española (1936–1939). Aportaciones desde la Antropología Forense." *Munibe (Antropologia-Arkeologia)* 65 (2014): 269–288.

Ezkieta Yaben, Fermin. *Los fugados del Fuerte de Ezkaba*. Pamplona-Iruñea: Pamiela, 2013.

García Colmenares, Pablo. "Los usos públicos de la Historia: La memoria de la represión de la guerra civil en Palencia (1936–1939)." *Publicaciones de la Institución Tello Téllez de Meneses* 76 (2005): 121–239.

Gatti, Gabriel. El detenido-desaparecido. Narrativas posibles para una catástrofe de la identidad. Montevideo: Ediciones Trilce, 2008.

Gil Andrés, Carlos. "Vecinos contra vecinos. La violencia en la retaguardia riojana durante la Guerra Civil." In "Nuevas miradas sobre la Guerra Civil." *Historia y Política*, no.16 (2006): 109–130.

González-Ruibal, Alfredo. "El último día de la batalla del Ebro. Informe de las excavaciones arqueológicas en los restos de la guerra civil de Raïmats, La Fatarella (Tarragona)." https://digital.csic.es/bitstream/10261/47780/1/2012_Informe%20La%20Fatarella%202011_Gonzalez.pdf.

Ferrándiz, Francisco. "Exhuming the Defeated: Civil War Mass Graves in 21st-Century Spain." *American Ethnologist* 40, no.1(2013): 38–54.

———. "Exhumar la derrota." In *Políticas de memoria y construcción de ciudadanía*, 255–263. Madrid: Postmetrópolis Editorial, 2015.

———. "From Tear to Pixel: Political Correctness and Digital Emotions in the Exhumation of Mass Graves from the Civil War." In *Engaging the Emotions in Spanish Culture and History (18th Century to the Present)*, edited by María Elena Delgado, Pura Fernández and Jo Labanyi., 242–261. Nashville: Vanderbilt University Press, 2016.

Ferrándiz, Francisco and Silva, Emilio. "From Mass Graves to Human Rights: The Spanish Disappeared in a Transnational Context." In *Missing Persons: Multidisciplinary Perspectives on the Disappeared*, edited by Derek Congram, 74–101. Toronto: Canadian Scholars' Press Inc., 2016.

Ferrándiz, Francisco. "Afterlives: 'A Social Autopsy of Mass Grave Exhumations in Spain.' " In *Legacies of Violence in Contemporary Spain: Exhuming the Past, Understanding the Present*, edited by Ofelia Ferrán and Lisa Hilbink, 23–43. New York: Routledge, 2017.

———. "Death on the Move: Pantheons and Reburials in Spanish Civil War Exhumations." In *A Companion to the Anthropology of Death*, edited by Antonius C. G. M. Robben, 189–204. Oxford: Wiley-Blackwell, 2018.

Herrasti, Lourdes and Francisco Etxeberria. "Exhumación y análisis de los restos del cementerio del Sanatorio penitenciario de San Cristóbal en el monte Ezkaba (Ansoain, Navarra)." In *El Fuerte de San Cristóbal en la memoria: de prisión a sanatorio penitenciario. El cementerio de las botellas*, 113–152. Pamplona-Iruñea: Pamiela, 2014

Herrasti, Lourdes, Jimi Jiménez, and Francisco Etxeberria. "Abordaje integral para el análisis y estudio de una fosa común de la Guerra Civil Española." *ROMULA* 17, no. 9 (2018): 41–57.

Herrasti, Lourdes, Alberto J. Sampedro, Joseba Diéguez, Jon Etxezarraga, Alfredo Irusta, Jimi Jiménez, Iñaki

Rebolledo, Alberto Sardón, Eduardo Sardón, and Francisco Etxeberria. "Placas de identificación de combatientes de la Guerra Civil española (1936–1937), recuperadas en exhumaciones de escenarios bélicos en el País Vasco." *Munibe (Antropologia-Arkeologia)* 65 (2014): 289–312.

Maroto García, Mariano. "La Memoria histórica de los vencedores de la Guerra Civil." In *Ciudadanas y ciudadanos por el cambio en Leganés*. 02-16-2012. http://www.ciudadanosporelcambio.com/mantenimiento/ficheros/memoria.pdf.

Moreno Gómez, Francisco. Los desaparecidos de Franco. Un estudio factual y teórico en el contexto de los crímenes internacionales y las comisiones de la verdad. Madrid: Editorial Alpuerto, 2016.

Solé i Barjau, Queralt. "Inhumados en el Valle de los Caídos. Los primeros traslados desde la provincia de Madrid." *Hispania Nova: Revista de Historia Contemporánea*, no. 9 (2009): 9.

NOTES

1 Maroto, La memoria histórica de los vencedores de la guerra civil.
2 García, "Los usos públicos de la Historia," 121–239.
3 Solé i Barjau, "Inhumados en el Valle de los Caídos," 9.
4 Moreno, Los desaparecidos de Franco, 237–238.
5 "The war resulted from the failed military coup, but the victims from places where the revolt was successful died because of the coup rather than the war." "La guerra fue el resultado del fracaso del golpe militar, pero, allí donde no fracasó, las víctimas corresponden al golpe militar, no a la guerra." Espinosa, *Violencia roja y azul*, 64.
6 Espinosa, "La memoria de la represión."
7 Order PRE/2568/2011, of September 26, which Announces the Agreement of the Council of Ministers of September 23, 2011, which Mandates the Publication in the Spanish Official State Gazette of the Scientific Protocol for the Exhumations of Victims of the Civil War and the Dictatorship.
8 To learn more about the exhumation process, see Etxeberria F (ed.). *Las exhumaciones de la Guerra Civil y la dictadura franquista 2000–2019. Estado actual y recomendaciones de futuro*. Madrid. Ministerio de Presidencia, Relaciones con las Cortes y Memoria Democrática, Madrid, 2020.
9 Herrasti et al. "Placas de identificación de combatientes de la Guerra Civil Española," 289–312.
10 Alfredo González-Ruibal "El último día de la batalla del Ebro." https://digital.csic.es/bitstream/10261/47780/1/2012_Informe%20La%20Fatarella%202011_Gonzalez.pdf.
11 Ezkieta, Los fugados del Fuerte de Ezkaba.
12 Gatti, *El detenido-desaparecido*, 53.

six

Primal Violence

Antoni Segura i Mas

The aerial bombings of Gernika (Guernica) and Durango in 1937 and Barcelona in 1938 would now constitute war crimes, or crimes against humanity, had the attempts of the Basque government-in-exile to define them as such at the Nuremberg trials (1945–1946) been successful. The carpet bombings that British and American air forces carried out against several German cities, including Dresden in 1945, were not deemed apposite examples of war crimes, even when the raids did not strictly aim at military targets. While these were the first air attacks to be codified as crimes against humanity under the Rome Statute of the International Criminal Court, a few others had paved the way before World War II—primarily chemical bombings used in colonial operations with a blatant animosity toward the indigenous populations. Italy attacked Abyssinia and Libya in 1911; the British raided Burma, India, and the Kurdish community in Iraq during the 1920s and 1930s; France bombed Syria and Morocco around the same time; Spain, the Rif; and Japan, China. With Russia's invasion of Ukraine in 2022, saturation bombings used to terrorize civilians, demoralize troops, and erode the capabilities of the resisting forces established in Ukrainian cities have unfortunately made headlines again.

In the introduction to Antoni Batista's *Voces sobre Euskadi*, I wrote:

> Every Basque family harbors one or more repositories of memories, of truth, of pain, of an unreconciled past that impedes the normalization of the political present. History is not just the analysis, organization, interpretation and assessment of data. The lives of peoples and societies are far too

rich and complex to abridge them to a single "politically correct" discourse that fails to explain anything. The histories of peoples are also made up of collective imaginary—or imaginaries—and memories. They hold the past accountable, removing the obstacles that keep the community from understanding the present and living in freedom. There is not one single truth, but multiple versions of it, juxtaposing, overlapping, and interconnecting with each other.

The multiplicity of truths that existed in the Autonomous Community of the Basque Country (BAC) ultimately turned into a "heavy burden after years of violence, death, and unresolved conflict."

Thus, "in the beginning was Gernika. The brutal bombing by the Condor Legion of a town of high symbolic value in the collective imaginary of the Basque people. It was market day, a day where the town doubled in population."[1] It was such an inexplicable act of violence, so atrocious and inhumane, even in the context of a civil war, that the fascist authorities tried to deny any responsibility for the tragedy by shifting the blame onto the Republican forces, alleging they had blown the town up with the help of anarchist miners who later abandoned it, or by asserting that Gernika's horror was the product of the Basque government's imagination. The Kremlin has used similar arguments to deny the war crimes committed by the Russian ground troops and air force in Bucha, Mariupol, and Kharkiv. Despite Franco's, and now Russia's, attempts to obscure the facts, the bombings of Gernika, and of Barcelona in January and March 1938, were real, and remain painfully real in the memories of the people who lived through them. The chronicle by American historian Herbert R. Southworth on Gernika and the report by British commander Noel de Putron MacRoberts on Barcelona were some of the first recorded efforts to denounce the historical events.[2]

These two locations became testing grounds for a new war tactic known as saturation bombings or carpet bombings. This kind of terror bombing involves the release of a large quantity of unguided bombs—often in combination with a string of incendiary bombs—into a specific area or city with the intent to level it or damage the population's morale, and indirectly, that of the troops on the battle front, who are faced with the frustration of being incapable of protecting the civilians in the rear guard.[3] Gernika and Barcelona have the sad privilege of being the first to suffer this kind of bombardments, but, with the onset of World War II, other cities soon followed: the German Luftwaffe attacked Warsaw on September 25, 1939, Rotterdam on May 14, 1940, and Coventry on November 14, 1940; the British and American air forces raided Hamburg between July 24 and August 3, 1943, Dresden on February 13–15, 1945; and US planes bombed Tokyo on March 9–10, 1945. Later, during the Vietnam War, the US Air Force engaged in extensive carpet-bombing operations with chemical bombs loaded with napalm, poisoning farmlands and rendering them unusable. In recent times, Russia has repeatedly resorted to this terror practice: first, during the Second Chechen War, against Grozny in 1999–2000; then, during the Syrian war, against Aleppo in September 2016 and the outskirts of Damascus; and now, against Kharkiv in Ukraine.[4]

According to Richard Weitz, director of the Center for Political-Military Analysis at Hudson Institute in Washington, DC, "what we are seeing [in Ukraine] is a strategy that the Russian military had already implemented during the Chechen War." It is known as "the Grozny doctrine (. . .) a strategy consisting of heavy bombardments that seek to destroy as much as possible, cause the greatest damage within reach of bombs, terrorize the civilian population, force everyone to flee, and then attack by land the enemy forces that remain on the ground." Essentially, "what Moscow did in 1999 was to recover a strategy used in a different context during World War II: the initial destruction of a city by air, to allow ground troops and heavy artillery to march into the territory afterwards."[5] Weitz's description closely resembles the considerations exposed by MacRoberts in 1938:

> The Iberian Peninsula was the first theater of war where aerial bombings were launched in a massive and systematic way against the civilian population of the rear guard. Madrid, followed by Durango and Gernika, became symbols of airborne terror. But, unlike these locations, where their proximity to the combat zone allowed a variety of justifications as for the nature and targets of the bombings, Barcelona and the Catalan coast, located hundreds of miles away from the front, offered no justification for their attack.

The goal behind the attacks was "to cripple, at any cost, the morale and physical strength of the enemy's rear guard by making their lives so unbearable that authorities would feel compelled to capitulate to the opposing side." This marks the moment when the war shifted from traditional battlefields to urban settings, causing civilian casualties to join the ranks of military losses. "Soldiers in the trenches had now to fear for their lives and the lives of their families in the rear guard."[6]

Before March 1938, Barcelona was raided by air only on occasion, and most of the attacks were strategic bombings planned by Francoist intelligence. Strategic bombings sought to destroy specific targets of military significance, including military stations, military and political headquarters, gas and power production facilities, command centers for radio and telegraph communication, as well as supply depots, and munition factories. Among the last category were Casa Elizalde, an aircraft engine manufacturer at 302 Valencia Street, which was hit by air and sea on February 13, 1937; and Maquinista Terrestre y Marítima, collectivized by the *Generalitat de Catalunya* (Government of Catalonia) and transformed into a military equipment manufacturing plant.[7] Throughout the Spanish Civil War, the port was subjected to the highest number of sustained raids of all of Barcelona; it was shelled no less than ninety-five times between November 1936 and January 1939. Starting in early 1937, the port and the adjacent neighborhoods of La Barceloneta and El Poble-Sec suffered at least an air strike virtually every month until the end of the war.[8] Strategic bombings ultimately seek to diminish access to resources—whether political, material, or military—and to debilitate the enemy's ability to wage war as a way to demoralize troops and precipitate capitulation.

At the beginning of 1938, as the decisive battle of Teruel raged on, air attacks against the city of Barcelona intensified in the ominous months leading up to the March massacre. Just in January, the city was air bombed fourteen times, in contrast to the entire year of 1937, where the attacks amounted to sixteen aerial bombings against various targets and six cannon blasts from the sea against the port, Casa Elizalde, and the surrounding districts.[9] The bombings of January 30, foreshadowing the March onslaught, were certainly the deadliest. They were brought on by the failed negotiations to end the air raids against the civilian population and the urban areas held by the Republican forces. Adhering to such an agreement was out of the question for the rebel side, which had allowed the German and Italian air forces to experiment with this new kind of warfare on Spanish ground. In Barcelona alone, more than three thousand buildings were damaged by their bomb tests.[10] The *Crònica diària de la Generalitat de Catalunya* (the daily chronicle issued by the government of Catalonia) provides a description of the January 30 bombings:

> Airborne terror. This Sunday morning, Barcelona was hit with two ruthless air offensives. The first one took place a few minutes after nine, when six planes from Majorca, grouped into two squads, and flying at an altitude of eighteen thousand feet at a high speed, released a string of bombs over the downtown area of the capital city. At eleven in the morning, an additional nine airplanes from Majorca, grouped into three squads and flying at an even higher altitude, dropped another round of bombs over heavily populated areas of the city, and, like their leading counterparts, flattened a few houses.
>
> The victims. The number of casualties as of ten at night totals to: deaths: 153, 47 of them are children; injuries: 63 men and 45 women. The most devastated areas by the attacks are the streets leading into Nova Square, Sant Felip Neri Square, Canuda, Duc de la Victòria, and Palla streets, and other points of District I.[11]

The target of the January 30 air raids was the *Palau de la Generalitat*, the seat of the presidency of the government of Catalonia. The bombs landed within a three-hundred-to-thousand-foot radius northeast of the Sant Jaume Square, badly damaging

Sant Domènec del Call, Palla, Pi, Duc de la Victòria, Capellans, Escudellers Blancs, Avinyó, and Canuda streets, and the surrounding area of Nova Square. The Sant Felip Neri Square also suffered damage, with three bombs destroying the cloister of a convent that served as a shelter for children displaced from regions occupied or in imminent danger of being occupied by the insurgents. Outside of this radius, the bombs fell on Casp Street, the Gran Via de les Corts Catalanes, the Passeig de la República (Passeig de Sant Joan), the Morrot station, and the La Maquinista factory in the neighborhood of La Barceloneta.[12]

The neighbors of the cathedral still remembered the January 30 bombings long after the war was over. The shrapnel pockmarks left by the bombs in the front wall of the Sant Felip Neri church immortalized the events for generations to come. Left in a state of ruin for decades, the rubble could be seen from Palla Street on the backside of the square. One of the two buildings decimated by the bombs was finally removed in the late 1950s for the school of l'Oratori de Sant Felip Neri, which opened in 1959. Next to the new school, the city transplanted the fronts of two old guild buildings from other areas of Barcelona. One was the guild of boilermakers (presently, the school's front wall), originally on Bòria Street, and later, on Lesseps Square. The other was the guild of shoemakers, first located in front of the cathedral on Corríbia Street. That street was affected by the bombings and later replaced to make room for Avinguda de la Cathedral Avenue. The horrific bombings of January 30, 1938, were burned into the memories of the locals, who still remembered them in the 1960s and '70s. Several of the bombs destroyed the sacristy of the convent, killing about sixty of the children who had fled their hometowns. Eyewitnesses mentioned that people recalled small broken bodies surfacing as volunteers frantically shoveled rubble out and cleared debris. The Basque government's new headquarters on 60 Passeig de Gràcia in Barcelona led to the assumption that many of the deceased children were Basque. But professor Joan Villarroya i Font's research on the last names of the victims indicated it is likelier that the children had traveled from Madrid or Málaga.[13] Today, vestiges of the tragic events still dot the neighborhood: the tiny Manuel Ribé Square replaced the empty space left by the toppled buildings of Sant Domènec del Call and Arc de Sant Ramon del Call streets, where sixteen people died;[14] the Villa de Madrid Square and the Nova Square, next to the cathedral, grew with the disappearance of some of the buildings on the adjoining streets.

With a fleet of 764 aircraft, including almost two hundred bomber planes, the Italian Legionary Air Force roared down with all its fury on Barcelona and other Catalan cities. Many of these bombers were responsible for the raids over Catalonia. Majorca became a rebel bastion as soon as the military coup against the Republican government of Spain broke out in July 1936. A month later, in August 1936, the Republican column of the Balearic Islands, formed by four thousand soldiers and commanded by Captain Alberto Bayo, was stopped in its tracks and forced out of the archipelago when it disembarked on the Manacor coast, following a stopover in Menorca and the successful liberation of the islands of Formentera, Eivissa (Ibiza), and Cabrera. By the first quarter of 1937, Italy's air force was using Majorca as a natural aircraft carrier for their bombing campaigns against Catalonia.[15] As a result, Barcelona became the first major city to be systematically bombed; throughout the war, it suffered more than 190 aerial attacks and just short of two thousand bomb collisions. MacRoberts referred to the bombings as "massive terrorism from the air" directed at the city's civilian population. News of the attacks, particularly those March 16–18 shook the world. England deployed MacRoberts to Barcelona with orders to write a report on the bombings that decimated the Catalan population. Out of the 5,200 people who died in Catalonia throughout the entire civil war, about a thousand died in Barcelona because of the bombs.[16]

According to Jordi Pons i Pujol, John Langdon-Davies, working as a war correspondent for the *News Chronicle,* wrote of the March 16–18 bombings:

> The Italian Air Force introduced the groundbreaking method of the silent approach: planes flew to very high altitudes, stalled their engines and glided down a few thousand feet to their target. The planes went undetected by the anti-aircraft system. Such unexpected attacks, along with the use of highly explosive bombs, had the desired effect of spreading panic and chaos among the population. The planes went undetected by the anti-aircraft system (. . .) Other authors have also paid notice to the new tactic the Italians tested in Barcelona: instead of launching the bombs in a concentrated manner, like it had been done until then, the Italians staggered their attacks. The city's air-raid sirens were rendered ineffective, because citizens did no longer know if the sirens were announcing the beginning or the end of an attack. People lived in a constant state of danger for three consecutive days.[17]

We now know that the bombings were a direct order from Mussolini, who wanted to experiment with a new tactic of war.[18]

At the time of the March 1938 bombings, Paola Lo Cascio and Susana Oliveira explain, Barcelona was home to three legitimate governments: the government of La Generalitat, the Basque government, and the government of the Spanish Republic. The latter two relocated there in the fall of 1937.

> The concentration of political power in Barcelona critically influenced the decision of the rebel authorities and their Italian allies to intensify and focus their air raids on the city center (. . .) By March 1938, Catalonia's capital city had become the center of operations of the Republican military and political leaders; it was the place of publication of major Republican

newspapers; and where foreign observers gathered to keep informed about the course of the war. In a way, an assault on Barcelona was an assault on the Republic and on everything it represented.[19]

About the same time, refugees coming from regions occupied by the rebel forces or within the combat zone, such as Madrid, Andalucía, Extremadura, and the BAC, constituted 16 to 18 percent of Barcelona's total population. Attacking Barcelona was a way to strike terror into the communities fleeing from other places of the Spanish state.

Lo Cascio's and Oliveira's observations are a good reminder that, over those three days of March, Barcelona, a city of one million people, lived through the most brutal bomb raids of the entire war. The Savoia–Marchetti SM.79 bombers had built-in cameras to capture the damage of the bombs they released:

> Bombs rained on the people of Barcelona for 41 interminable hours: constant attacks, often less than three-hours apart, paralyzed the city and filled the population with panic. The Italian planes dropped as much as 44 tons worth of bombs over the city center, on a section of the city sitting between the streets of Córcega, Marina, and Entenza. The area had no military value and the attacks were directed at civilians indiscriminately. The aftermath was devastating with close to a thousand people dying over the span of three days. The Spanish Civil War earned the sad title of being the first war in modern history where the count of civilian fatalities exceeded that of military casualties.[20]

The night of March 16, Barcelona sounded the air-raid sirens at ten o'clock, and eight minutes later the first "of a tragic sequence of bombardments struck the city. The campaign lasted two days and two nights, leaving the local community in a complete state of terror and with a profound feeling of helplessness." Fire crews put out fires on 7 Passeig de la Marina, on 363 València Street and on Casp, Consell de Cent, Riera Alta, and Girona streets. Twenty nine impacts on buildings and streets of the city center were recorded. A total of 14 people died, and 43 people suffered injuries. A second raid followed soon after, and a third one struck at 1:36 in the morning. The Savoia bombers took to the skies again at 7:36 a.m. March 17, then at eleven in the morning, and then again at two-thirty in the afternoon. The pilots were earnestly following Benito Mussolini's orders to "hammer" Barcelona down. "Begin violent attacks over Barcelona tonight, hammer the city down with attacks spread in time," stated a telegram sent by Giuseppe Valle, the Italian vice minister of the air forces, to the Italian Legionary Air Forces based in Majorca. The message is evidence that Barcelona was the laboratory where a new military tactic was put to the test: the spread of panic and commotion, and the crippling of the alert systems by means of spread-out attacks on the civilian population. The city suffered the worst kind of bombings of any region during the war.[21]

The bombers returned in the early hours of the morning of March 17. Starting at 7:36 a.m., they bombed the city every three hours until shortly before two in the afternoon. Attacks resumed at night and did not stop until the next morning.

> Their target was still the civilian population. They charged against them indiscriminately with the sole purpose of disseminating panic, terror, and confusion, and of demoralizing the Republican troops. (. . .) In the afternoon the toll was 252 deaths and 525 injured people. By that night, it had climbed to 400 deaths and 600 injured people. (. . .) The deadliest attack happened at two in the afternoon on the intersection of the Gran Vía de les Corts Catalanes and Balmes Street. One of the bombs released by the five Savoia 79s executing the raid landed on a TNT-filled truck that was pulled over at a security checkpoint. In the truck were 23 Republican soldiers and Corporal Jaume Laporta. They, and the people in close proximity to the truck, died. The vehicle blew up in a violent explosion creating an 820-feet tall column of smoke. The Italian pilots captured the impact in the built-in cameras of their SM.79s (. . .) [The fire department] recorded 45 trips between 7:45 a.m. and 4:40 p.m.[22]

Of the close to one thousand victims killed during the March bombings,[23] including those who lost their lives to the bomb that struck the TNT truck, one stands out for its historiographic importance. Julia Gay Vives, the mother of writers Juan, Luis, and José Agustín Goytisolo, and her unfortunate death, led the biographer of the brothers to soldier Juan P., an exceptional witness of the events that unfolded on the intersection between the Gran Vía de les Corts Catalanes and Balmes Street.

> They arrived at the [Montjuic] Castle at eleven in the morning and they loaded the vehicles with a total of ten tons of explosives: three on his Chevrolet, and seven on the other driver's big truck. (. . .) As the squad of Italian bombers flew over Castelldefels, soldier Juan P. arrived at Plaça de España. Short after, approaching Urgel Street, he heard the air-raid sirens go off and stepped on the gas pedal. His assistant suggested they pulled over, but he was set on executing the orders he had been given. Then, the Republican soldier told him something that stuck with him all these years: "Juan, if we are hit by a bomb, the entire city will blow up with us." In response, Juan P. ordered him to stand on the running board and clear the way with a flag and a whistle. The Chevrolet raced down the Gran Vía through the crowds of people that were rushing to the bomb shelters . . . As they drove past the Ritz Hotel, Juan P. heard a deafening explosion behind them. He saw an enormous cloud of smoke enveloping the Coliseum theater from the rearview mirror. The Gran Vía stretch going from Balmes Street to Passeig de Gràcia had vanished in an instant. (. . .) The clock

hanging by the entrance to the Unión Suiza Relojera store stopped at 1:55 in the afternoon. (. . .) Ten minutes after two o'clock in the afternoon, soldier Juan P. arrived in the La Sagrera station driving a Chevrolet filled with explosives. His ears were still ringing from the massive explosion at the Coliseum when the official asked him about the whereabouts of the other truck that made up the small military unit. It was then when Juan realized they would never see that truck again. One of the enemy bombs had struck the vehicle and pulverized it. Everyone had perished in the attack: the driver, his assistant. (. . .) That day, a 550-pound Italian projectile activated seven tons worth of melinite cargo. (. . .) So devastating were the effects of the deflagration, that rumors of a new explosive used by the Italian Army rapidly spread across Barcelona, people talked about a powerful bomb made of "liquid air" of unprecedented destructive power. Only Juan and a few other army members knew the truth, which was never revealed for military reasons. Until Juan P. told me the story fifty years later. (. . .) News of the ghastly scenes at the Coliseum propagated immediately: an uncle of soldier Juan vaporized along with a group of people waiting at a streetcar stop; the patrons sitting at the patio of the Oro del Rhin café evaporated; the passengers inside a streetcar carbonized to death too quickly to be helped out; cars were howling uncontrollably, and a headless man walked upright for several feet after the explosion decapitated him. The pictures taken minutes after the tragedy are horrifying, monstrous, and like Gernika, they foreshadow Hiroshima's holocaust. (. . .) That evening of March 17 the mother of the Goytisolos did not return home.[24]

Some experts believe Barcelona suffered the worst bombings of the civil war. Never had a big city been bombed with such violence. Only in the span of that week, the Italians launched thirteen air raids causing over a thousand casualties, hundreds of injured victims, and substantial damage to the city center, where "the existence of a military target was beyond the bound of possibility," a contemporaneous issue of the Catalan paper *La Vanguardia* read. The international community, in a somewhat self-righteous fashion, strongly condemned the attacks, which went on to become a passage of the universal history of infamy. Prime Minister Winston Churchill referred to them years later, when London was raided by Nazi air bombers: "I do not at all underrate the severity of the ordeal which lies before us; but I believe our countrymen will show themselves capable of standing up to it, like the brave men of Barcelona." This valuable quote serves as a reminder that the tragedy of 1938 was the result of the same fascist hatred that struck Madrid and Gernika, which are often awarded the sad and *exclusive* honor of having suffered this kind of savage bombings.[25]

I would like to end this chapter with historian Laia Gallego Vila's reflections on the attacks:

> The bombing of Barcelona left a lasting scar on the collective memory of the people of Barcelona, who still remember the raids today. This is a sign of the serious and profound impact the events had on the lives of the survivors, whose families transmitted their experiences from generation to generation. Today, the memory of the bombings, encapsulating the pain of the victims as well as the coming together of a community to defend its city, constitutes a defining element of Barcelona's identity. Unfortunately, Franco's dictatorship silenced the reality of the attacks for forty years, defending the theory that the raids were strategic bombings directed at military targets. The identities of the actors behind these crimes were never revealed and the memory of the victims was left out of the official narratives and hidden from public spaces.[26]

The term *primal violence* is often used by the Basque separatist left to refer to the violence that predated ETA's[27] and that was inflicted by the Spanish state on Basque society, during the Carlist wars and the Francoist dictatorship, in particular.[28] Primal violence is faithfully represented in the war crimes committed by the fascist air forces during the Spanish Civil War, or the German, British, and American air forces in the context of World War II. This is a violence that goes beyond targets of military value and that, as we saw, after Gernika and Barcelona, spilled into Warsaw, Rotterdam, Coventry, Hamburg, Dresden, Tokyo, Hiroshima, Nagasaki, Vietnam, Grozny, Aleppo, Damascus, Kharkiv, and several other locations around the world. The historical discourse bears the responsibility to not only explain the past, but, to the extent possible, expose the perpetuation of this kind of violence in the present, and restore the memory of the victims who were killed by "massive terrorism coming from the air" as MacRoberts described it.

In conclusion, we should learn from the lessons of our past and, as Westerners, rid ourselves of the sense of complacency and superiority with which we tend to judge the histories of nations we deem "underdeveloped or under civilized." We should not forget that the same eras that produced the Age of Enlightenment and human rights birthed the most terrible monsters of reason and primal violence.

NOTES

1. Antoni Segura. "Introduction" in *Voces sobre Euskadi*, 13–21. Barcelona: Plaza & Janés, 2004. Xabier Irujo Ametzaga's work offers key insights on the bombing of Gernika. *Gernika: 26 de abril de 1937*. Barcelona: Crítica, 2017.
2. Herbert R. Southworth. *La destrucción de Gernika*, edited by Ángel Viñas. Granada: Comares, 2013; Noel de Putron MacRoberts. *Lliçons de Barcelona (Informe britànic sobre els bombardeigs*

de la ciutat, 1938), edited by Jordi Pons i Pujol, 4. Barcelona: Fundació Carles Pi i Sunyer d'estudis autonòmics i locals. Documents d'Història, 2008. https://www.academia.edu/3696670/Lli%C3%A7ons_de_Barcelona_informe_brit%C3%A0nic_sobre_els_bombardeigs_de_la_ciutat_1938 (in Catalan).

3   Horst Fischer. "Bombardeo de àrea o de alfombra" in *Crimenes de guerra: lo que debemos saber*, edited by David Rieff and Roy Gutman, 105–107. Barcelona: Debate, 2003.

4   Jeremy Bowen, "Rusia y Ucrania | De Grozni a Alepo: la brutal táctica de bombardeos con la que Moscú responde a la resistencia." *BBC News | Mundo*. Kyiv, March 8, 2022: https://www.bbc.com/mundo/noticias-internacional-60635767.

5   Lioman Lima. "Qué es la doctrina Grozni, la estrategia de ataque rusa detrás de los bombardeos que han dejado centenares de muertos en la región siria de Guta Oriental." *BBC News | Mundo*. February 27, 2018: https://www.bbc.com/mundo/noticias-internacional-43163662.

6   Noel de Putron MacRoberts. *Lliçons de Barcelona (Informe britànic sobre els bombardeigs de la ciutat, 1938)*, edited by Jordi Pons i Pujol, 12-13. Barcelona: Fundació Carles Pi i Sunyer d'estudis autonòmics i locals. Documents d'Història, 2008.

7   For the targets Francoist intelligence set in Barcelona, see Víctor Hurtado, Antoni Segura, and Joan Villarroya, *Atles de la Guerra Civil a Catalunya*. Barcelona: Edicions Dau, 2010. Map 17.3 (454–455). Maps 17.8 and 17.13 (462–465) show the most destructive bombings that hit Barcelona between 1937 and January 24 1939. Joan Villarroya i Font focuses on the timeline (date, and starting and ending times) and the details (death toll, injured victims, total number of bombs, and observations—emplacement and targets) of the naval and air bombings that ravaged Barcelona between December 26, 1936, and January 25, 1939, in *Els bombardeigs de Barcelona durant la Guerra Civil (1936–1939)*, appendix no. 3 193-210. Barcelona: Publicacions de l'Abadia de Montserrat, 1999.

8   See Víctor Hurtado, Antoni Segura, and Joan Villarroya, *Atles de la Guerra Civil a Catalunya*. Barcelona: Edicions Dau, 2010. Map 17.14 (465); Joan Villarroya i Font, *Els bombardeigs de Barcelona durant la Guerra Civil (1936–1939)*, appendix no. 3 193–210. Barcelona: Publicacions de l'Abadia de Montserrat, 1999. Oriol Dueñas Iturbe's contributions are indispensable: *El port de Barcelona: objectiu militar durant la Guerra Civil (1936–1939)*. Barcelona: Museu Marítim de Barcelona, 2016; and *L'ocupació de Catalunya*, 47. Barcelona: Rosa dels Vents, 2021.

9   Joan Villarroya i Font, *Els bombardeigs de Barcelona durant la Guerra Civil (1936–1939)*, appendix no. 3 193–197. Barcelona: Publicacions de l'Abadia de Montserrat, 1999.

10 Oriol Dueñas Iturbe, *L'ocupació de Catalunya*, 111. Barcelona: Rosa dels Vents, 2021.

11 Govern de la Generalitat/Josep Tarradellas. *Crònica de la Guerra Civil a Catalunya*, Vol. 2, 1094–1095. Barcelona: Edicions Dau, 2009.

12 Govern de la Generalitat/Josep Tarradellas. *Crònica de la Guerra Civil a Catalunya*, Vol. 2, 1094–1095. Barcelona: Edicions Dau, 2009; Joan Villarroya i Font, *Els bombardeigs de Barcelona durant la Guerra Civil (1936–1939)*, 50–53. Barcelona: Publicacions de l'Abadia de Montserrat, 1999. The then Passeig de la República—presently, Passeig de Sant Joan—started at Plaça del Arc de Triomf and ended at Plaça de Mossèn Jacint Verdaguer. *1935, Pla de la ciutat de Barcelona 1:10 000*. Institut Cartogràfic de Catalunya: https://www.historiadebarcelona.org/el-teu-carrer/.

13 Antoni Segura i Mas. "Sant Felip Neri." *Avui* (June 9, 1999); Joan Villarroya i Font, *Els bombardeigs de Barcelona durant la Guerra Civil (1936–1939)*, appendix no. 3 230–235. Barcelona: Publicacions de l'Abadia de Montserrat, 1999.

14 Ajuntament de Barcelona. "Ciutat Vella recorda les víctimes dels bombardejos de la Guerra Civil" https://ajuntament.barcelona.cat/dretsidiversitat/ca/noticia/ciutat-vella-recorda-les-victimes-dels-bombardejos-de-la-guerra-civil_476679 (Accessed April 26, 2022).
15 Laia Gallego Vila. "Els bombardeigs de Barcelona durant la guerra civil: historiografia i memorialització." In *Índice Histórico Español*, no. 130 (2017): 15–17.
16 Josep Maria Solé i Sabaté and Joan Villarroya. *Catalunya sota les bombes (1936–1939)*, 235. Barcelona: Edicions 62, 1985.
17 Noel de Putron MacRoberts. *Lliçons de Barcelona (Informe britànic sobre els bombardeigs de la ciutat, 1938)*, edited by Jordi Pons i Pujol, 14–15. Barcelona: Fundació Carles Pi i Sunyer d'estudis autonòmics i locals. Documents d'Història, 2008.
18 Laia Gallego Vila. "Els bombardeigs de Barcelona durant la guerra civil: historiografia i memorialització." In *Índice Histórico Español*, no. 130 (2017): 16–17.
19 Paola Lo Cascio and Susanna Oliveira. *Tres dies de març*, 15. Girona: El Punt, 2009.
20 Paola Lo Cascio and Susanna Oliveira. *Tres dies de març*, 69. Girona: El Punt, 2009.
21 Paola Lo Cascio and Susanna Oliveira. *Tres dies de març*, 70–73. Girona: El Punt, 2009.
22 Paola Lo Cascio and Susanna Oliveira. *Tres dies de març*, 76–77. Girona: El Punt, 2009.
23 Joan Villarroya i Font, *Els bombardeigs de Barcelona durant la Guerra Civil (1936–1939)*, 100. Barcelona: Publicacions de l'Abadia de Montserrat, 1999.
24 Miguel Dalmau. *Los Goytisolo*, 112–115. Barcelona: Anagrama, 1999.
25 Miguel Dalmau. *Los Goytisolo*, 117. Barcelona: Anagrama, 1999.
26 Laia Gallego Vila. "Els bombardeigs de Barcelona durant la guerra civil: historiografia i memorialització." In *Índice Histórico Español*, no. 130 (2017): 29.
27 Short for *Euskadi Ta Askatasuna* (Basque Country and Freedom) ETA was a Basque separatist organization that sought an independent Basque state by means of terrorism.
28 In words of Iulen Madariaga, Basque politician and cofounder of ETA: "The way I see it, if we accept that primal violence triggered a secondary form of violence—that of ETA—if we accept that the invasion and subsequent permanent occupation are historical facts, then, I believe, as a Basque *abertzale* (patriot), that primal violence will always be fueling other forms of violence, so long as the right to self-determination is not fully recognized, and Basque society is not allowed to revert to the *status quo ante*." Iulen de Madariaga, *Deia*, November 8, 1992; Antoni Batista. *Madariaga de las armas a la palabra*, 143–144. Barcelona: RBA, 2007.

seven

The "Gernika" Case in the German Historical Military Writing of the Postwar Years and the Denial of Culpability

Ángel Viñas

I never understood why professor Manfred Merkes's seminal books on the Nazi intervention in the Spanish Civil War were not translated into Spanish or English. The first one, published in 1961, was an adaptation of his PhD dissertation, while the second one, in 1969, expanded his earlier work to include additional research which led the way to his winning a chair in history. These books are must-reads for anyone interested in the subject. One can easily find references to both, particularly the second one, in German publications. They have also been mentioned in English and Spanish literature. In my case, they have been loyal and lasting companions ever since they were published.

Merkes, whose name I never saw in Wikipedia in German, English, French, or Spanish, was a true trailblazer. He was the first historian to analyze the Nazi archives that the Allies had returned to the Federal Republic of Germany (FRG) in the 1950s. He examined the diplomatic, military, and political road map that the Nazis followed during their intervention in the Spanish Civil War. When total silence reigned in Franco's Spain, he was one of the very few foreign authors to have forged ahead doing primary research.

Merkes's second book was an absolute tour de force. It weighed in on virtually every aspect he had not been able to explore in his PhD dissertation. At the time of his publication, however, he had consulted fewer sources than he had wished, as he himself acknowledged. This was not because of censorship, but because the FRG still had to sort out and reclassify the collections returned by the Allies.

In his second book, Merkes offered an overview of how German- and English-speaking scholars had approached the Spanish Civil War in the decades following the conflict. And, while he shed light on some interesting details, which later were helpful in the development of this topic , his research efforts on the bombing and destruction of Gernika were unsubstantial.

In the case of Gernika, it was not until 1975 that a well-documented monograph by German Air Force commander Klaus A. Maier was published.[1] It was translated into Spanish and published the following year. Although still a fundamental read, the book is not impervious to the passage of time nor to the work of historian Herbert Rutledge Southworth, who was working on the same area of research at the time, and whose findings were expanded by other scholars later.

BACKGROUND

Merkes indicated that the Nazi leaders very early showed concern about how the German intervention in Spain would be portrayed. The ministry of aviation, spearheaded by Hermann Göring, commissioned Werner Beumelburg,[2] a famous war writer, to publish a book about the Condor Legion (CL). Beumelburg visited Spain in August 1937 and again in November 1938. Upon his return, the German army provided him with inside information. The resulting work is known as *Kampf in Spanien. Die Geschichte der Legion Condor* (Fight in Spain. The History of the Condor Legion). It was published in 1939 when the war was finished. It instantly became a classic. It inspired several other works of variable quality, including pieces of journalism, life stories, and propaganda.[3] From the little I know about them, they were not much concerned with the Gernika case.

Furthermore, before the end of the Spanish Civil War, the chief of staff of the Wehrmacht, taking a more serious approach, commissioned two academic articles on the war in Spain and the Sino-Japanese War from the Department of Military History. Merkes found no evidence of the existence of either article.

This is when the work group "War in Spain" (*Kämpfe in Spanien*) from the Luftwaffe Department of Military History stepped in. *General der Flieger* (three-star General) Karl-Friedrich Schweickhard, chief of the Luftwaffe training department, ordered several officers who had served in Spain to write down their memories and send them to the aforementioned department. The idea was not so much to publish an academic report of the events but to expand the available evidence. (The department had already written an academic report in March 1940, while Germany planned its offensive against France.) Substantial archival material was available to the participants. However, they did not deal with the political nature or the background of the Nazi intervention in Spain.

Their work brought forth a known multivolume collection of essays that has been referenced by several authors (including myself) with a particular focus on the first two volumes.[4]

The present contribution is concerned with a later historiographic exercise made after the defeat of the National-Socialist dictatorship. However, months before the end of the war in Europe, the relevant archives suffered a major loss. The building where many of the documents were sent to and received by the CL, namely, instructions from Berlin and the Legion's replies to the capital, was destroyed by an Allied bombing on February 3, 1945. Some of the documents were saved, because in August of the same year, after the Third Reich's capitulation, records were found in the repositories of other archives of the Ministry of Aviation. Merkes wrote he was unable to locate them. Present-day historians have recovered some.

After the war, Americans became historiographers of the Luftwaffe. In 1946, the Historical Division of the US Air Force was tasked with developing the Rhode Project, later renamed the Karlsruhe Project. A working group focused on research in air warfare analyzed the Spanish case. Members of the former Luftwaffe, many of whom served in the CL, were summoned. The project took several years to complete.

The resulting report, *Die deutsche Luftwaffe im Spanischen Bürgerkrieg* (The Luftwaffe in the Spanish Civil War), was prepared under the direction of the former *general der flieger* Karl Drum.[5] It was never published, and only exists as a manuscript. Merkes used part of the text for his second book. The report showcased a compilation of documents from the wartime period, intertwined with recollections and accounts from numerous individuals with various military backgrounds.

As far as I know, this final report has never been used in Spanish scholarly work, let alone in relation to the destruction of Gernika. As for scholars outside of Spain, I cannot say. Merkes, and certainly Maier, drew from it. I made a copy in 1973. It was kept at the branch of Military Records[6] of the German Federal Archives in Freiburg, catalogued under Number N176/22-25 when I found it. Under number LW 107/1, one can consult the compendium of partial research studies of the investigation undertaken at the time. The total product was a collection of documents adding up to about five hundred pages.

THE DRUM REPORT: POLITICAL AND IDEOLOGICAL FOUNDATIONS

The summary of the case, which I will refer to as the Drum Report, is 265 pages. The editor, Drum, signed the last page on April 12, 1957. He later added a seven-page appendix comprising two brief essays penned by former four-star general Erwin Jaenecke.[7] In it, he described some of the political intrigues which developed after the Third Reich accorded "Francoist Spain" diplomatic recognition in November 1936. In addition, he explained the reasons why, in his—not so accurate—opinion, Hitler had decided to intervene in Spain. The first part centers on the, at times, serious frictions between the CL commander, General Hugo Sperrle,[8] and the first Nazi chargé d'affaires, later ambassador, General Wilhelm Faupel.[9]

Faupel's appointment at the instigation of the Nazi Party temporarily disrupted professional diplomat Eberhard von Stohrer's plans to become Germany's future envoy to Spain. Stohrer's designation had been confirmed before the advent of the civil war, but it was only officially realized after Sperrle and Faupel returned to Germany.

The report is divided into four chapters. The first one provides a brief overview of the period preceding the Civil War, its outbreak, and Hitler's decision to aid Franco. The second chapter details the training, equipment, command structures, and coordination of the CL as well as its supply and operational relations with home. Chapter three is the most interesting for this chapter: the Condor Legion's collaboration in Spain against "Communist control" (sic). It is also the longest one. The final chapter reflects on the experiences and the lessons learned from the CL deployment. It contains valuable information, but it is irrelevant here. The final pages reflected on how the knowledge gained in Spain regarding the management and leadership of the Luftwaffe influenced World War II. Analyzing the compendious Drum report would exceed the narrow scope of the present chapter.

While Franco attempted to conceal the actions of the CL in the first publications about air warfare in Spain, the information that the attacks had had on the international scene was inescapable. Especially after the bombing and destruction of Gernika.

Following Southworth's trail, professors Xabier Irujo, Sir Paul Preston, and I have worked to refute the broad range of—sometimes far-fetched—accounts of the air strikes that took place in Spain as they were portrayed during the Franco dictatorship. They still survive in a kind of apologetic pro-Francoist literature in today's Spain.

My intention in this chapter is to present a brief but crucial clarification that will help decipher the political and ideological nature of the Drum Report. Written by officers of the former Nazi Wehrmacht, it dealt primarily with military issues. To fully understand it, one must consider three factors: the state of affairs of the Federal Republic of Germany when the report was drafted; the strategic approach of the United States government in general and the US Air Force in particular toward Franco; and the relations between Spain and the FRG. No report of this nature could have been written in a political and ideological vacuum, especially between 1953 and 1957.

As for the first factor, a new state had emerged on the political map in 1949: the Federal Republic of Germany (FRG). The circumstances surrounding its birth are broadly familiar: the rapid deterioration of the relationship between the Soviet Union and the Western allies; the Berlin blockade; the formation of the two German political entities, one ruled by the Soviet Union and the other by the British, American, and French. The areas governed by the three Western powers quickly sought to form a new state with limited independence. Furthermore, the FRG soon started a limited rearmament program in response to the pressing demands of the Cold War and the need to form a common front after the 1954 Paris Agreement, according to which West Germany's future military would join NATO. This decision came amid heated debates during the early 1950s. As it happened, numerous units of the Wehrmacht, the Luftwaffe, and the Kriegsmarine (the navy of the Nazi regime) were assimilated into the new Bundeswehr (the Armed Forces), accelerating after the FRG implemented a mandatory military service. The contributors to the Drum Report lived through all of this. And yet, there is no evidence that they joined the new Bundeswehr.

The US Air Force was in no position to be reticent because, for years, Washington had been negotiating with Franco a way to establish permanent military bases in Spain. The Iberian Peninsula was a crucial strategic area for the United States. First, because it was the farthest rearguard area from the Central European front to which Allied forces could retreat in case of an armed conflict in Europe. Second, because it could act as a base for contingents coming from across the Atlantic for a future recovery of invaded territories.

Since the strategic plans of the US involved contributing to the enhancement of the strategic position of Spain, the Pact of Madrid of 1953 implied the acceptance of the Spanish political regime, although politically half-heartedly. The pacts, considered executive agreements, did not need the approval of Congress. The US Air Force, which had exalted the strategic qualities of the Iberian Peninsula long before the end of the war in Europe, achieved its goals.

The readiness of Germany and the United States to approve of Franco's regime may be explained by a common anti-Communist sentiment, which, in the Drum Report, served as the defining factor for all subjects discussed beyond military matters. Hitler's anti-Communist vein, defended by the Wehrmacht until the bitter end in Eastern Europe, was no surprise to the soldiers and airmen who had waged an all-out war against their new common enemy: the USSR.

This objective confluence of perceptions, interests, and needs unraveled in the few pages explaining the years leading up to the Spanish Civil War. General Drum and his contributors turned to structural factors, such as the substantial disparity between the wealthy and the poor, and the revolutionary tendencies of the lower classes, to allege that, even if the conflict was not the direct consequence of the Second Republic, it had opened the door to "certain actors" who instigated the war. Francoist literature and the interpretations collected by the leaders of the CL placed the blame of the war on the *radicals*, who had endorsed the weaponization of the working class to expand a *new red army* that would eventually support a revolution.

The Third Reich had showed a shallow understanding of the Spanish social and political context in the 1930s. The Republic, in that view, had wanted to deplete and destroy the Spanish army, dissolving entire units and distributing weapons among its own supporters. Some of the sentences in the report mirrored the trite expressions the Nazis had picked up in Spain because of their close collaboration with Franco. "Ships loaded with war supplies sailed the oceans" even before the coup (from the USSR, it was claimed). The former soldiers, now impromptu historians, parroted errant nonsense without checking their sources. Today, Spanish army veterans continue to produce drivel for Spanish right-wing publications of substandard quality.[10] The Communists were preparing a revolution in Spain.

I find it unnecessary to highlight the numerous factual errors the former Nazi soldiers committed. Suffice it to say they thought José Antonio Primo de Rivera and José Calvo Sotelo had been killed at the same time. Hitler was portrayed as acting in response to the military aid lent by the French Popular Front to their Spanish left-wing counterparts. The following paragraph portrays the opinions that Drum's contributors held on the immediate internationalization of the Spanish conflict:

> Germany and Italy were fully immersed in a fascist order. With the triumph of Franco and the Fascists, France would become surrounded by three authoritarian states. There would be no place for safety. *The defeat of Democracy should be avoided at all costs.*

I suspect that many US military historians kept up with Drum's writings, and I find no reason why they would have objected to such claims, especially to the most crucial part of them which I have highlighted in italics. The German soldiers who had defended the Third Reich morphed fascism and authoritarianism into a particular form of non-democracy. They added, however, that France felt compelled to protect democracy.[11] Didn't the United States fight for the same cause in World War II? The contributors to the Drum Report seemed to be distancing themselves from Hitler, although with extreme care. The reference to authoritarian states is truly touching.

Their political and strategic interests led the German military writers in the 1950s to contend that the British stance, abiding by the ancient tenet of the European balance of power, put London between a rock and a hard place: on the one hand, there was the risk of losing important investments in Spain if Soviet-like republics gained power; on the other, the convenience of supporting Franco's victory. This justified Britain's nonintervention policy, which was implemented undeterred by the opposition of other powers and aimed at keeping Spain in a state of helplessness. It ultimately favored the insurgents' victory. This translated into security for France and protection for the British Empire.

It is unlikely that the strategic conception of the decorated members of the Wehrmacht who embraced democracy in the mid-1950s differed much from that of Hitler's, at least in relation to the claims spread by national-socialist propaganda.

Undoubtedly, Drum and his collaborators believed that the Soviets were the villains of the story. The USSR was alleged to have followed a defined course of action: stop the Popular Front from making too many mistakes; mobilize the international Communist community; send instructors, weapons, and munition to the Republican army; and faithfully support the Spanish Republic politically and logistically (but, luckily, one may think, the fascists and Francoists contained them).[12]

In addition, the contributing authors of the Drum Report painted Hitler's intentions with Spain in softer tones. In their view, Hitler thought of Spain as another chapter of his concern to re-arm Germany and break loose from the bonds of Versailles, like other military leaders had done before him. He was anxious about Germany's relations with the French, who were heavily armed and infected with the virus of communism. He worried about the fallout on France of communist Spain and decided to take action to prevent it. He would respond to the Spanish crisis by intervening in the Iberian Peninsula. This retrospective interpretation of the German generals and officers was enhanced by the new setting of the Cold War. I believe some of them were under the impression that the Western allies should be grateful for the Third Reich's actions in Spain.

GERNIKA IN THE DRUM REPORT

The Drum Report treated the bombing and destruction of Gernika in a rather peculiar manner. The matter was discussed in less than a single page. Maier maintains in his book that the passage was apparently based on a text by Erwin Jaenecke. Appendix 17 of Maier's book includes a copy of it.

General Jaenecke argued that the Luftwaffe target was a stone bridge, which was to be destroyed over the estuary flowing through Gernika. (It remained intact, and this "explanation" was provided almost right after the attacks). He also stated that people fled the town after the impact of the first bombs. (Nothing was said about how those who fled were machine-gunned.) Jaenecke, probably to minimize the "tactical ambitions" of the Luftwaffe, added that the Italians targeted the same bridge. In this case, their bombing techniques were unfit for the target, but proved successful in the town center, which had already been abandoned. In other words, the glorious "Germanic knights of the air" placed most of the blame for the town's destruction on their former fascist allies. These "explanations" are nothing but downright lies.

A group of experts on the countless bombings that struck the world during the World War II would write—and the Americans would accept—such a load of hogwash only if their goal were to cloak the events and rewrite the memory of the world's consternation when the news of the attack broke in 1937. Maybe Gernika's was a trivial episode for Drum because he was preoccupied with the general approach of the Nazi military intervention in the Spanish Civil War. Or, maybe, because, as opposed to the effects of aerial weapons between 1940 and 1945, the destruction of a small town, and the violent death of close to two thousand people, was deemed inconsequential in comparison.

Former colonel Hans-Henning von Beust explored the attacks in one of the essays annexed to the report. It is dated 1955. Maier included von Beust's text in appendix 12 of his book. According to this document, the bombing was carried out by six four-plane air squads, flying at an altitude of approximately 11,500 feet (incorrectly, as I will explain later). The bombs of the first squad led to a large cloud of dust and smoke that concealed the ground and the targeted bridge over the estuary. Blinded by the cloud, the rest of the squads could only estimate the location of the target, and because of strong winds, the bulk of the bombs fell over the town center.

The fact that von Beust was given the green-light to write this in 1955 is proof of at least three things:

a) The authors did not think the Drum Report would ever be published.
b) They sought to mislead their readers, even audiences with a sophisticated understanding of bombardments, like the US Air Force.
c) They intended to paint the Luftwaffe pilots as "knights of the air."

None of von Beust's claims were correct. In his essay, he postulated that the officers of the CL were under the supervision of the Spanish military, and/or operating at its request (this is correct), and that the offensive had been highly destructive, but not launched by the *rojos* (communists), as the Francoist regime had repeatedly asserted since the time of the bombing.

CONTEMPORARY NAZI SOURCES

As far as I know, Merkes, in his 1969 book, was the first historian to address the issue on a documentary basis. It was in appendix nine. I do not know of any Francoist historian who used his findings. Merkes indicated that, although there were some discrepancies about the way the attack had been executed, the German primary sources confirmed that the attack was done by the CL, and that they all mentioned a single target.

There were three of those sources: the preliminary and final versions of *Die Kämpfe im Norden* (DKiN); *Auswertung Rügen,* a general assessment of the lessons learned in Spain; and the report by Wilhelm Meise, a colonel in charge of combat engineers, written about his trip to Spain in March 1938.

The preliminary version of DKiN maintained, among other things, that the raid was launched by nine planes (note the sharp decrease in numbers), at an altitude of 7,500 feet (much lower that what von Beust stated); that they dropped nine 330-pound bombs and one-hundred and fourteen 110-pound bombs, and that none of them landed on the stone bridge; there was bad visibility because of the thick smoke coming from the burning town; the pilots were following orders. and the *rojos* had started fires before the air strikes. All this was a pack of lies. The final version insisted that the town had been destroyed *before* the bombing. It also announced a special report on the matter which was never produced.

In a report countersigned on July 11, 1938, by his commanding officer, General Hugo Sperrle, Colonel Wolfram von Richthofen denied any responsibility for the town's destruction. The offensive on Gernika had been successful because it helped thwart the enemy's retreat efforts. The advance of the somewhat reluctant "Nationalist forces" made this possible.

Note the lack of analysis and the deflection of blame. Except for a few sources, this was the common denominator of the documents moving through the Nazi official channels during the Civil War and World War II.

There were, obviously, additional sources. The identification of the course of events which happened in 1937 was a recurring topic in the research published in the years after the publication of Merkes's book, perhaps following Ranke's principle of *wie es eigentlich gewesen* (how it actually happened)—today displaced by new historiographic trends. However, identifying and assessing the facts in both Germany and Spain, and even in publications in other countries, was controversial.

Southworth spent many years exploring the facts. His conclusions regarding Francoist culpability—Franco's and General Emilio Mola's—have stood the test of time. Other German authors, such as Stefanie Schüler-Springorum, have contributed newly found contemporaneous documents that had previously gone unnoticed. One of the documents, signed by a family member of von Richthofen who went by von Richthofen II to avoid misunderstandings, elucidated many of the objectives of the CL. Among them was the analytical reconstruction of the destructive operations conducted in the Basque Autonomous Community. According to the analysis by von Richthofen II, the Luftwaffe sought to identify the most destructive combination of break-up bombs, incendiary bombs and other munition that could be used to attack urban areas of similar size in Germany's neighboring countries.[13]

It has now become broadly known that the Nazis had acted following orders. Solid evidence has become available that the CL leaders had previously clashed with the Francoist military authorities and with Franco himself.[14] The notion that they would act independently in those circumstances on Gernika is a Francoist legend. I started to investigate the culpability issue back in 1975. Despite my findings and the more substantial contributions made by professor Irujo, the copious fallacies propagated during the Francoist dictatorship, fostered by Franco's ardent defenders such as Ricardo de la Cierva, or Air Force Major General Jesús Salas Larrazábal, proved difficult to lay to rest.

The myths surrounding Gernika, and the actors behind its destruction, have persisted from their inception on April 26, 1937, to our days, displaying a strange form of resilience. These myths are founded on one of the guiding principles of historiography, or what pro-Francoist scholars come to understand as history: the intent to portray controversial episodes of Spanish history from 1931 to 1975 according to a fundamental, unequivocal, and permanent exercise of continuous projection, i.e., the need to consider one's own behavior as typical of the enemy's. History turned on its head.

DENIAL OF CULPABILITY

That Franco's Spain avoided any confrontation with evidence-based historical research is understandable. Any study that would have delved into the events of the time would have revealed unpleasant truths for the emerging dictatorship. Given that the decimation of Gernika had caused international commotion and that Franco had slandered the Basque *lehendakari* (president) Jose Antonio Aguirre, accusing the Basque people and the miners from Asturias of having set fire to the town, Franco imposed a head-in-the-sand policy to deny any kind of involvement in the tragedy.

The Spanish authorities forced the CL to fabricate a version of the events that would clear the names of both regimes. National interests were at stake, so the Nazis went ahead with the task. By 1937, a pressing need for mutual protection had arisen between Franco and the fascist dictators, although each harbored disparate reasons. As expected, it was General Sperrle who suffered the consequences. By then, Franco had taken a profound dislike to him for other reasons.

Despite Germany's and Spain's vested interest in perpetuating the myth that the Basque attacked their own people, the story did not hold water. Drum, and even Merkes, stuck to their guns. But the myth became indefensible afterward. The theory Maier proposed was untenable. His work was one of the last embodiments of the languishing anti-Communist, anti-Republican, and anti-liberal current in German historiography on the Spanish Civil War.

The final nail in the coffin came in 1977, when the people of Gernika set out to find the truth about the events. On April 26, Walter Scheel, the president of the Federal Republic of Germany, received a telegram from Spain. On the fortieth anniversary of the bombing, Scheel was asked to intercede with the Spanish government to advocate for a Spanish-German joint committee that would mainly focus on establishing culpability. As far as I know, democratic Spain never took a stance on the matter, but the wheels started to turn in Germany. By then, the German military archives were wide open to the public, and they exposed a different version of the story.

The Basque organizing committee was right. Several disputed aspects were finally clarified thanks to a combination of Spanish, German, Italian, and other sources. The CDBG and professor Irujo have been working relentlessly to enrich the German and Spanish data pool with documents from observer countries, including Britain, the United States, France, and Belgium. Using their own archives and data from contemporaneous information outlets, historians have managed to construct an accurate understanding of the ebbs and flows of the debates that occurred within government bureaucracies, parliaments, the media, and the general public.

Integrating sources from multiple countries has yielded positive results in that we have been able to document facts that had remained unconfirmed until recently. Contrary to the statements made by General Kindelán, chief of the Air Force during the Spanish Civil War, in his fallacious memoirs, upon its arrival in Spain, the CL adhered to the standard procedures established for cooperation between foreign air forces and the rebel air forces. A few records from the collections of the Air Force Historical Archives attest to it.[15]

I find myself among those who believe that the collections might have been "looted," likely before their transformation into a formal archive in 1972.[16] The bombing of Gernika triggered the reaction of various authorities in 1937, with the result that only a few sources have been preserved in the new archive. However, sufficient material has survived to cast doubt on the traditional narrative dating back to Franco's regime.

Breaking away from the epitome of blame deflection that was the Drum Report and its appendixes, scholars gradually started holding the involved parties responsible for their actions, in a trend that required some additional years to materialize. The most noteworthy episodes came after Maier's book. In Spain, it was not until some years after Franco's death.

That said, one can finally laugh at the verbal gymnastics performed by certain Western historians, mainly German, French, British, and American. Southworth harshly criticized them for their hypocrisy, for turning a blind eye on the growing evidence, and for their reluctance to investigate one of the greatest lies of the Spanish dictatorship.

BIBLIOGRAPHY NOT CITED IN THE NOTES

Dávila Álvarez, Rafael. *La guerra civil en el Norte. El general Dávila, Franco y las campañas que decidieron el conflicto*, Madrid: La esfera de los libros, 2021.

Irujo, Xabier. *La verdad alternativa. 30 mentiras sobre el bombardeo de Gernika*, Donostia-San Sebastian: Txerkoa, 2018.

———. *26 de abril de 1937. Gernika*, Barcelona: Crítica, 2017.

———. *El Gernika de Richthofen. Un ensayo de bombardeo de terror*, several Edtioins. Gernika-Lumo: Centro de Documentación del Bombardeo de Gernika.

Maier, Guernica. 26.4.1937. *La intervención alemana en España y el "caso Guernica,"* Madrid: Sedmay ediciones, 1976.

Merkes, Manfred. *Die deutsche Politik im spanischen Bürgerkrieg, 1936–1939*, Bonn: Ludwig Röhrscheid Verlag, 1969.

———. *Die deutsche Politik gegenüber dem Spanischen Bürgerkrieg, 1936–1939*, Bonn: Ludwig Röhrscheid Verlag, 1961.

Salas Larrazábal, Jesús. *Guernica. El bombardeo La historia frente al mito*, Valladolid: Galland, 2012.

———. *Guernica*, Madrid: Rialp, 1987.

Schüler-Springorum, Stefanie. *Krieg und Fliegen. Die Legion Condor im Spanischen Bürgerkrieg.* Schöningh, Paderborn, 2010. *Abridged version in Spanish: La guerra como aventura. La intervención de la Legión Cóndor en la guerra civil española 1936–1939,* Madrid: Alianza Ensayo, 2014.

Southworth, Herbert R. *La destrucción de Guernica. Periodismo, diplomacia, propaganda e historia,* Granada: Comares, 2013.

NOTES

1 *Guernica, 26.4.1937. Die deutsche Intervention und der "Fall Guernica,"* Freiburg: Rombach Verlag, 1975.
2 The German Wikipedia entry on Beumelburg reviews his professional career. The book is only mentioned in passing. https://de.wikipedia.org/wiki/Werner_Beumelburg.
3 For example, Dagobert von Mikusch, *Kampf um Spanien. Die Geschichte der Condor Legion,* and above all, Adolf Galland, *Die Ersten und die Letzten,* translated into several languages.
4 *Das Unternehmen Feuerzauber* (The Fire Magic Exercise) and *Die Kämpfe im Norden* (The Battles in the North) (DKiN), which covered the period up until April 29, 1937. Nine more volumes were produced. The first two are available at the Documentary Center of the Bombing of Gernika (CDBG). I mentioned them frequently on my blog www.angelvinas.es, most recently, on my posts of March 31; April 7, 14, 21, 28; and May 5, 2015; and of May 15, 16, and 23; and July 25, 2017. The latest post is from April 26, 2020. Several authors have drawn from those volumes, including myself for my edition of Southworth's *Guernica, 26.4.1937.*
5 See https://de.wikipedia.org/wiki/Karl_Drum. The entry mentions this study. His career, decorations, and destinations are reported in https://www.oocities.org/~orion47/WEHRMACHT/LUFTWAFFE/General/DRUM_KARL.html. Some of his works can be found in https://www.abebooks.co.uk/book-search/title/airpower-and-russian-partisan-warfare/author/general-der-flieger-a-d-karl-drum/. Drum's contributions are discussed in a book edited by Sebastian Cox and Peter Gray in 2002. *Air Power History: Turning Points from Kitty Hawk to Kosovo,* London-Portland: Frank Cass, 2002.
6 Bundesarchiv-Militärarchiv (Federal Archives-Military Archives) in Freiburg. Freiburg was also the former home of the Militärgeschichtliches Forschungsamt (Military History Research Office), but it was relocated to Potsdam and integrated into other research institutions. https://de.wikipedia.org/wiki/Milit%C3%A4rgeschichtliches_Forschungsamt.
7 https://de.wikipedia.org/wiki/Erwin_Jaenecke. He was chief of staff of the *Sonderstab W* (undercover name for the operation as managed from Berlin) during the bombing of Gernika; he followed the contingencies and oversaw the actions of the air unit from the German capital. He is mentioned later in this chapter.
8 https://de.wikipedia.org/wiki/Hugo_Sperrle. The data provided in the Wikipedia entry regarding the death toll of the bombing of Gernika are incorrect.
9 https://de.wikipedia.org/wiki/Wilhelm_Faupel.
10 The work by retired three-star general Dávila Álvarez is the latest example I know.
11 I hope my translation is accurate (p. 7): „Deutschland und Italien hatten sich bereits zu der neuen Lebensordnung des Faschismus bekannt. Wenn nun auch noch mit einem Sieg Francos und der Falangisten Spanien folgte, dann sah sich Frankreich von drei autoritär geführten

Staaten umklammert. Wo blieb da seine Sicherheit? Folglich musste die Demokratie in Spanien mit allen Mitteln vor einer Niederlage bewahrt werden". Thus is the original.
12   This is explained in detail on page 8 of the report.
13   Read my Spanish translation of their analysis on my blog post of May 23, 2017.
14   In the epilogue I wrote for the Comares edition of Southworth's book.
15   This reference can easily be found in my blog post of July 26, 2017.
16   https://ejercitodelaire.defensa.gob.es/EA/archivohistorico/historia.html.

Index

Note: Photographs and associated captions are indicated by f following the page number. End note information is indicated by n and note number following the page number.

aerial bombings
   of Barcelona, 115–24
   casualties of, 109, 118–19, 121–23
   denial of, 116, 130, 135, 136–37
   German historical military writing on, 127–37
   of Gernika, 109, 115–17, 128, 133–37
   goals and objectives of, 117–18, 120–22
   as primal violence, 124
   as saturation or carpet bombings, 115, 116–17
   of TNT-filled truck, 122–23
   as war crimes or crimes against humanity, 115
AGLA group (Guerrilla Group from Levante and Aragón), 111
Aguilera, Gonzalo, 98–99
Aguirre, Jose Antonio, 136
Ahaztuak association, 54
Amnesty Act (1977), 2, 3–4, 5, 9, 15
Amonarenean kea—Humo en casa de la abuela (Smoke at Grandma's House), 58–59
Anda, José Ramón, 53
Andueza, Eneko, 36–37
Aragón, 5, 49–51, 111
Aranzadi Society of Sciences *(Sociedad de Ciencias Aranzadi)*, 9, 25, 27, 44–45, 58, 97
Arroyo, Agustín Joaquín, 46–47
Artolazabal, Beatriz, 31
Asociación de Familiares de Fusilados de Navarra AFFNA36NAFSE (Navarre's Association of Family Members of Execution Victims), 44, 54, 66n8
Asociación para la Recuperación de la Memoria Histórica (Association for the Recovery of Historical Memory, ARMH), 97
Auschwitz (Poland), 73–74, 75, 78–79
Auswertung Rügen, 134
autosomal short tandem repeat marker testing, 45–46
Aznar, José María and administration, 6

Babesaren Muga (Iriarte), 49
BAC. *See* Basque Autonomous Community
Barcelona, 106, 115–24
Barcones, 101
Barrera, Eduardo, 28
Barriro, Carmelo, 36–37
Basque Autonomous Community (BAC)
   aerial bombings in (*see* aerial bombings)
   exhumations in (*see* exhumations)
   Franco dictatorship in (*see* Franco dictatorship)
   German historical military writing on, 127–37
   Historical Memory Act of 2022 of, 24–38, 47, 112
   Spanish Civil War in (*see* Spanish Civil War)
   Statute of Autonomy of, 3, 24, 30
   structure of, 38n1
   UNESCO heritigization policies in,

67–87
Basque Country, structure of, 38n1. *See also specific autonomous communities*
Basque National Party. *See* EAJ
Basque Socialist Party (PSE-EE), 28, 36
battlefield casualties, 109–10
Bayo, Alberto, 120
Beazley, Olwen, 81
Belaustegi, Unai, 1
Berruezo, Reyes, 50
Beumelburg, Werner, 128
Bilbo-Bilbao, 1, 20–21n37, 37, 109
Bizkaia (Vizcaya), 9, 20–21n37, 109–10. *See also* Gernika
Blanco, Miguel Ángel, 7
bombings. *See* aerial bombings
Botellas de la Libertad, Las (Bottles of Freedom) hike, 59–60, 64
Buried. Early Exhumations in Navarre *(Lur Azpian-Bajo Tierra. Exhumaciones tempranas en Navarra),* 63, 64

Calvo Sotelo, José, 132
Cameron, Christina, 81
Camino a Gurs-Gurserako bidea (Destination: Gurs), 51
Camuñas, Ignacio, 36
Captive City, The. Detention Centers in Pamplona-Iruñea, 1936–1945 *(Ciudad de los cautivos, La. Centros de detención en Pamplona, 1936–1945),* 63
Casa Elizalde, 117, 118
Casanova, Julián, 99
Castile and León, 10–11, 97, 106
Castilla la Mancha, 5
Catalonia
  aerial bombings in, 115–24
  exhumations in, 109
  genetic identification program in, 47
  historical memory support in, 34
  reparation stance in, 5, 6
  retreat from defeated, 51
Cementerio de las Botellas (Cemetery of the Bottles), 44, 60, 61–62, 64, 110
Chueca, Josu, 50

Churchill, Winston, 123
Cierva, Ricardo de la, 135
Cinco de la Nava, Los association, 44
Ciudadanos, 28, 36, 37
Ciudad de los cautivos, La. Centros de detención en Pamplona, 1936–1945 (The Captive City. Detention Centers in Pamplona-Iruñea, 1936–1945), 63
Concrete Borders *(Fronteras de Hormigón),* 64
Condor Legion (CL), 128–32, 134–37
Convention Concerning the Protection of the World Cultural and Natural Heritage (1972), 67–68, 71–81, 85–87

Deconstruir el franquismo—Frankismoaren dekonstruzioa egiten (Deconstructing Francoism), 53
Democratic and Historical Memory Act of 2022. *See* Historical Memory Act of 2022
Destination: Gurs *(Camino a Gurs-Gurserako bidea),* 51
Deutsche Luftwaffe im Spanischen Bürgerkrieg, Die (The Luftwaffe in the Spanish Civil War) (Drum), 129–34, 137
Diéguez, Claudio Doroteo, 46
Die Kämpfe im Norden (DKiN), 134–35
Directorio Revolucionario Ibérico de Liberación (Iberian Revolutionary Liberation Directory, DRIL), 14
DNA banks and genetic information, 15, 27, 33, 45–47, 105–6, 111
documentary heritage protection
  on exhumations, 64, 95–96
  by Gogora, 33, 34 (*see also* Historical Memory Documentary Center)
  Navarre's Documentary Center for, 43, 50, 62–64
  UNESCO Memory of the World Program for, 84–85, 84*f*
Donde el bosque se espesa (Where the Woods Thicken), 57, 66n14
Donostia-San Sebastian, 1, 14
Drum, Karl, 129–30, 136
Drum Report, 129–34, 137
Durango, 115, 117

EAJ (Euskal Alderdi Jeltzalea), 6, 7, 28, 37
education
    Historical Memory Act on, 33, 37–38
    ikastola instructors in, 8, 32
    Navarre's Escuelas con Memoria program on, 43, 50, 56–62
EH Bildu (Euskal Herria Bildu), 28, 37
Elkarrekin Podemos-IU, 28
Escuelas con Memoria (Schools with Memory, EM) program, 43, 50, 56–62
Espacios de memoria—Memoria Guneak (Memory Sites), 55–56
Espinosa, Francisco, 99
ETA (Euskadi Ta Askatasuna), 7, 11, 14, 15, 36–37, 126nn27–28
European Commission European Heritage Label, 81, 83–84
Euskal Alderdi Jeltzalea (EAJ), 6, 7, 28, 37
Euskal Herria Bildu (EH Bildu), 28, 37
Ex ESMA Museum and Site of Memory (Argentina), 78, 78*f*
exhumations, 95–112
    analysis of graves and, 101–6
    anthropological analysis from, 104
    associated artifacts recovered in, 102–4, 105*f*
    biological profile from, 104
    cause of death identified from, 104
    chronology of, 106, 107*f*
    delivery of remains following, 111
    DNA banks and genetic information with, 33, 45–47, 105–6, 111
    documentary heritage protection on, 64, 95–96
    early, 44, 50, 51, 53, 61, 63, 64, 96
    Escuelas con Memoria program on, 58–59, 61
    events creating graves for, 98–99
    by Francoist regime, 95–96
    grave morphology and, 101–2
    Historical Memory Act of 2022 and, 24–25, 33, 35, 47, 112
    human rights violations exposure with, 112
    integrated reports on, 105–6
    in Navarre, 43–48, 49–50, 53, 58–59, 61, 63, 64, 65n2, 96–97, 110
    overview of, 95–97
    penalties for improper, 35
    reparations and, 9, 10–11, 20–21n37
    repression and, 97, 99–100, 111
    sites of memory tied to, 53–54
    typology of mass graves and, 107–11
exile, victims in, 6, 31, 49–51, 55, 60–61, 64
"Exile, Art, and Memory" program, 51
extrajudicial executions, 37, 108
Ezkaba 1938-2018 exhibit, 64
Ezkieta, Fermín, 45, 110–11

Fascismo y lugares de memoria (Fascism and Sites of Memory), 52, 57
Faupel, Wilhelm, 130
Federación Española de Municipios y Provincias (Spanish Federation of Towns and Provinces, FEMP), 106
Fernández, Jovino, 59
Ferrándiz, Francisco, 28
Fight in Spain. The History of the Condor Legion *(Kampf in Spanien. Die Geschichte der Legion Condor)* (Beumelburg), 128
First Conference of the Inter-Regional Network Advocating for Historical Memory, 47
Fort San Cristóbal
    documentary heritage protection on, 64
    Escuelas con Memoria program on, 57, 59–60, 61–62
    exhumations near, 44–46, 59, 101, 110–11
    sites of memory near, 53–54, 55, 59
Franco dictatorship, 1–16
    establishment of, 1
    exhumations by, 95–96
    exhumations of victims of (*see* exhumations)
    exile due to (*see* exile, victims in)
    German historical military writing on, 127–37
    Gogora's role in remembrance of (*see* Gogora)

human rights violations by (*see* human rights violations)
Institute of Memory of Navarre on, 42–65
legislation regulating memory of, 2–16, 17–18, 24–38 (*see also specific legislation*)
penalties for exaltation of, 35–36
perpetrators in, 100–101
places of memory for victims of (*see* places of memory)
removal of symbols of, 13, 26, 34, 43, 51–53
reparations for victims of (*see* reparations)
repression chronology of, 99–100
Spanish identity under, 2
Transition following (*see* Transition)
violence embraced by, 98–99
Fregenal, 102
Fronteras de Hormigón (Concrete Borders), 64

Gabarda, Vicente, 109
Gallego Vila, Laia, 124
Gamarra, Eneko, 58
García de Albizu, Balbino, 44
García Fernández, Javier, 68–69
Gastón Aguas, José Miguel, 42
Gatti, Gabriel, 112
General Directorate of Peace, Coexistence and Human Rights, 43–45, 48–49, 52, 54, 62, 64
genetic data. *See* DNA banks and genetic information
German historical military writing, 127–37
background for, 128–29
contemporary Nazi sources for, 134–36
denial of culpability in, 136–37
in Drum Report, 129–34, 137
on Gernika bombings, 128, 133–37
political and ideological foundations for, 129–33
research on, 127–28
Gernika (Guernica)
aerial bombings of, 109, 115–17, 128, 133–37

German historical military writing on, 128, 133–37
Gernika Peace Museum in, 33
Gipuzkoa (Guipuzcoa), 1
Gogora (Institute for Memory, Coexistence, and Human Rights)
Action Plans of, 14, 15, 27
administration of, 35
documentary heritage protection by, 33, 34 (*see also* Historical Memory Documentary Center)
educational initiatives of, 33
exhumation by, 33, 35
Francoist symbols removal by, 34
Historical Memory Act role of, 28, 32–36
historical memory advocates advice from, 35
legislation creating, 14–15, 26–27, 28, 35
mission and goals of, 26, 35
moral reparations/recognition under, 14, 15, 27, 33
penalties administration by, 35–36
right to justice advocacy by, 32
right to truth advocacy by, 32
González, Felipe and administration, 5
Gorée (Senegal), 73
Gran Fuga, La (The Great Escape), 57
grave exhumations. *See* exhumations
Greiff, Pablo de, 13
Grozny doctrine, 117
Grupo Paleolab, 111
Guernica. *See* Gernika
guerrillas, repression against, 111
Guipuzcoa (Gipuzkoa), 1
Gurs concentration camp, 49, 50–51, 60–61

Haro González, Ramón, 47
heritigization policies. *See* UNESCO heritigization policies
Herrasti, Lourdes, 95
Hiroshima (Japan), 73, 74, 79
Historical Memory Act of 2007, 7, 12–14, 25–26, 106
Historical Memory Act of 2017, 27

Historical Memory Act of 2022, 24–38
  beneficiaries and eligible victims under, 31–32, 36–37
  chapters and provisions of, 30–36
  context for enactment of, 24–28, 37–38
  DNA banks in, 27, 47
  documentary heritage protection in, 33, 34
  draft bill for, 28–36
  education, research, and documentation through, 33, 37–38
  exhumations and, 24–25, 33, 35, 47, 112
  Francoist symbols removal in, 34
  goals and objectives of, 28–29, 30–31
  Gogora's role in, 28, 32–36
  importance of, 37–38
  international humanitarian law integration in, 29–30
  penalties under, 35–36
  places, itineraries, and spaces of memory in, 33–34, 35
  political positions on, 28, 35–37
  public registry of historical memory advocates in, 34–35
  reparations in, 30–31, 32–33
  right to justice in, 32
  right to truth in, 32
  transitional justice in, 30
Historical Memory Archives of Navarre, 52, 57, 63
Historical Memory Documentary Center, 12, 26, 33, 34
Historical Memory Sites of Navarre, 54–56, 64. *See also under* places of memory
History and Memory in the Classroom *(I Historia con Memoria en la Educación)* international conference, 61
Hot Terror period, 99
Hristova, Marije, 28
human rights violations
  Escuelas con Memoria program on, 58
  exhumations exposing, 112
  Gogora on (*see* Gogora)
  heritigization of sites of, 67, 69, 73, 81–84, 86

Historical Memory Act addressing, 29–32, 36, 37–38
Navarre General Directorate addressing, 43–45, 48–49, 52, 54, 62, 64
penalties for exaltation of, 36
reparations recognizing, 10–11, 13–16, 26–27
sites of memory recognizing, 53
transitional justice addressing, 30

Ibáñez, Ana, 58
Ibarretxe, Juan José and administration, 7, 11
Iberian Revolutionary Liberation Directory *(Directorio Revolucionario Ibérico de Liberación, DRIL)*, 14
ICOMOS, 67, 74–76, 77–81, 82
ICSC (International Coalition of Sites of Conscience), 79–80
I Historia con Memoria en la Educación (History and Memory in the Classroom) international conference, 61
ikastola instructors, 8, 32
Imágenes con Memoria (Images with Memory), 63
Institute for Memory, Coexistence, and Human Rights. *See* Gogora
Institute of Memory of Navarre, 42–65
  challenges for, 42–43
  context for founding of, 42–43
  Documentary Center of, 43, 50, 62–64
  Escuelas con Memoria program by, 43, 50, 56–62
  exhumation records by, 43–48, 49–50, 53, 58–59, 61, 63, 64, 65n2
  Francoist symbols removal by, 43, 51–53
  goals and objectives of, 42, 43, 63, 65
  identification and location of victims by, 43–48
  reparation and recognition advocacy by, 43, 48–51, 54
  sites of memory protection and recognition by, 43, 49, 51, 53–56, 59–60, 64
International Coalition of Sites of Conscience (ICSC), 79–80

International Covenant on Civil and Political Rights (1966), 29
International Covenant on Economic, Social, and Cultural Rights (1966), 29
International Memory of the World Register, 84, 85*f*
Iriarte, Mikel, 49
Irujo, Xabier, 24, 130, 136
itineraries of memory, 34, 35, 55–56
Iturrate, Inigo, 37–38
Izarra, Josean, 36

Jaenecke, Erwin, 130, 133, 138n7
justice
   right to, 32
   transitional, 30, 81

Kampf in Spanien. Die Geschichte der Legion Condor (Fight in Spain. The History of the Condor Legion) (Beumelburg), 128
Kindelán, General, 137
Kowasch, Amaia, 64

Laharie, Claude, 50
Langdon-Davies, John, 120
Larrasoaña, 101
Layana Ilundain, César, 42
Libertad's Memory *(Memoria de Libertad—Libertaden Memoria)*, 57–58
Linzoain, Paulina, 101
Lizarraga, Gerardo, 57, 64
Lo Cascio, Paola, 120–21
López, Francisco and administration, 13
Luftwaffe in the Spanish Civil War, The *(Die Deutsche Luftwaffe im Spanischen Bürgerkrieg)* (Drum), 129–34, 137
Lur Azpian-Bajo Tierra. Exhumaciones tempranas en Navarra (Buried. Early Exhumations in Navarre), 63, 64

MacRoberts, Noel de Putron, 116, 117, 120, 124
Madariaga, Iulen, 126
Maier, Klaus A., 128, 129, 133–34, 136
Majuelo, Emilio, 50

Maquinista Terrestre y Marítima, 117–18
maquis, repression against, 111
Maraña, Maider, 67
Martínez, Amaia, 36
Martirena, Dani, 58
mass grave exhumations. *See* exhumations
Mazorra Hill, La, 108
McDowell, Sara, 70
Meise, Wilhelm, 134
Memoria de Libertad—Libertaden Memoria (Libertad's Memory), 57–58
Memoriaren Bideak (Paths of Memory) association, 44, 54, 55, 60
Memorias de la objeción de conciencia y la insumisión en Navarra (Memories of Conscientious Objectors and Draft Dodgers in Navarre), 63
memory. *See* remembrance
Memory Acts. *See* Historical Memory Act entries
Memory of the World Program, 84–85, 84*f*
Memory Sites *(Espacios de memoria—Memoria Guneak)*, 55–56. *See also* places of memory
Merkes, Manfred, 127–28, 129, 134, 136
mitochondrial DNA testing, 46
Mola, Emilio, 98, 135
monetary penalties, 35–36
monetary reparations
   Historical Memory Act on, 32
   legislation on, 3–10, 14, 16, 19n6, 25, 32
   Navarre's support for, 8, 43
moral reparations/recognition
   Historical Memory Act on, 32–33
   legislation on, 5, 10–16, 26–29, 32–33
   Navarre's support for, 43, 48–51, 54
Mostar Old Bridge Area (Bosnia and Herzegovina), 80

Nasertic, 45
Navarre
   exhumations in, 43–48, 49–50, 53, 58–59, 61, 63, 64, 65n2, 96–97, 110
   General Directorate of Peace,

Coexistence and Human Rights in, 43–45, 48–49, 52, 54, 62, 64
Institute of Memory of Navarre in, 42–65
reparation stance in, 8, 43, 48–51, 54
Navarre's Association of Family Members of Execution Victims *(Asociación de Familiares de Fusilados de Navarra AFFNA36NAFSE)*, 44, 54, 66n8
Navarro, Marysa, 50
Nora, Pierre, 53

Oliveira, Susana, 120–21
Oroibidea, 51, 55, 57, 62–63

Palacios Belloso, Cristina, 58
Palencia, 97
Pamplona-Iruñea, 44, 45, 51, 55, 63, 64, 101
Parent, Michel, 73–74
Partido Popular (PP)
  exhumation decline under, 106
  on Historical Memory Act, 28, 36, 37
  reparations under, 6, 7, 13, 27
Paths of Memory *(Memoriaren Bideak)* association, 44, 54, 55, 60
Pedraja, La, 102, 104
penalties and sanctions, 35–36
pensions, 3–5, 25, 95
Pérez, Esperanza, 97
Pérez Barriuso, Plácido, 103
Picón de Valdeabejas, 108
Pinochet, Augusto, 11
Pintor en el exilio (Gerardo Lizarraga. Painter in Exile), 57
places of memory
  Historical Memory Act protecting, 33–35
  Navarre's protection and recognition of, 43, 49, 51, 53–56, 59–60, 64
  penalties for desecration of, 35
  UNESCO heritigization policies on, 67–87
Podemos, 11
Pons i Pujol, Jordi, 120
PP. *See* Partido Popular
Preston, Paul, 130
Priaranza del Bierzo (León), 10–11, 97, 106
primal violence, 124, 126n28. *See also* aerial bombings
Primo de Rivera, José Antonio, 132
prisoners
  documentary heritage protection on, 64
  Escuelas con Memoria program on, 57, 59–60, 61–62
  exhumations of, 44–47, 101, 103, 108, 110–11
  Historical Memory Act on, 31
  monetary reparations for, 3–4, 5, 8–10, 25
  moral reparations for, 49
  sites of memory honoring, 53–55, 59–60
PSE-EE (Basque Socialist Party), 28, 36
PSOE (Spanish Socialist Party), 5, 7, 13, 25, 27
Pueblo de Viudas association, 54, 66n8

Rajoy, Mariano and administration, 27, 37
Ramírez Barace, Oskia, 58
Registry of Vital Records, 95–96, 111
remembrance
  of aerial bombings (*see* aerial bombings)
  exhumations and (*see* exhumations)
  in German historical military writing, 127–37
  Historical Memory Act of 2022 on (*see* Historical Memory Act of 2022)
  Institute of Memory of Navarre on, 42–65
  of Spanish Civil War and Franco dictatorship (*see* Franco dictatorship; Spanish Civil War)
  UNESCO heritigization policies and, 67–87
reparations
  heritigization policies based on, 82
  Historical Memory Act on, 30–31, 32–33
  monetary, 3–10, 14, 16, 19n6, 25, 32, 43
  moral, 5, 10–16, 26–29, 32–33, 43, 48–51, 54
  Navarre's support for, 8, 43, 48–51, 54
  transitional justice including, 30
Requejo Requejo, Tomás, 103
Resolution 18/7 (UN), 30

Resolution 60/147 (UN), 29–30
Rhode Project (later Karlsruhe Project), 129
Robben Island (South Africa), 73, 74
Rodríguez Senosiain, Irantzu, 58
Russia, aerial bombings by, 115, 116, 117

Sainz Plaza, Máximo, 59
Salas Larrazábal, Jesús, 135
Salinas, Tomás, 47
Sartaguda, Memory Park of, 49–51, 54–55, 60, 64, 66n8
Scheel, Walter, 136
Schools with Memory (Escuelas con Memoria, EM) program, 43, 50, 56–62
Schüler-Springorum, Stefanie, 135
Schweickhard, Karl-Friedrich, 128
Segura i Mas, Antoni, 115
Shaheed, Farida, 81–83
Silva, Emilio, 97
Simbología dictatorial. Arte y espacio público (Symbols of Dictatorships. Art and Public Space), 52
sites of memory. *See* itineraries of memory; places of memory; spaces of memory
Smoke at Grandma's House *(Amonarenean kea—Humo en casa de la abuela)*, 58–59
Social Security contributions, 3, 8
Sociedad de Ciencias Aranzadi (Aranzadi), 9, 25, 27, 44–45, 58, 97
Southworth, Herbert R., 116, 128, 135
spaces of memory
    Historical Memory Act protecting, 33–34, 35
    Navarre's protection and recognition of, 43, 49, 51, 53–56, 59–60, 64
    penalties for desecration of, 35
    UNESCO heritigization policies on, 67–87
Spanish Civil War, 1–16
    aerial bombings in (*see* aerial bombings)
    archives and documentation on, 2, 6, 7, 13, 26, 33
    casualties of, 99
    exhumations of victims of (*see* exhumations)
    exile due to (*see* exile, victims in)
    German historical military writing on, 127–37
    Gogora's role in remembrance of (*see* Gogora)
    human rights violations in (*see* human rights violations)
    Institute of Memory of Navarre on, 42–65
    legislation regulating memory of, 2–16, 17–18, 24–38 (*see also specific legislation*)
    perpetrators in, 100–101
    places of memory for victims of (*see* places of memory)
    reparations for victims of (*see* reparations)
    repression chronology in, 99–100
    violence central to, 98–99
Spanish Constitution, 2, 24, 32, 96
Spanish Federation of Towns and Provinces *(Federación Española de Municipios y Provincias, FEMP)*, 106
Spanish Socialist Party (PSOE), 5, 7, 13, 25, 27
Sperrle, Hugo, 130, 135, 136
Stohrer, Eberhard von, 130
Suárez, Adolfo and administration, 2
summary executions, 100, 104, 109
Súñer, Ramón, 109
symbols, Francoist, removal of, 13, 26, 34, 43, 51–53
Symbols of Dictatorships. Art and Public Space *(Simbología dictatorial. Arte y espacio público)*, 52

teachers, 8, 32, 50, 57. *See also* education
Teatro con Memoria (Theater with Memory), 61
Tejera Hill, La, 108
Tejiendo redes-Sareak ehortzen. Mujeres solidarias con los presos del Fuerte de San Cristóbal (1934–1945) (Weaving Nets. Women in Solidarity with the Runaways of Fort San Cristóbal) (Kowasch), 64
terrorism
    aerial bombings as, 124
    by ETA (*see* ETA)

Historical Memory Act on victims of, 36–37
penalties for exaltation of, 36
reparations for victims of, 7, 14, 15
Theater with Memory *(Teatro con Memoria)*, 61
Tongariro National Park (New Zealand), 79
Torrero cemetery, 49–51, 64
tourism, 56, 70–71, 80
Transition
    Amnesty Act during, 2, 3–4, 5, 9, 15
    exhumations during, 44, 50, 53, 96–97
    monetary reparations during, 3–10
    moral reparations questioning
    reconciliation in, 12
transitional justice, 30, 81
truth, right to, 32
Txinparta-Fuerte de San Cristóbal association, 44, 54

Uluru-Kata Tjuta National Park (Australia), 79
UNESCO heritigization policies, 67–87
    criteria for site consideration in, 70, 73, 82
    debate over, 71–81
    evolution of discourse on, 68–71
    expert opinions and action plans to modify, 77–81
    foundations of, 71–77
    Memory of the World Program in, 84–85, 84f
    other international institution policies vs., 81–85
    overview of, 67–68, 85–87
    for sites of conflict, 67–87
    terminology influencing, 67, 71, 76, 77, 79
    World Heritage Committee administering, 67–68, 72–77, 74f, 82, 87
    World Heritage Convention guiding, 67–68, 71–81, 85–87
    World Heritage List and, 67, 72, 73, 76–77, 80–82, 83, 86
United Nations Human Rights Council heritigization policies, 81–83
Universal Declaration of Human Rights (1948), 29

Urbasa Plains, 44, 53
Urkullu, Iñigo, 28–29
Urroz, Begoña, 14

Valley of Cuelgamuros (formerly Valley of the Fallen), 15, 33, 82, 96
Vietnam War aerial bombings, 116–17
Villarreal, Enrique ("El Drogas"), 60
Villarroya i Font, Joan, 119
Viñas, Ángel, 127
Vives, Julia Gay, 122
Vizcaya (Bizkaia), 9, 20–21n37, 109–10. *See also* Gernika
von Beust, Hans-Henning, 134
von Richthofen, Wilfram, 135
Vox, 28, 36, 37–38

war crimes, aerial bombings as, 115
Weaving Nets. Women in Solidarity with the Runaways of Fort San Cristóbal *(Tejiendo redes-Sareak ehortzen. Mujeres solidarias con los presos del Fuerte de San Cristóbal (1934–1945))* (Kowasch), 64
Weitz, Richard, 117
Where the Woods Thicken *(Donde el bosque se espesa)*, 57, 66n14
World Heritage Committee, 67–68, 72–77, 74f, 82, 87
World Heritage Convention (1972), 67–68, 71–81, 85–87
World Heritage List, 67, 72, 73, 76–77, 80–82, 83, 86. *See also* UNESCO heritigization policies
World Tourism Organization, 70–71
World War I Funerary and Memorial sites, 67, 74–76, 82
World War II aerial bombings, 116, 124

Yagüe, Jesús, 98
Y chromosome testing, 46

Zapatero, José Luis Rodríguez and administration, 10–13, 106

Þingvellir National Park (Iceland), 73

About the Authors

JOSÉ MIGUEL GASTÓN

José Miguel Gastón is a PhD in history from the Public University of Navarre. He is the director of the Navarre Institute of Memory. His primary research has focused on the study of conflict over land ownership and use in Navarre during the 19th century and the first third of the 20th century, as well as public memory policies in Navarre. He is the author of various articles in specialized journals and several books. Among these are "¡Vivan los Comunes! Communal Movement and Corralito Incidents in Navarre, 1896-1930" and "No Time for Russian Dances. The Good Press of Navarre Facing the Bolshevik Revolution (1917-1923)."

CÉSAR LAYANA

César Layana holds a PhD in history from the Public University of Navarre. He is the Head of the Documentation Section at the Navarre Institute of Memory and also an associate professor at the Public University of Navarre. His fundamental research lines are directed toward the repression of the war and post-war period in Navarre, especially economic repression, and public memory policies in Navarre. He has authored numerous articles on these topics in specialized publications. In 2021, he published "Plunder and Punishment. Economic Repression in Navarre, 1936-1945."

MAIDER MARAÑA

Maider Maraña is the director of the Baketik Foundation, an organization dedicated to human rights, promoting dialogue, and conflict resolution. As an independent consultant, she promotes the incorporation of human rights and non-discrimination into various public policies for international organizations—like UNESCO or the European Union, local governments, and associations. With a degree in history, she is part of the UNESCO Chair on Cultural Landscapes and Heritage at the University of the Basque Country and has specialized in cultural rights: her research addresses policies on cultural heritage, mainstreaming a rights-based approach, gender equity, and social participation. Regarding memory sites, she recently published the article "Sites Linked to Conflicts as a Heritage Category: Analysis from the Current Debate in UNESCO (2021)" and coordinated the study "Leveraging the Potential of Tourism at Historical Conflict Sites to Promote Peace (2020)," and we can also mention "Heritage and Human Rights (2015)."

ÁNGEL VIÑAS

Ángel Viñas is an emeritus professor of the Complutense University of Madrid (UCM), former EU Ambassador to the United Nations in New York, former Director of External Relations at the European Commission, former executive advisor to ministers Fernando Morán and Francisco Fernández Ordóñez, former Vice Chancellor of the Universidad Internacional Menéndez Pelayo (UIMP) and the Universidad Nacional de Educación a Distancia (UNED). He ranked first in his class and was awarded the Extraordinary Prize in his doctoral degree in Economic Sciences by the UCM. He has been honored with the Grand Cross of Civil Merit and is Doctor honoris causa by the University of Alicante (UA). As an Adoptive son of Las Palmas de Gran Canaria and co-recipient of the Gernika Prize for Peace and Solidarity 2019, his latest books are *Who Wanted the Civil War?* (Crítica, 2019) and *The Great Mistake of the Republic* (Crítica, 2021).

ANTONI SEGURA I MAS

Antoni Segura i Mas is a professor of contemporary history at the University of Barcelona (UB). He works on conflict analysis and the history of the current world, including the civil war and Francoism, and, in relation to the presentation, has published: *Atlas of the Civil War in Catalonia* (with Joan Villarroya); *The Autonomous University of Barcelona: History, Memory, and Commitment; Chronicle of Catalanisme. From Autonomy to Independence; Euskadi, Chronicle of Despair; Views on Euskadi; The Question of Historical Memory in Spain and Catalonia: Between 2002* and 2017, he was the Principal Investigator (PI) of various projects of the Ministry of Justice of Catalonia such as *The Early Years of Francoism in Catalonia (1938-1953), Francoism in Catalonia: Institutionalization of the Regime and Organization of the Opposition (1938-1979), The Spanish Civil War,* and Three Decades of "War in Europe: Legacies and Consequences (1914-1945/2014) and of the Generalitat of Catalonia as Research and Analysis Group of the Current World" and *Recovery of the Historical Memory of the Struggle for Democracy in the Context of Catalonia.*

XABIER IRUJO

Xabier Irujo is the director of the Center for Basque Studies at the University of Nevada, Reno, where he is a professor of genocide studies. He was the first Guest Research Scholar of the Manuel Irujo Chair Fellowship at the University of Liverpool, William Douglass visiting lecturer at the University of Massachusetts Amherst, and Eloise Garmendia Chair at Boise State University. With BA and MA degrees in philology, history, and philosophy, he holds two doctorates in history and philosophy. He has directed numerous doctoral theses and is part of the scientific committees of five academic and university publishers. He is the author of more than twenty books and a number of articles in specialized journals and has received awards and distinctions at the national and international levels, including the Gernika Prize for Peace and Solidarity in 2019. He has dedicated the last two decades to studying the bombing of Gernika and has collaborated with the Gernika Documentation Center in searching for archival material about the bombing. As a result of these investigations are his trilogies on the bombing of Gernika and the political exile. Among his latest books, we highlight the trilogy on the bombing of Gernika: *Gernika: Genealogy of a Lie* (Sussex Academic Press, 2019), *The Bombing of Gernika* (Center for Basque Studies Press - University of Nevada, Reno, 2018), *Gernika: April 26, 1937* (Crítica, Barcelona, 2017) and *Legal History of the Basque Language* (HAEE, Bilbao, 2015).

LOURDES HERRASTI

Lourdes Herrasti holds a PhD in history and is a Secondary Education teacher. Archaeologist and osteoarchaeologist in excavations of historical periods, both in prehistoric sites and medieval and modern era necropolises. She has specialized in field intervention and laboratory analysis. Archaeologist of the "Humanitarian Project Plan for the Identification of Argentine Soldiers Buried in the Darwin Cemetery Malvinas-Falklands." (ICRC/CICR) (2017), she participated in the exhumation and analysis of five clandestine graves in the Liberated Territories of Western Sahara (2013-2018). She has participated, directed, and/or coordinated the exhumation of more than 200 graves from the War in the Basque Country, Catalonia, and Spain (2000-2021). Her current main line of research is the analysis of the graves and study of repression and political violence during the War of 1936 and Francoism. She has collaborated in collective publications: *The Cemetery of Bottles, Underground. Exhumations in Navarre (1938-2019), Lemoatx, 1936,* and *Exhumations of the Civil War in Euskadi.* She has organized several exhibitions: "Exhuming Graves, Recovering Dignities," "Let What is Buried Surface (Cemetery of Ezkaba Prison)" (both itinerant), "Facing Death" (at the San Telmo Museum).

UNAI BELAUSTEGI

Unai Belaustegi was an adjunct professor at the Department of Contemporary History of the University of the Basque Country (EHU) since 2016, and an associate professor since 2022. He currently is the Secretary of the Section and Coordinator of the Teaching Team of the Department of Contemporary History in Vitoria-Gasteiz. Graduated in history from the EHU (2006), he holds a Master in contemporary history from the University of the Basque Country (2007) and a Master in teacher training for compulsory secondary education by the EHU (2007). He holds a PhD in contemporary history (2014) with international mention and extraordinary award (2016). He received a predoctoral scholarship from the Basque Government in the 2009 call, with a stay as a visiting researcher at the University of Nevada, Reno (2013). Afterward, he obtained two other postdoctoral scholarships at the EHU that allowed him to develop his research at the University of Santa Barbara, California (2015-2016). He has also been a Visiting Researcher at the University of Messina (Italy, 2017).

www.ingramcontent.com/pod-product-compliance
Lightning Source LLC
Chambersburg PA
CBHW071849230426
43671CB00012B/2117